INSIDE THE CRIMINAL MIND

ALSO BY STANTON E. SAMENOW

Straight Talk About Criminals

Before It's Too Late

In the Best Interest of the Child

With Samuel Yochelson, M.D.

The Criminal Personality: Profile for Change

The Criminal Personality: The Change Process

The Criminal Personality: The Drug User

Videotape Series and Workbooks by Stanton E. Samenow

Commitment to Change: Overcoming Errors in Thinking

Commitment to Change: Tactics

Commitment to Change: The Power of Consequences

INSIDE THE CRIMINAL MIND

REVISED AND UPDATED EDITION

STANTON E. SAMENOW, PH.D.

CROWN PUBLISHERS

NEW YORK

364.3
Sa44

Published by Crown Publishers, New York, New York.
Member of the Crown Publishing Group, a division of Random House, Inc.
www.crownpublishing.com

CROWN is a trademark and the Crown colophon is a registered trademark of Random House, Inc.

Originally published in slightly different form by Times Books, a division of Random House, Inc., in 1984.

Printed in the United States of America

Design by Leonard Henderson

Library of Congress Cataloging-in-Publication Data
Samenow, Stanton E., 1941–
Inside the criminal mind / Stanton E. Samenow—Rev. and updated.
Includes bibliographical references and index.
1. Criminal psychology. 2. Juvenile delinquents—Psychology. 3. Conduct disorders in adolescence. I. Title.
HV6080.S22 2004
364.3'01'9—dc22   2003019505

ISBN 1-4000-4619-X

10 9 8 7 6 5 4 3 2 1

Revised Edition

In memory of Dr. Samuel Yochelson,
who taught and inspired me so many years ago.

ACKNOWLEDGMENTS

I thank Ed Schuman and Richard Stromberg
for reading the manuscript and making excellent suggestions.

CONTENTS

CONTENTS

A CAUTION

TO THE READER

IN MY EARLIER writings, I received the following criticism. Readers understood the characteristics of the criminal that I described in detail. However, some developed a case of "medical students' disease." That is, they saw themselves in what they were reading. Thus they thought, "Gee, my wife does some of these things. My son does, too. For that matter, so do I. Am I a criminal by Samenow's definition?" It is true that we all have lied at times. We have hurt other people, if not deliberately, then by displaying insensitivity. We have become angry when we felt mistreated or when a situation did not meet our expectations. Occasionally, we have put off an obligation inconveniencing or hurting others. And so forth. So it is understandable that one might ask whether I am stating or insinuating that anyone who is irresponsible is a "criminal." In fact, a reviewer of the 1984 edition of *Inside the Criminal Mind* wondered whether my description of criminality didn't embrace most of the population.

Another issue that arose in some readers' minds was the following: One can reasonably argue that the definition of criminality depends on whether an individual violates a law. And laws change. A person might engage in behavior that is considered a crime in one state but not in another. Even within the same jurisdiction, laws change. Marijuana use might be against the law today but not tomorrow. Thus the argument is that criminality is relative to place and time.

If I was not clear before, now is the time to address these issues. My work during the past thirty-four years does not deal just with violations of laws. It focuses on the minds of human beings and how they live. There are people who would be "criminals" no matter where they live. These are individuals for whom to be someone in life is to do the forbidden, whatever the forbidden might be. One man said that if rape were legalized, he wouldn't do it, but he declared that he would certainly do something else that was just as exciting and forbidden. The criminal thirsts for excitement and a buildup at the expense of others. No matter what the laws, mores, and customs of a particular society are, he will violate them and leave a trail of injury behind.

Let's talk about whether, by my framework, we are all criminals. Let's do this by looking at several aspects of the criminal mind. Responsible people occasionally lie to spare themselves embarrassment or to show themselves in a favorable light. There are the lies that grease the wheels of social interactions. I might ask whether you like the tie I am wearing. You might think it is hideous but reply that it is good looking because you don't want to hurt my feelings. I submit that there is a major difference between the person who tells an occasional lie and an individual who lies as a way of life. The criminal lies to cover his tracks (he has a lot to conceal) and to get out of a jam that he has created for himself. However, he also lies about the most minuscule matters even when there is no ostensible reason. He'll say that he went to one store when he really went to another. Some people in the mental health field will conclude that this is pathological or compulsive. This is not the case. The lie that makes no sense does make sense when you understand the mentality of the liar. The criminal lies in order to preserve a view of himself and the world. He derives a sense of power from lying, in believing he is pulling the wool over the eyes of others.

The same is true with the other characteristics. They exist along a continuum, just like lying. For example, at times we put off meeting obligations or ignore them completely. Others are harmed by this behavior. The criminal has no concept of obligation! Everything is about him—what he wants and when he wants it. Failing to put himself in the place of others except for the most self-serving purposes, the criminal constantly defaults on obligations because he doesn't recognize that he has them to begin with.

Occasionally, we have hurt other people inadvertently or perhaps out of vindictiveness. Usually, we have regrets. The criminal leaves carnage in his wake as he pursues the excitement and the power and control that he constantly craves. To him, injury is leaving a person lying in a pool of blood. He has no idea of the physical, financial, and emotional impact on his immediate victims and the ripple effect on others. No matter how many victims he has and how much damage he does, the criminal has little, if any, remorse and continues to regard himself as a good person.

As you read *Inside the Criminal Mind,* it is important to bear in mind that, as with so much else in life, the characteristics described exist by degree. Thus, there is a spectrum—from the person who rarely engages in the thinking and behavior being cited to the individual for whom that thinking and behavior has become part of his way of life. If a man, woman, or youngster is extreme in all the characteristics I am describing, the whole is greater than the sum of the parts. The result is a human being who holds a radically different view of himself and the world from a person who lives a basically responsible life.

I ask the reader to keep the above in mind as he reads this book and enters into the mind of the criminal.

PREFACE TO THE NEW EDITION

COLLEAGUES AND FRIENDS have asked me why I am writing this book twenty years after the first edition was published. Have I changed my views, they wonder. In short, what's new?

A change has occurred in the public's attitude toward crime, in that there is a greater demand to hold offenders accountable, regardless of age, and impose appropriate punishment, including banishment for some of the worst to new "super-max" facilities. When a shocking crime grabs the headlines, the "why" question continues to remain foremost in the public mind. When crimes of a less sensational nature are committed, the perpetrator still is someone's son, daughter, relative, friend, student, or co-worker. The same questions arise. Why did the person act as he did? Why is he the way he is? Then, out from under the rocks comes crawling a conventional wisdom that has been around for decades purporting to answer that very question: Why?

There still is an undying adherence to the view that environment and mental illness cause people to commit crimes. This is based on a belief that the criminal is basically a good guy who is pushed by adversity into doing terrible things. Clinging to this premise, proponents are perpetually coming up with new factors that they think propel otherwise decent people into crime. Thus the conclusion that the criminal is as much a victim as a victimizer. If the criminal didn't have enough excuses of his own for his heinous acts, society supplies more. Policies and programs still are based on this conventional wisdom and, as before, they continue to fail. I shall discuss how this happens. Moreover, I shall also describe how, by adhering to the conventional wisdom, parents, educators, counselors, employers, and others make their own jobs even more difficult than they already are.

What is new in the search for causal factors are studies suggestive of a genetic or other biological basis for criminal behavior. Research into the functioning of the brain, the role of neurotransmitters, and other biological factors may shed light on the origins of criminal behavior. People have been wary of such research and the implications of its findings. We still lack conclusive evidence about a link between biological factors and criminality. Even if such a connection were established, it would not portend that human beings are destined from birth to end up in the penitentiary. Biology need not be destiny. I have given some attention to this subject in this new edition of my book.

After spending more than three decades evaluating and treating offenders, my understanding of the criminal mind has been confirmed repeatedly. The person who makes crime a way of life has a radically different way of thinking from the individual who behaves responsibly. The two mentalities are so different, it's as though the criminal were a different breed.

I have been asked repeatedly about the extent to which the concepts in the first edition of this book apply to female offenders. Between 1990 and 2000, the number of females in prison has more than doubled.[1] Clearly, human nature has not changed, but judicial philosophy and penal practices have. Female offenders were often diverted to programs outside the criminal justice system, especially if they had children. With increasing emphasis on equal rights and opportunities for women in all areas of life, females who break the law are now treated more like their male counterparts. Whatever the prevailing philosophy and practices have been toward female offenders, the thinking patterns that give rise to criminal behavior are identical in both sexes.

The criminal seeks excitement by doing the forbidden at the expense of others. Living a life that requires effort to overcome adversity, considering the impact of one's own behavior on others, and listening to one's conscience are totally alien to him. The criminal perpetually maneuvers to prop up an ever-precarious image of himself as unique and powerful. In his ongoing attempts at self-aggrandizement, he cares not whom he hurts. To him, the world and its people are to be controlled like pawns on his own personal chessboard. Although he envies the trappings of success, he rejects taking a responsible path to earn them. "Take my crime away, and you take my world away," said one offender.

After spending hours interviewing men and women who have committed a vast array of offenses, ranging in seriousness from petty shoplifting to serial murder, I am now able to draw upon hundreds of new cases for this revised edition. I shall devote attention to arenas in which the criminal mind functions were either briefly addressed or not included before: stalking, domestic violence, hate crimes, so-called white-collar crime, and abuse of legitimately gained authority and trust by professionals. Criminals have related how they take advantage of new technology in casing out people and places to pursue their objectives.

I devote an entire chapter to the effects of mind-altering substances on individuals with a criminal mind. The criminal is far more addicted to a way of life than to a particular substance. If he were to cease all drug use, his criminal mentality would remain operative. I take issue with the "disease" concept of addiction in that it interposes a major barrier to change in dealing with the criminal.

Mental health professionals are frequently involved in the evaluation of offenders who commit bizarre or seemingly out-of-character crimes. At issue is whether such depraved individuals should be held responsible for their offenses. New controversies have arisen over whether offenders suffer from a "bipolar disorder"; whether repeat offenses by the same perpetrators stem from compulsions perhaps resulting from brain dysfunction; and what criteria to use in determining whether an offender is truly mentally retarded and thus not responsible. I address these matters in chapter 9, "Getting Over on the Shrinks."

Writing about crime after September 11, 2001, it is impossible to ignore the implications of my studies with respect to terrorism. After all, criminals are terrorists. Serial rapists, arsonists, wife batterers, and perpetrators of numerous other crimes terrorize people, whether they keep an individual in a state of constant fear or spread fear throughout a community. I have not interviewed heads of states who terrorize their own citizens, nor have I interviewed international terrorists. However, it is not much of a stretch to surmise that many such individuals have criminal minds that they disguise by promoting their "cause." I have devoted a separate new chapter to this subject.

I continue to urge that in order to think clearly about crime, we must return to basics and understand what criminals are really like. We must discard labels and diagnoses, and cease the fancy theorizing we use to convince ourselves that we are clever when actually we are far more clever than correct. A basic understanding of who criminals really are continues to be lost in a fog of theoretical speculation and political rhetoric often promulgated by people who have no clue how criminals think.

Public opinion about the feasibility of rehabilitating criminals remains deeply divided. While some voices clamor for ever-tougher punishment, others strongly advocate providing offenders with extensive opportunities for change. Correctional institutions reflect different philosophies, with some serving as little more than human warehouses while others are multimillion-dollar facilities that involve offenders in a multitude of programs throughout the day. I have discovered over the years that professionals working in juvenile and adult correctional programs throughout the United States who endeavor to help criminals change have incorporated my approach to identifying and correcting thinking errors.

I hope that new readers who discover this book will find it informative. And I hope that readers of the 1984 edition who return for an update will find enough new to make another reading worthwhile.

Stanton E. Samenow
Alexandria, Virginia
March 2004

IT WAS 1968, and I had received my doctorate in clinical psychology. My internship had been spent in an adolescent psychiatric unit in Ann Arbor, Michigan. Eager and idealistic, I went to work at my first full-time professional job, serving as chief psychologist in a young-adult unit at Northville State Hospital near Detroit. My clinical training had led me to become a dyed-in-the-wool Freudian.

In my new position at Northville, I was asked to diagnose and treat eighteen- to twenty-year-olds both from Detroit's inner city and from its suburbs. Many of these youths had been in trouble with the courts for antisocial behavior, but had been regarded as sick rather than as delinquents. I plunged into treating them, applying the concepts and techniques I had studied in graduate school and picked up by being a patient in psychoanalysis. I was repeatedly exposed to some rather raw slices of life, but I didn't see much improvement in my patients, who stubbornly clung to their disordered ways of thinking and acting. As I approached the termination of my work at Northville, it was time to decide what I wanted to do next.

Several years before, my father had introduced me to Dr. Samuel Yochelson, a friend of his from college days. At age fifty-five Dr. Yochelson had given up a large, successful private practice in Buffalo, New York, to begin what he regarded as a "second career" in psychiatry. From treating well-to-do corporate executives, he had moved to Washington, D.C., to direct a research project in which he would study and treat people who had committed serious crimes. His work was based at St. Elizabeths Hospital, an immense federal psychiatric facility in Washington, D.C.

Knowing that I was pondering whether to remain in Michigan or go elsewhere, Dr. Yochelson invited me to become his associate in the Program for the Investigation of Criminal Behavior. Because I had no interest in criminals, I turned him down. Nevertheless, Yochelson asked me to visit St. Elizabeths with an open mind to see what he was doing. I had come to know this man well during the past six years. I had heard him speak with great passion about his work and found him enormously likable, brilliant, and fascinating. I read some of his clinical notes and talked with a young man who, having been treated by Yochelson, had changed drastically since setting fires that had done millions of dollars' worth of damage. It seemed to me that I was being offered a singular opportunity. Yochelson told me that if I joined him, I would come to understand why I had failed in my treatment efforts with so many adolescents in Michigan. While job hunting, I had visited a number of East Coast and West Coast psychiatric centers that had adolescent units. At all of them I saw corroboration for my observation that a shift was taking place in the type of adolescent being referred for treatment. No longer did psychotic or intensely neurotic youths populate the wards in large numbers. More and more, psychiatrists and psychologists were being asked to treat teenagers who were truants, thieves, and drug users. These kids were in conflict with society, not suffering from internal psychological conflicts.

Confidently, Dr. Yochelson predicted that by working with him I would become equipped with concepts and techniques that would be more effective with such people than anything else I had learned. Still, I wasn't too keen on the idea of committing myself to a project that entailed studying and eventually treating murderers, bank robbers, rapists, and drug traffickers. I think I regarded them as a pretty hopeless bunch. Why not devote myself to people who were desperately asking for help and who would change, I thought. Finally, though, admiration for Dr. Yochelson as a human being was the decisive factor. He clearly had embarked on a radically different path and was having some success with men whom others had given up on. In late January 1970, I moved to Washington and reported for work at St. Elizabeths as a clinical research psychologist.

When I began this work, I believed that criminal behavior was a symptom of buried conflicts that had resulted from early traumas and deprivation of one sort or another. I thought that people who turned to crime were victims of a psychological disorder, an oppressive social environment, or both. From my work in Michigan with inner-city youths, I saw crime as being almost a normal, if not excusable, reaction to the grinding poverty, instability, and despair that pervaded their lives. On the other hand, I thought that kids who were from more advantaged backgrounds had been scarred by bad parenting and led astray by peer pressure.

When it came to understanding Yochelson's "crooks," as he referred to them, I discovered that I had to unlearn nearly everything I had learned in graduate school. Only reluctantly did I do so, debating many points along the way. But Dr. Yochelson told me that he had had to do exactly the same thing. His decades of psychiatric practice had left him unequipped to deal with these difficult patients. As he abandoned what he had long thought and practiced, he developed new methods to understand and treat people who had made crime a way of life.

During the six and a half years that I was Dr. Yochelson's associate, he and I worked on a three-volume technical work. We titled the first chapter of Volume 1 "The Reluctant Converts," disclosing our extreme reluctance to abandon our sacred theoretical cows and how he, and later I, gradually led those sacred cows to pasture and slaughtered them. We then presented in detail an entirely new approach to understanding and changing criminal behavior.

The essence of this approach is that criminals choose to commit crimes. Crime resides within the person and is "caused" by the way he thinks, not by his environment. Criminals think differently from "responsible" people. What must change is how the offender views himself and the world. Focusing on forces outside the criminal is futile. We found the conventional psychological and sociological formulations about crime and its causes to be erroneous and counterproductive because they provided excuses. In short, we did a 180-degree turn in our thinking about crime and its causes. From regarding criminals as

victims we saw that instead they were victimizers who had freely chosen their way of life. Dr. Yochelson piloted a set of procedures that
resulted in career criminals willingly changing their thinking so that
they lived without injuring others and became responsible members of
society.

Dr. Yochelson first had contact with these men at a time in their lives
when things were going badly for them. They were about to be sentenced by the court, were already locked up, or had been faced with
the loss of something valuable to them, such as a family or a career. In
his initial interview, Yochelson asked few questions of the criminal, but
instead presented him with so accurate a picture of himself that the
criminal could do nothing but agree. From then on, his objective was
to teach these men to examine and change patterns of thinking that in
the past had led to criminal behavior. Dr. Yochelson taught the criminals to become aware of and write down their day-to-day thinking
without editing it in a self-serving manner. Daily, in small groups, the
criminals reported that thinking, and Yochelson identified the "errors"
and taught them corrections. He also instructed them in how to deter
the massive amount of criminal thinking that occurred daily.

As the men saw themselves realistically, they became fed up with
their old ways and made efforts to change. Their progress was not rapid
or smooth, for even though they did not want to return to crime, they
did not find living responsibly particularly appealing either—at least not
for a while. The criminals had been accustomed to instant results in
whatever they undertook, and these were not forthcoming. As they
developed new patterns of thought and behavior, they slowly found
that there were rewards, tangible and intangible. They did not have to
look over their shoulders for the police, and they felt "clean." The
criminals discovered that effort, competence, and reliability were usually rewarded and that they could accomplish worthwhile things without deception or intimidation. Responsible people, especially members
of their families, began to trust them and react to them differently. The
men were promoted in their jobs and began to acquire material possessions honestly. Gradually, criminal patterns were abandoned, and
they acquired a new set of values by which they could live responsibly.

Dr. Yochelson did not live to see his work receive national recognition in the media and in professional circles. On his first out-of-town

speaking trip, his heart failed and he died. After Dr. Yochelson's death, I stayed at St. Elizabeths to complete the project. I then left the hospital to enter private practice, but continued to evaluate and treat antisocial people. I worked with adult offenders while also pursuing my earlier interest in adolescents. But now, as Yochelson had predicted, I was in a position to see adolescent crime in a new light.

In the St. Elizabeths study, our subjects were 255 adult men, half of whom were patients hospitalized as not guilty by reason of insanity or incompetent to stand trial; the others came to us through agencies such as probation, the courts, mental health, and social service. In my clinical practice during the last five years, I have evaluated and treated several hundred offenders referred to me by courts, schools, lawyers, mental health centers, and word of mouth. Although I have treated and evaluated female offenders, they represent no more than 10 percent of my clients. In this book, I have chosen to speak in terms of male offenders, the group with whom I have had more experience. However, my clinical work with female offenders, limited as it is, leads me to conclude that the same thinking patterns underlie the criminal behavior of both male and female offenders. I have also been told by people who work in correctional centers for females that the concepts of Dr. Yochelson's work are totally applicable.

Throughout the United States and Canada, interest in the St. Elizabeths work increased. I was asked to talk about this work and consult with people in a variety of fields. Next to the economy, crime has been the number-one social issue. I found inquiries pouring in not only from criminal justice and mental health professionals, but also from lawyers, judges, law enforcement agencies, educators, clergymen, and citizens' groups. Crime was escalating to new heights not only in the cities but also in the suburbs and rural areas. Fears that crime was engulfing our civilization had led to a crisis attitude of "do something now, and fast."

Federal monies were pouring into law enforcement and correctional programs, with billions of dollars provided annually by the now-defunct Law Enforcement Assistance Administration. Criminal justice programs proliferated at America's colleges, and professional training programs expanded. The 1960s had been an era of prison reform, and there was a surge of interest in rehabilitating offenders rather than just locking them up and "warehousing" them. Offenders were offered a smorgasbord of opportunities to develop skills and change their lives. In the 1970s, attempts were made to assess how effective rehabilitation was, and then the rehabilitative bubble burst. "Nothing works" was the grim conclusion of many evaluations, and the death knell of rehabilitation sounded. The courts were seen as having gone soft on criminals, and other parts of the criminal justice system were accused of coddling criminals. The cry came for stiff determinate sentencing, firmer parole guidelines, habitual offender laws that mandated long sentences, preventive detention, reinstitution of the death penalty, and trying as adults teenagers who committed violent crimes.

Sensing the mood of their constituents, politicians began to talk more of "law and order," less of rehabilitation. The political pendulum was swinging to the right on this issue as well as others. If the rehabilitation movement wasn't already terminal, a troubled economy and a new consciousness of limited resources dealt it a nearly lethal blow. But the desire to help criminals change was never totally snuffed out. And it is a good thing, because every man, woman, or child who is under court supervision for committing a crime will one day be released unless he has a sentence of death or life without parole. Studies show that most repeat offenders, even after prison, will continue to prey upon the community, and the costs, not measurable in dollars alone, will continue to be astronomical. Society cannot afford to give up looking for ways to help criminals become responsible, productive citizens.

While working with Dr. Yochelson, I saw impressive results as hardcore criminals changed 180 degrees to become responsible citizens. Dr. Yochelson's approach was a radical departure from anything I knew of that was being done in the United States.

In discussing this work in the United States, Canada, and England, I have been perceived both as a dewy-eyed, liberal reformer and as a hard-line reactionary, although I am neither. Dr. Yochelson's work can be responded to in political terms, but it is apolitical. It is a new approach that warrants serious attention.

I look back and realize that when I began this work I had beliefs and preconceptions about crime and criminals. I discovered that years of study and training both at Yale University and the University of

Michigan had been valuable to me in treating people who were neurotic and psychotic. But most of what I had learned had to be discarded to deal with a different type of person—the individual who makes crime a way of life. Only when I understood with whom I was dealing could I be effective in helping some criminals change. It is this knowledge that I want to share. I want you to consider what I have to say with an open mind. I ask you to bear in mind our nation's many failures to cope with criminals. In writing this book, I have as background thirteen years of experience. I am drawing not just on the St. Elizabeths study but most heavily on my observations during the last four years as I have evaluated and treated dozens of offenders. I am also drawing on the hundreds of conversations I have had with prison wardens, mental health professionals, correctional officers, law enforcement agents, court services workers, judges, educators, clergymen, social service workers, politicians, and adult and juvenile offenders and their families. In crossing this country many times to talk with and train people, I have found that most of them have not abandoned hope. They fervently desire to come to terms with this problem, which threatens to destroy the very fabric of our society. I hope this book will reinforce that hope and help them and others to see what can and must be done.

Stanton E. Samenow
Alexandria, Virginia
April 1983

INSIDE THE CRIMINAL MIND

1

THE BASIC MYTHS

ABOUT CRIMINALS

IN NEARLY A HALF-CENTURY, little has changed in terms of deeply ingrained beliefs about the causes of crime. In the classic, still often performed, 1957 musical *West Side Story,* Stephen Sondheim parodied what then was the current thinking about juvenile delinquency in the song "Gee, Officer Krupke." Delinquents were punks because their fathers were drunks. They were misunderstood rather than no good. They were suffering from a "social disease," and society "had played [them] a terrible trick." They needed an analyst, not a judge, because it was "just [their] neurosis" acting up. In short, their criminal behavior was regarded as symptomatic of a deep-seated psychological or sociological problem. In this chapter I shall briefly discuss this proposition. In subsequent chapters I shall examine them in greater detail and show that the prevalent thinking about crime has been and still is loaded with fundamental misconceptions resulting in devastating consequences for society.

A man abducts, rapes, and murders a little girl. We, the public, may be so revolted by the gruesomeness of the crime that we conclude only a sick person could be capable of such an act. But our personal gut reaction shows no insight into, or understanding of, what really went on in this individual's mind as he planned and executed the crime. True, what the perpetrator inflicted upon this child is not "normal" behavior. But what does "sick" really mean? A detailed and lengthy examination of the mind of a criminal will reveal that, no matter how bizarre or repugnant the crime, he is rational, calculating, and deliberate in his actions—not mentally ill.

Criminals know right from wrong. In fact, some know the laws better than their lawyers do. But they believe that whatever they want to do at any given time is right for them. Their crimes require logic and self-control.

Some crimes happen so fast and with such frequency that they appear to be compulsive. A person may steal so often that others become convinced that he is the victim of an irresistible impulse and therefore a "kleptomaniac." But a thorough mental examination would show that he is simply a habitual thief, skilled at what he does. He can case out a situation with a glance, then quickly make off with whatever he wants. A habit is not a compulsion. On any occasion, the thief can refrain from stealing if he is in imminent danger of getting caught. And if he decides to give up stealing for a while and lie low, he will succeed in doing so.

The sudden and violent crime of passion has been considered a case of temporary insanity because the perpetrator acts totally out of character. But again, appearance belies reality.

A man murders his wife in the heat of an argument. He has not murdered anyone before, and statistical trends would project that he will not murder again. It is true that the date, time, and place of the homicide were not planned. But an examination of this man would show that on several occasions he had shoved her and often wished her dead. In addition, he is a person who frequently has fantasies of evening the score violently whenever he believes that anyone has crossed him. He did not act totally out of character when he murdered his wife. He was not seized by an alien, uncontrollable impulse. In his thinking, there was precedent for such a crime. An individual with even worse problems, but with a different personality makeup, would have resolved them differently. For example, one man whose family I evaluated during a child custody dispute discovered that his wife was spending hours on the Internet involved with a man whom she met and had sex with, then announced her plan to spend the rest of her life with him.

Although her husband was emotionally devastated and irate, he neither threatened nor attacked her. He proceeded through the legal system toward divorce and obtaining custody of his daughter.

If criminals are not mentally ill, aren't they nevertheless victims of poverty, divorce, racism, and a society that denies them opportunities? Since the late nineteenth century, there has been a prevalent opinion that society is more to blame for crime than the criminal. But criminality is not limited to any particular societal group, as the 3.2 million arrests during 1999 demonstrate.[1]

Sociologists assert that the inner-city youngster responds with rage to a society that has excluded him from the mainstream and put the American dream beyond his reach. Some even contend that crime is a normal and adaptive response to growing up in the soul-searing conditions of places like Watts and the South Bronx. They observe that correctional institutions contain a disproportionately large number of inmates who are poor and from minority groups. These inmates are seen as casualties of a society that has robbed them of hope and virtually forced them into crime just so they can survive.

Suburban delinquents are also regarded as victims—of intense pressures to compete, of materialism, of parents who neglect them or push them to grow up too fast, or are overly protective. These adolescents are perceived as rebelling not only against their parents but against middle-class values, seeking meaning instead through kicks and thrills.

If it isn't grinding poverty that causes crime, then its opposite—overindulgence—is cited as the cause. As developing nations become increasingly industrialized and their citizens become prosperous, crimes that were rare burst into headlines. In a *Bangkok Post* article about two tragic shooting sprees, the writer conjectured that "Western-style teenage crime" was emerging in Thailand because Thai children were so indulged that they would "snap" when confronted by life's hardships.[2] Whether a child is deprived or pampered tells us nothing about how he will turn out. Most children who grow up in poverty and most indulged children become independent, resourceful, and responsible.

What of the observation that a disproportionate number of people incarcerated for crimes are both poor and from minority groups? Does this make a commentary on those groups? Or does it prove that the criminal justice system is racist? To whatever extent inequities exist, they need to be corrected. During the past thirty-three years I have focused on individuals, not groups. While interviewing and evaluating members of various ethnic and racial groups, I have found that in nearly every case members of the offender's own family have been law-abiding. The critical factor in becoming a criminal justice statistic is not race or ethnicity; it is the character of the individual and the choices he makes. It is unwarranted and racist to assume that because a person is poor and black (or brown, red, or yellow) he is inadequate to cope responsibly with his environment and therefore can hardly help but become a criminal.

Peer pressure is seen as a critical factor in the lives of youngsters from all social classes who turn to crime. Experts point out that some subcultures reward being daring and tough, and not living by a work ethic. Kids learn about crime from one another; they are schooled in the streets and go along with the crowd in order to acquire self-esteem and a sense of belonging. The belief that crime is contagious like a disease is more than a century old.

Every social institution has been blamed for contributing to crime. Schools have been singled out as forcing into crime youngsters who don't fit the academic mold. Churches have been accused of not providing leadership to wayward youth and to the community at large. Newspapers, television, and the movies have been charged with glamorizing crime. American business and advertising have been accused of contributing to distorted values and therefore to crime.

Economic hard times have been associated with an increase in crime. But then so have good times. Financial setbacks are said to push despondent people over the edge. But then, when times are booming, it has been thought that the gap between the "haves" and "have nots" widens and the latter, out of resentment, turn to crime. Economic pressures are also seen as contributing to crime by forcing mothers to go to work, further weakening the family. Their children have less supervision and guidance than before, and are even more vulnerable to peer pressure.

Economic adversity affects us all. We may be pushed to work longer hours or to take a second job. Women who prefer to be at home may have little choice but to go to work. Families may have to make do with less and watch goals slip further out of reach, and people on fixed incomes bear a special burden. The responsible person responds to economic pressures by sacrifice and hard work. Even for him, temptation may be stronger to step outside the law as the economic squeeze grows tighter. Ultimately, however, it comes down to how each person chooses to deal with the circumstances he faces.

Sociological explanations for crime, plausible as they may seem, are simplistic. If they were correct, we'd have far more criminals than we do. Criminals come from all kinds of families and neighborhoods. Most poor people are law-abiding, and most kids from divorced parents are not delinquents. Children may bear the scars of neglect and deprivation for life, but most do not become criminals. The environment does have some effect. For instance, it can provide greater or fewer opportunities for crime to occur—greater or lesser deterrence. But people perceive and react to similar conditions of life very differently. A family may reside in a neighborhood where gangs roam the streets and where drugs are as easy to come by as cigarettes. The father may have deserted and the mother may collect welfare. Yet not all the children in that family turn to crime. In suburbia, a family may be close emotionally and well off financially, but that is not enough to keep one of the youngsters from using drugs, stealing, and destroying property. In an area where firearms and drugs are readily available, most residents choose to use neither. The criminal seizes upon opportunities that others shun. More critical than the environment itself is how the individual chooses to respond to whatever the circumstances are.

We have seen other instances of when a major change in the environment suppresses crime or permits it to flourish even throughout an entire country. When totalitarian governments with their despots fall from power and are replaced by democratic regimes, the citizenry has more freedom. The responsible person has opportunity to develop his talents and pursue interests that he couldn't before. The person who is criminally inclined also has greater freedom and will pursue whatever interests him. This in part explains the surge in crime reported in countries that previously had oppressive governments.[3]

Criminals claim that they were rejected by parents, neighbors, schools, and employers, but rarely does a criminal say why he was rejected. Even as a young child, he was sneaky and defiant, and the older he grew, the more he lied to his parents, stole and destroyed their property, and threatened them. He made life at home unbearable as he turned even innocuous requests into a battleground. He conned his parents to get whatever he wanted, or else he wore them down through endless argument. It was the criminal who rejected his parents rather than vice versa.

Not only did he reject his family, but he rejected the kids in the neighborhood who acted responsibly. He considered them uninteresting, their lives boring. He gravitated to more-adventurous youngsters, many of whom were older than he. Crime is not contagious like chicken pox. Even in crime-infested neighborhoods, there are youngsters who want no part of the action. Sure, there is the desire to belong to the crowd, but the question is which crowd. Criminals are not forced into crime by other people. They *choose* the companions they like and admire.

The school does not reject the antisocial youngster until he is impossible to deal with. Many criminals have no use for school whatsoever. Some remain in school, then use their education to gain entree into circles where they find new victims. More commonly, delinquent youngsters use the classroom as an arena for criminal activity by fighting, lying, stealing, and engaging in power plays against teachers and other pupils. Basically, for them, school is boring, its requirements stupid, the subjects meaningless. Just as the criminal rejects his parents, he does the same to his teachers. It is neither incompetent teachers nor an irrelevant curriculum that drives him out. In fact, the school may offer him an individually tailored program, but no matter what he is offered, it does not suit him. Finally, he is expelled for disruptive behavior or grows so bored that he quits.

The notion that people become criminals because they are shut out of the job market is an absurdity. In the first place, most unemployed people are not criminals. More to the point, perhaps, is that many criminals do not want to work. They may complain that without skills they can't find employment. (Of course, it was their choice not to remain in school to acquire those skills.) But, as many a probation officer will observe, usually jobs of some sort are available, but criminals find them too menial and beneath them.

Some criminals are highly educated and successful at their work. Their very success may serve as a cover for crime. If a person has a solid work record, he is generally regarded as responsible and stable. But even legitimately acquired money, recognition, and power are not sufficient incentives for a criminal to live within the law. The point is that what a person's environment offers or lacks is not decisive in his becoming a criminal.

The public often criticizes the media for making crime enticing by glorifying both specific crimes and criminals. There has long been intense concern about the high incidence of violence in television programs that reach children. In the aftermath of school shootings during the 1990s, television again came under scrutiny for its effect on children. One highly publicized study released in 2000 claimed to support the contention that television causes aggression.[4] But millions of people who frequently watch violence on television dramas, films, documentaries, and newscasts do not enact what they see.

A person already thinking about committing crimes may pick up ideas from the media, or become more confident about the feasibility of a particular crime. Fascinated and excited by the prospect of imitating and getting away with what he has watched on television or in a movie, he perpetrates what has come to be called a "copycat crime." Critical, though, is not what plays on the screen but what lies in the mind of the viewer. Television, movies, video games, magazines, or books will not turn a responsible person into a criminal. To believe otherwise is again to subscribe to the erroneous premise that external events easily shape human character.

So far, I have said that criminals are not mentally ill or hapless victims of oppressive social conditions. But psychiatrists, psychologists, counselors, and social workers still contend that a person is what he is largely because of his early experiences. They regard criminal behavior as "symptomatic" of conflicts that are rooted in childhood and remain unresolved.

Too long have the social sciences promulgated the view that a human organism comes into the world like a lump of clay to be shaped by external forces. This view renders us all victims! What it does accomplish is to offer a facile but erroneous explanation of behavior. If any of us had taken a criminal path, something could be found in our past to explain why we turned out as we did. If your child has problems, you will be faulted for your child-rearing practices, whatever they were. If you were strict, you will be told that your child has been affected by your harshness. If you were permissive, you will be accused of being too indulgent. If you were relatively democratic, you might be considered wishy-washy or even indifferent. Worst of all, you might be tagged as inconsistent, something that we are all guilty of to some extent. Psychology always has a clever theory about any bit of behavior, and offers an explanation, but only *after the fact*. There's the old line that if a patient arrives late for his psychotherapy appointment, he's resistant. If he's early, he's anxious. If he's on time, he's compulsive. Although sincere in trying to explain why we are the way we are, social scientists are often incorrect.

In varying degrees, all human beings suffer trauma as they grow up. But if a domineering mother or an inadequate father produces delinquent children, why is it that most children who have such parents aren't criminals? Psychologists stress the importance of parents as role models, especially fathers for their sons and mothers for their daughters. Yet many children with weak or irresponsible role models become honest, productive adults. Conversely, some children with strong, positive role models become criminals.

Am I saying that it doesn't matter what kind of role model a parent is? Hardly! We need to be the best role models possible. Most of our children will internalize the values that we attempt to inculcate in them. However, being a responsible role model does not guarantee the choices a child will make. Probably every reader knows a family where the parents are nurturing, caring, and responsible. These superb role models may have three children, two of whom have internalized what they have endeavored to teach them. But one child skips school, hangs out with troublemakers, uses drugs, then lies about his activities. This child has chosen to reject all that he has been taught, and embarks on an agenda of his own.

When interviewed after being apprehended, criminals invariably relate a litany of horrors about their early lives. They seize upon hardships, real or made up, to justify their acts against society. Portraying themselves as victims, they seek sympathy and expect to absolve themselves of culpability.

Some of society's chronic lawbreakers do come from volatile, conflict-ridden families where they have suffered abuse. But that is likely to be only part of the story. In their accounts, they relate only what others inflicted upon them, omitting what they did to make a bad situation even worse. A man may describe savage beatings by a maniacal father, but he never discloses how he provoked such treatment. He conceals the fact that he taunted, deceived, and defied his parents to the point that his frustrated father finally lashed out at him physically. A complete account might reveal that the criminal was the only child in the family to have received severe corporal punishment, whereas his siblings were generally well-behaved. This is not to defend harshness in discipline. It is, however, to suggest that we ought not to limit our inquiries to what parents have done to children, but strive to determine what children have done to their parents. Criminals contend that their parents did not understand them and failed to communicate with them. They are often believed, and as usual, the deficiency is attributed almost entirely to parents. If we could be invisible observers in the homes of delinquent youngsters, we might reach a different conclusion. As a child, the criminal shuts his parents out of his life because he doesn't want them or anyone else to know what he is up to. When a teenager skips school, hangs out at an arcade, joyrides, drinks, smokes pot, and steals from stores, it should be no surprise that he tells his parents little about his day's activities. In fact, he will respond to parental interest and concern with accusations that the parent is prying into his business. No matter how hard they try, mothers and fathers cannot penetrate the secrecy, and they discover that they do not know their own child. He remains the family mystery.

I want to make it very clear what I am saying. Probably most children who are mistreated suffer long-range effects, but not all are criminals. Some children are abused through no fault of their own by parents who are themselves criminals. Some of these children will become depressed, blaming themselves. Some will become anxious and withdrawn. Some may become aggressive. Although being abused has its aftermath, the fact is that most children have tremendous resilience. Behavioral scientists finally have taken note of this and researched the subject. For his book *Back to the Family*, Dr. Ray Guarendi interviewed members of what he calls America's happiest families.[5] He observed that some excellent parents had suffered abuse while growing up. Determined to learn from what happened to them, they did not repeat their own parents' harshness when they had children. Their "reverse resolve" inspired them to be excellent parents.

In short, psychological theory, in its current state, is more misleading than illuminating in explaining why people become criminals. Child raising is not a one-way street. The criminal shapes others more than they do him.

During the nineteenth century, many experts believed that people were born criminals. Attempts to identify criminals on the basis of facial or other physical features were discredited. However, the "bad seed" hypothesis never died. In the 1960s, for example, a controversy arose over whether criminals had special chromosome patterns. Evidence for an "XYY syndrome" or other chromosomal anomaly remains inconclusive.

Another belief long held by many in the professional community is that perhaps criminals suffer from a physiological dysfunction that may be hereditary or may result from physical trauma. The notion that some people are born criminals or are in some sense "constitutionally inferior" goes back to the nineteenth century. Currently, brain lesions or tumors, temporal lobe epilepsy, blood chemistry changes, glandular abnormality, hypoglycemia, low heart rate, and birth trauma are among the organic factors that have been linked to criminality, but conclusive evidence of such a linkage is still lacking. Of the many people who are afflicted with these conditions, few become criminals. The question of whether there might be a genetic predisposition toward criminality remains unanswered.

Another theory is that criminals are *inherently* less intelligent than the general population. One might think that this notion had been laid to rest long ago. Not so! In 1985 two Harvard professors declared, "There appears to be a clear and consistent link between criminality and low intelligence."[6] Empirical studies of criminals and noncriminals simply do not support such a proposition. For the most part, criminals are remarkable in their capacity to size up their environment in order to pursue objectives important to them. Their mental acumen and resourcefulness are striking to anyone privy to their complex, well-thought-out schemes. However, these attributes often do not translate into high scores on intelligence tests, which, in part, test mastery of basic information that most people acquire in school.

The alleged link between antisocial behavior and attention deficit hyperactivity disorder (ADHD) has received major attention during the past decade. This disorder, characterized by extreme difficulty in concentration and attention, is thought to arise from a brain malfunction that has a hereditary base. ADHD, if not a direct contributory factor to criminal behavior, has been cited as placing a youngster at risk for engaging in criminal acts.

This concept is flawed. No method exists to diagnose ADHD definitively, whether by a brain scan or some other test. I have interviewed antisocial children and adults wrongly considered to have ADHD. They proved perfectly able to concentrate on whatever interested them; they simply failed to pay attention to academic subjects that they found difficult or boring. Of course, it is possible for a person to have an attention problem and be a criminal, just as he can have cancer and heart disease and be a criminal. One condition does not cause the other.

Formulating conclusions about cause and effect can be extremely complicated, and it is inherently difficult to make a definitive finding. One claim is that suffering head injuries during childhood (e.g., through falls or bicycle accidents) has a causal relationship to a youngster's becoming a delinquent and a criminal.[7] John Douglas, a former head of the Federal Bureau of Investigation's Serial Crime Unit, commented about this issue, "You have to ask yourself—did this particular young man grow up to become a killer because he had a brain injury in childhood? Or did he sustain a brain injury in childhood because he was a reckless, aggressive kid?"[8]

No factor or set of factors—sociological, psychological, or biological—has proved sufficient to explain why a person becomes a criminal. So far, the search to pin down causation has been futile. But this does not stop people from coming up with ever more explanations, some seemingly plausible, others just plain kooky. We continue to be inundated by theories that offer excuses but explain nothing. Far more disturbing is that programs, laws, policies, and decisions about how to deal with criminals continue to be based upon these theories. The result: a tremendous waste of resources while crime continues in epidemic pro-portions.

What is clear is that criminals come from a wide variety of back-grounds—from the inner city, suburbia, rural areas, and small towns, and from any religious, racial, or ethnic group. They may grow up in close-knit families, unstable homes, or foster homes. They may be grade-school dropouts or college graduates, unemployed drifters or corporate executives. In most cases they have brothers, sisters, and next-door neighbors who grew up under similar circumstances but did not become criminals.

Despite a multitude of differences in their backgrounds and crime patterns, criminals are alike in one way: *how they think.* A gun-toting, uneducated criminal off the streets of Southeast Washington, D.C., and a crooked Georgetown business executive are extremely similar in their view of themselves and the world. This is not to deny individual dif-ferences among criminals in their aesthetic tastes, sexual practices, reli-gious observance, or favorite sports team. But all regard the world as a chessboard over which they have total control, and they perceive peo-ple as pawns to be pushed around at will. Trust, love, loyalty, and team-work are incompatible with their way of life. They scorn and exploit people who are kind, trusting, hardworking, and honest. Toward a few, they are sentimental but rarely considerate. Some of their most altruis-tic acts have sinister motives.

More than seventy years ago, the noted psychologist Alfred Adler observed, "With criminals, it is different: they have a private logic, a private intelligence. They are suffering from a wrong outlook upon the world, a wrong estimate of their own importance and the importance of other people." Adler went on to say that the criminal's crimes "fit in with his general conception of life."[9] Implied throughout Adler's writ-ing is the idea that people choose to be criminals, that they are in fact a different breed. Even in 1930, Adler's was a lone voice.

An argument has been made that evolution, favoring the survival of the fittest, evokes criminality that is innate to primates, humans being no exception. However, Dutch biologist Frans de Waal, observing chimpanzees and other apes for thousands of hours, watched these ani-mals getting along. Commenting on the implications of de Waal's work for people, Richard Conniff pointed out that, although a "quarrelsome species," humans are "endlessly working out the business of living together." Mankind has "a long history of empathy, reconciliation, cooperation, and morality."[10]

Psychology and sociology have long advanced the view that the criminal is basically like everyone else, but has turned antisocial because he has been traumatized or blocked by others in fulfilling his aspirations. Thus the criminal is perceived as a victim of forces and circumstances beyond his control. Those who hold such a view go a step further, asserting that we are all, in a sense, criminals because we lie, lust, and yield to temptation. But it is absurd to equate the rare small lie of the responsible person with the gigantic network of lies of the criminal. It is equally absurd to equate a child's pilferage of a candy bar with a delinquent's stealing practically everything that isn't nailed down. At some point we and the criminal are very different. He is far more extreme in that, for him, crime is a way of life, not an occasional aberration. It is misleading to claim that the criminal wants what the responsible person wants, that he values the same things a responsible person values. Both may desire wealth, but only one will work steadily and earnestly to acquire it and then use it responsibly. The criminal believes that he is entitled to it and grabs it any way he can, not caring whom he injures, and then thirsts for more. Both may desire a family life, but the responsible person shows the give-and-take, the empathy, and the selflessness that family life requires. The criminal pays lip service to love while demanding that his spouse and children cater to his demands and fulfill his wishes.

By taking the position that the criminal is a victim, society has provided him with excuses for crime and thereby supported his contention that he is not to blame. Partly to atone for its alleged injustices to the criminal, society has offered him countless opportunities to "rehabilitate" himself and enter the mainstream. Surprise has given way to despair as the criminal rejects the very opportunities that he rejected before (work, school, counseling), or else shamelessly exploits them while continuing to commit crimes.

Attempts to improve the environment, no matter how worthwhile, have not altered the criminal's personality. Psychological methods have been equally unsuccessful because therapists have mistakenly utilized concepts and techniques suited to patients with a very different character structure. In the more distant past, castration, lobotomy, and drugs were employed in hopes of altering biological forces within the criminal, but to little avail. The search for an effective medical treatment continues, but none has yet been found to be effective in changing the criminal's thinking so that he becomes a responsible human being.

The death knell of rehabilitation having sounded, the pendulum has been swinging the other way—to "lock 'em up and throw away the key." Given the high recidivism rate of criminals who were considered rehabilitated, such a sentiment is understandable.

What about the function of punishment? Arrest alone or confinement undoubtedly deters some offenders, but contact with the criminal justice system has little lasting impact on habitual offenders. Warehousing a criminal in an institution gets him off the streets for a while, but one day he will be released to wreak havoc again in society. Because prison is expensive—costing taxpayers the equivalent of a year's college tuition for every prisoner incarcerated—and because many prisons are dehumanizing, alternatives to incarceration are sought. What is termed "community-based corrections" features a smorgasbord of offerings—vocational training, schooling, counseling, psychotherapy—as well as accountability to a probation officer. Restitution and community service programs have proliferated as society considers finally not just criminals but people who are truly victims.

The more things change, the more they stay the same. The criminal's motivation is to avoid confinement. He sees his probation officer once every couple of weeks for a brief appointment. He may attend some programs if they are mandated by the court. And he may make restitution. But his personality does not change.

And so the criminal comes up against a world that either bleeds for him because he is a victim or else wants to remove him from the earth. Criminals have been imprisoned, educated, counseled, preached to, and even executed. All too often, decisions are made on the basis of misconceptions in an atmosphere of "do something now and do it fast."

A surprising number of people who deal with criminals do not know how criminals think. How a person behaves is determined largely by how he thinks. *Criminals think differently.* If we are thoroughly familiar with how they think, we are in a far better position to draft legislation, formulate policies, administer programs, render more informed decisions, and be more effective in direct contacts with criminals both in the institutions and in the community.

There is even a ray of hope that we can help some criminals change and become responsible citizens. But to undertake this task, we must see the criminal as the problem rather than single out society as the culprit for turning people into criminals. Our approach to change must be to help the criminal radically alter his self-concept and his view of the world. Some criminals can be "habilitated," that is, helped to acquire patterns of thinking that are totally foreign to them but are essential if they are to live responsibly.

2

PARENTS DON'T TURN
CHILDREN INTO CRIMINALS

DELINQUENT YOUNGSTERS COME from all social classes and from all kinds of homes. The variation in their upbringing is enormous. They differ from one another physically, in their talents and capabilities, and in many aspects of their personalities. Despite these differences, they are strikingly alike in that they all display the patterns that will be described in this chapter. This is true regardless of whether they come from the suburbs or the city, from well-to-do or poor parents, or from two-parent families or divorced parents, and regardless of whether their parents were strict or indulgent. Each of them thinks and acts differently from responsible members of his own family. At an early age, such a child begins making a series of choices to live a life that he considers exciting, a life in which he is determined to do whatever he wants, a life in which he ignores restraints and eventually turns against his family and scoffs at those who live responsible lives. He complains about unfair treatment and is perceived by others as a hapless victim of his parents' pathology or of a malfunctioning family unit. But this is not the case. The theories that purport to explain delinquency by blaming parents are misleading and potentially harmful. Such youngsters *choose* the life they want.

★   ★   ★

Many boys and girls defy their parents, tell lies, fight, succumb to temptation, and steal a candy bar or some other small item. However, this behavior does not become a way of life. The criminal child's departure from parental and societal expectations involves more than isolated acts. Beginning as early as the preschool years, *patterns* evolve that become part of a criminal life style. As a child, the criminal is a dynamo of energy, a being with an iron will, insistent upon taking charge, expecting others to indulge his every whim. His appetite for adventure is voracious. He takes risks, becomes embroiled in difficulties, and then demands to be bailed out and forgiven. No matter how his parents try to understand and guide him, they are thwarted at every turn. This youngster is unlike most other children, including his own sisters and brothers. While the others are seeking recognition through schoolwork, sports, or social activities, this child thumbs his nose at it all. He establishes himself by doing what is forbidden. His mother and father do not perceive a pattern unfolding, but assume that his waywardness is merely a stage of development. This "stage," however, never ends. The parents become the first in the criminal's string of victims. Only it is not a one-time victimization. The emotional turmoil of seeing their child injure others and jeopardize himself is like a persistent searing pain. The parents' interminable struggle to cope with this wayward youngster saps their energy, drains their finances, weakens their marriage, and harms their other children. But the criminal child remains unmoved and unaffected.

Case studies of criminal youngsters differ in their particulars, but they all reveal common patterns. The case of Bill, fifteen years old, is an example. He is the youngest of four children from a middle-class family. Both his parents are teachers. But there are youngsters just like him from inner-city and upper-class families.

There is nothing unusual about Bill's appearance—scraggly, shoulder-length blond hair and intense blue eyes. Like his contemporaries, he dresses in baggy pants, a colored T-shirt bearing an insignia or design such as a motorcycle, and sneakers gray from wear. You might find him bantering with a friend as he tinkers with parts of an old car, or he may be alone, slumped in an overstuffed chair, transfixed before a television screen. A stranger would find him easy to talk to, in fact quite charming. Usually he is stuffing candy bars or junk food into his mouth, or else he is smoking a cigarette. Few people would suspect that this teenager is a liar, thief, vandal, fighter, and pot pusher.

Although Bill has spent all of his fifteen years with his mother and father, he has never been interested in them as human beings. To him they are merely vehicles to gratify his rapidly shifting desires. As a young boy he expected his mom and dad to buy whatever he wanted. When he spotted a shiny red bicycle, he not only took for granted that he would own it, but, in his mind's eye, he was already pedaling it down the block, receiving jealous stares from other kids. Bill's parents did not believe in overindulging their children, but it was tough to say no to Bill and hold their ground. When he didn't get his way, he'd erupt into a tantrum, then pout, and generally make life miserable. His mother recalled a time when her boy implored her to buy him a toy gun for $1.39. When she refused, he was heartbroken. Later he snatched the gun off the counter. As he scurried toward the door, he was grabbed by a clerk who detained him. His mother describes her reaction to Bill today as being what it was years ago: "He makes us feel so irrational, so guilty." At seven, it was a toy gun. At fourteen, Bill had his mind set on a room with thousands of dollars' worth of furnishings. His parents told him that if he started earning the money, they'd help him out. His idea of working was quite different from theirs—he became a vendor of marijuana.

Bill always tried to get his way through a process his parents termed "negotiating." This was a one-sided ordeal, more like extortion, in which Bill tried to force his mother and father to make concessions by grinding them down through endless argument. Bill relished an argument the way he enjoyed chess. He was positive that if he persisted long enough he would vanquish his opposition. When the power of argument failed, Bill became belligerent and, as he got older, verbally abusive, calling his mother an "old bitch" and berating his father as a "bastard" and a "stupid old fool." But perhaps his most effective ploy was to promise his parents good behavior in exchange for whatever he wanted. Implied or explicit was that if he did not get his way he would continue to do whatever he pleased. For example, his mother told him to remove nails that protruded from a pair of shoes. (Bill drove these nails in deliberately so that he could kick an adversary during a fight.)

His response was "I don't give a shit. I'll take the nails out if you'll take me where I want to go. I don't get any cooperation from you, so you don't get any from me. Here, I've also got my chain for fuckin' up people's faces." Bill's parents were in essence being blackmailed. Either they transported their son to whatever place he chose at any outrageous time, or he would persist in behavior they disapproved of. This was typical of Bill's attempts to manipulate them.

Constantly, Bill demanded things on his own terms because that was how he thought life should be. He pressed his mom and dad to justify even a simple request. When ordered to do something, he regarded it as an imposition. "I'm not going to be your little nigger," he'd snap. If he complied, he expected great fanfare. Not getting it, his attitude was "Those slobs don't appreciate all that I do." He put off a chore until his parents tired of waiting and did it themselves. He developed an amazing knack for forgetting. A request made of him would slip from memory in ten minutes, but recollection was sharp for something that he had asked for ten weeks previously.

The older Bill got, the more blatant became his defiance. When he spat out "Fuck you," his parents had all they could do to control themselves, but as their anger subsided, they'd begin to wonder if they had been unreasonable after all. When they yelled, they felt guilty afterward. But if they ignored misbehavior, they also felt guilty. Reasoning always seemed to fail; nothing succeeded.

Bill regarded everything his family owned as belonging to him. He was well acquainted with the inside of his mother's pocketbook, having often rummaged for change without asking permission. Money was missing so often that his mother began taking her purse to bed with her. Bill became similarly familiar with his father's wallet. The amount he took depended on how much money was in the wallet. Once, when greed outweighed judgment, he swiped two twenty-dollar bills. His father confronted him, but backed down when his son looked at him with his large blue eyes and seemed totally devastated by the accusation. Bill then realized that he had a powerful psychological weapon. He said to a friend, "The next time he accuses me, I'll act heartbroken the way I did before, and he'll feel so fuckin' guilty." When money was hidden, Bill would find it, pawing through drawers and forcing open locks on file cabinets during his search. He was quite practiced in this, for at nine he had begun sampling the family liquor supply and had introduced his friends to various beverages. A locked liquor cabinet posed no obstacle; he'd unscrew the hinges and remove the entire door.

Although Bill considered others' property to be his own, anything that legitimately belonged to him he deemed sacred. His parents had repeatedly asked him to clean up his messy room. One Saturday afternoon when Bill was out with friends, his parents, unable to stand it any longer, entered his room with the intention of throwing out the trash and cleaning up the litter. While hanging up his son's windbreaker, Bill's father heard something drop. He looked down and saw a pipe and a small plastic bag with a substance that he suspected might be marijuana. When he and his wife confronted Bill with their discovery, Bill vehemently denied knowing anything about it, and refused to discuss the matter. His face contorted with rage, he cursed his mother and father for daring to invade his privacy. Determined to prevent any further parental intrusion, he purchased a small, lightweight file box with a lock in which to stash and safeguard his drug paraphernalia.

All children are self-centered and shape their parents' behavior by acting in a particular manner to get what they want. In their egocentricity, they focus on what matters to them immediately and drag their feet about doing anything disagreeable. Their parents frequently have to badger or even coerce them to do things, but most of these children do not become criminals.

Bill's family was headed by two devoted parents, both of whom had placed their offspring's welfare highest in their priorities. They spent considerable time with their children, and got along well with each other. There was no indication of the maternal deprivation or paternal inadequacy that is so often cited as contributing to the character development of delinquents. Bill's mother was a warm, giving woman who displayed both idealism and common sense in bringing up her four children. She spent a lot of time at home, placing family ahead of her part-time teaching and other activities. Bill's father was gentle and even-tempered. Despite his career and many other interests, such as singing, he treasured time with his children. Yet Bill belittled him, rejected him as a model of behavior, and spewed forth contempt for his entire way of life.

It has been claimed that children become delinquent because their parents overindulge them to the point that they continue to expect the world to cater to them. But like neglect, "spoiling" leads to different outcomes. Whereas some overindulged children remain self-centered and dependent on others, they do not function criminally. Other pampered youngsters are jolted into reality once they leave home, and they learn to become self-sufficient. Perhaps more to the point is that when a counselor attributes delinquent behavior to an overindulgent attitude of the parents, it is often based on appearance. The counselor sees that the youngster is behaving outrageously and seems to be getting away with it. But the counselor may not realize that for years the child has thwarted nearly all parental attempts at disciplining him. Rarely is he acting irresponsibly because the parents gave him free rein.

One counselor advised Bill's mother and father, "You just need to be strong parents." He saw that Bill was doing whatever he wanted, and assumed that his parents had been weak. The counselor hypothesized that unconsciously Bill was begging for restraint. It made a good theory. But it was not true. Both mother and father had long believed in the importance of setting limits and in being consistent. With Bill, they found themselves being stricter than they had ever intended. When they tightened up, more of Bill's behavior went underground. Their determination to be "strong parents" with Bill had borne no fruit. They had even initiated a "point system" of rewarding responsible behavior by granting him privileges and restoring freedom that he had previously handled badly. But to no avail. It was Bill who modified his parents' behavior. So it is with any child of Bill's kind, regardless of social class or family structure. He dangles the incentive of good behavior in order to get what he wants. The promise of being good is effective bait, allowing him to extract trust, money, and material possessions. It is blackmail, a matter of the child dangling the prospect of peace while determining the price the parents will pay. As parental stamina and self-confidence wane, concessions mount.

It has been theorized that a child becomes delinquent despite parental discipline because, on an unconscious level, the parents are deriving vicarious gratification of their own forbidden wishes.[1] Repeated contact in a clinical setting with Bill's parents revealed self-aware human beings, people with integrity who were struggling to rear their children responsibly. If they seemed to condone some of their son's irresponsibility by occasionally looking the other way, it was because over the years they had grown weary of being forced by Bill into the roles of detective, prosecutor, and judge. This was a far cry from vicarious enjoyment of their son's deviance. If the theory about unconscious gratification is correct, what are its implications? Must parents of delinquents undergo years of intensive psychotherapy to get in touch with their unconscious? Even if they did, would that ensure a change in the child? The only result of such a theory is to shift responsibility from the child to the parents. The youngster's criminal behavior persists.

Family systems theory suggests that one member's problems are symptomatic of a disturbance in the entire family. Thus a child may become delinquent because he has become the scapegoat whom the family unconsciously selects to act out the other members' forbidden fantasies and impulses. It may well be that a disturbed family system can give rise to isolated cases of antisocial behavior, but there is as yet no convincing evidence from treating entire families that the disturbed system is the cause of a child's expanding and intensifying *patterns* of delinquent activity. In fact, what often happens in treatment is that the delinquent child scapegoats the family. While insisting that he is all right and does not require treatment, he blames the family for being "sick."

Bill's family entered family therapy, where it was assumed from the start that a disturbed child meant that mother and father had deep-seated problems. His parents felt as if they were on trial as Bill recited his list of grievances against them. Following the lead of the counselor, he was adept at shifting the spotlight to his mother and father in the quest to identify the cause of his behavior. With mom and dad becoming the focus, they had more problems because of the treatment than they ever before imagined, and consequently even more guilt, bitterness, anger, and despair. The most outrageous part of it was the counselor's assumption that because Bill was so clearly out of control, they were inadequate parents. Bill's mother still smarts from the sting of those sessions, which they endured while Bill quit. This left them with a counselor who offered no suggestions that were any different from what they had been doing for years. Bill's parents did not give up after this experience, but consulted other mental health practitioners. The results were usually the same. Bill could be bribed to attend one or two sessions, where he'd hurl accusations at them, and then they became the patients.

One clinician who evaluated Bill arrived at the following psychodynamic formulation: "Bill's behavior may be understood not so much as the product of indulgence but rather of subtle demands for high performance in the presence of role models portraying and expecting excellence." This was a complicated way of saying that his parents, who were teachers, set unrealistically high standards and applied too much pressure on their son. At first glance, this seems a plausible theory. But it had nothing to do with the facts. Like most parents, Bill's mother and father wanted their children to do well at whatever they undertook. But doing well did not necessarily mean that Bill had to be a straight-A student and later a teacher. His parents' aspirations were far more modest. They hoped that Bill would get along with other people and be competent at whatever life work he chose. As they discovered Bill's considerable mechanical aptitude and interest in electronics, they encouraged him and bought him equipment, to which he reacted first with a flash of enthusiasm and then with total lack of interest.

Bill was the biological offspring of two loving, devoted parents. Despite the devotion, love, time, energy, and money that his mother and father poured into their unending effort to help him, Bill turned out to be an adult criminal.

A significant number of offenders whom I have interviewed were adopted. I have talked with many counselors and therapists who believed that their clients' feelings about adoption were related to their antisocial conduct. They theorized that their clients resented (even if unconsciously) being abandoned by their biological parents, and always felt dispossessed and not totally accepted by their adoptive family. Anything is possible, but such theorizing represents still another forced effort to make sense of disturbing behavior, the proverbial jamming a square peg into a round hole. In different ways, children who are adopted come to terms with this aspect of their lives. Most adopted boys and girls accept what happened to them and are grateful to have been raised by loving parents. They grow up to be responsible human beings. I know a young man whose adoptive parents provided him love, guidance, a wonderful home and community in which to grow up, and, because of their affluence, more opportunities than many children, adopted or not, ever have. This youth rejected it all. While he was in residential treatment, a well-intentioned therapist did his utmost to convince this young man that his conflicts over being adopted lay at the root of his lying, stealing, and drug use. This emphasis diverted the focus from vital, even life-threatening issues and derailed the process of change.

A mental health professional can always fish for some underlying problem and spot conflict in any family. But to conclude that criminal behavior emanates from the family's psychopathology is a mistake. In a middle-class family from the same county as Bill, seven youngsters grew up with erratic, volatile, and often cruel alcoholic parents. With the exception of the fourth-born, all the offspring are now leading responsible lives. That one child is in jail for the sixth time, in this case for violation of parole. How easy it would be to account for his criminality by viewing him as the unfortunate victim of his parents' pathology. But what of the other six, who were exposed to the same unwholesome environment but are not in jail?

Many delinquent youngsters assert that their parents are too restrictive and distrustful. In reality, their mothers and fathers yearn to trust them, but find it difficult after they have been lied to and exploited repeatedly. Every time such a child asks for something, his parents are in a quandary. While endeavoring to blackmail them psychologically into acceding to his every request, their child is unresponsive to their pleas for cooperation. If his parents then deny his request, he berates and threatens them. Or he plays on their guilt for denying him something they know he wants.

The threats and "guilt trips" continue into adulthood as criminals intimidate their parents. Donald told me that he wanted no relationship with his father other than having him pay for his home and other living expenses. "It's his world, and I live in it. I have to depend on him," complained this able-bodied adult male who refused to work and succeeded in browbeating his father into providing for him financially. Why his dad constantly caved in, I came to understand. Although determined not to be manipulated, Donald's father was nonetheless terrified by his son's threats of suicide. He hoped that by preserving some sort of relationship, he might help Donald or, at the very least, keep him alive. While speaking with me, Donald spewed hatred for this parent, who was his very lifeline. Asked if he became angry enough to want to kill his dad, Donald retorted, "No! I'd rather he suffer with my death." As to how serious he was about ending his own life, Donald said, "I don't own a handgun, and I can't find a doctor who will give me a big enough prescription to do it." Clearly, Donald had no genuine intention of committing suicide, but it was evident that he would continue emotionally blackmailing and extorting large sums of money from his terrified father.

Occasionally the delinquent offspring deliberately sets out to convince his parents that he is trustworthy. He puts on a show of shouldering responsibility at home by fixing something that is broken, cleaning up a room in the house, and voluntarily helping with chores. This is a con job, a front designed to lull his family into thinking that he is changing his ways. At these times he has no such intention. Later he hearkens back to his good deeds, expecting them to blot out all misconduct.

Such a child puts his parents in a double bind. On the one hand, he perceives their kindness as weakness and exploits it. When they say yes, they are played for suckers. However, strictness sparks a new series of hostilities. Deprivation of privileges and restrictions breeds only more wrangling and bitter resentment.

When taken to counselors and therapists, delinquent youngsters complain that their parents do not understand them. The picture is not simply of a communications gap but of a yawning chasm that seems unbridgeable. Therapists conclude that the child's parents are aloof, uncaring, or perhaps irresponsible. But their assessments are based on hearing only one side of the story.

Most parents faced with such a difficult child make extraordinary efforts to talk to and understand their offspring. However, the child is the one who constructs an increasingly impenetrable barrier to communication. He lives a life that he is determined to hide. Although such youngsters blame their parents for poor communication, they are the ones who choose not to communicate and respond to questions with evasion or belligerence. "I communicate to the point it makes *me* happy," snapped one such teenager. "*They* need to communicate with *me*. I don't really want to hear anything they have to say. I don't have anything to say to them. We're just different kinds of people."

To the extent that it exists at all, dialogue between parent and criminal child is on the child's terms. Savvy enough to know that silence annoys others and makes them suspicious, the youngster may engage in polite conversation, tell his parents what is safe, and remain on neutral ground. When his parents speak to him, he hears but usually does not listen. He is highly practiced at screening out what is disagreeable. It is as though, with a flick of a button, the youngster controls which parental messages reach his ear. The communications gap exists all right, but not, as many experts suggest, one created primarily by indifferent or neglectful parents.

The delinquent youngster spins an increasingly intricate and sometimes tangled web of secrecy. Beginning as early as the preschool years, the child resorts to lies to worm his way out of trouble that he creates. He relates to his parents only part of the truth, omitting that which would incriminate him.

All children may lie at one time or another, but lying does not become a way of life. As they grow up, youngsters respond positively to social rewards for truthfulness. They desire to establish themselves as credible people. Occasionally they lie to cover up wrongdoing, to save face in an embarrassing situation, to avoid the disagreeable, or to protect their image. But they don't experience the tremendous excitement and sense of power that the delinquent gains from lying. In fact, quite the opposite is true. Normally, children are reticent about lying, and when they do lie, they suffer pangs of conscience afterward. For the child who becomes a criminal, lying conceals more and more forbidden and destructive activity. In contrast to a child who occasionally concocts a lie and whose guilty expression just about gives him away, the criminal child can look his parents straight in the eye and solemnly tell the most outrageous lies, his gaze never faltering, his voice never cracking. These children see nothing wrong with lying. Indeed, they view it as necessary to get away with all that they do.

Perhaps most distressing to the delinquent's parents is that so many of his lies seem to have no purpose. Their youngster delights in making fools of them by inventing things that never happened. Although his innumerable misrepresentations and embellishments appear senseless to his parents, they are purposeful to him. By deceiving his mother and father in matters even as trivial as whether he has taken a shower, the youngster believes he has gained the upper hand. Never knowing what to believe, his mother and father search for cues by scrutinizing his facial expressions and listening for a quaver in his voice, a quaver that rarely appears.

Two parents brought their sixteen-year-old son to me for counseling. Although the boy had done many things that alarmed them, his constant lying was driving them to distraction. The youngster had figured out that, in daily life, people usually regard others as trustworthy and truthful. If you seek directions, you trust that the person you've asked is directing you the best he can. If you buy fresh salmon in the grocery store, you trust that the advertising is truthful—the fish is fresh, not frozen. This sixteen-year-old sensed that he could exploit the trusting attitude of others. He explained that he lied "because it's so easy to get away with it." His only worry was that he had told so many lies to his buddies that he was afraid he would be ostracized once they discovered his conflicting stories.

The delinquent lies so often and has done so for so long that his lying appears to be compulsive. Yet the lying is totally under his control. He can readily distinguish truth from falsehood and is prepared to tell either, depending on which best serves his purpose. From the time he is in grade school, he develops and practices at home the deceptive methods he will use in dealing with the rest of the world. Neither his parents nor anybody else will penetrate the shield of secrecy long enough to really know him.

Brazen lying is hard for parents to tolerate, but equally distressing is the paralysis they experience while trying to dispel the fog of such a youngster's vagueness. He is tentative and global, hard to pin down. Even in situations that clearly call for a yes or no, he responds with "maybe," "perhaps," or "I guess." The delinquent youngster doesn't have to work at obfuscation; it is as automatic as his lying. Again, he is the one creating the bulk of the communication problem, not uncaring, indifferent, or hostile parents.

Although these children are exasperating to live with, they have a sensitivity and gentleness that is as genuine as their selfishness and destructiveness. They seem truly to have a Jekyll-and-Hyde personality. When their endearing qualities surface, they can be completely captivating. When the sunny side of these youngsters shines through their darker nature, parents find welcome relief from battle fatigue and once again grow hopeful.

Such phases are not always con jobs. Throughout his life, there are times when the delinquent is earnest about reforming. He resolves to do well at school, and he cooperates at home. The desire to shape up may last hours, days, or weeks. Then it seems to vanish. A life of going to school, working, staying around the house, and generally living like the "straight" kids is intolerable. The praise that others lavish on him for the positive changes pales in comparison with the excitement of the life he has been leading.

Although family members never know whether the child genuinely wants to change or whether it's all another hoax, they delight in every moment that he is thoughtful and considerate. Even during these relatively calm periods, his parents are reminded that he is troubled, because they are witness to his restlessness, irritability, and explosive temper. It may take a shockingly dramatic event to convince them that things are far worse than they ever imagined. This happened to the parents of a fifteen-year-old named Tom.

Tom's mother and father regarded him as moody but good at heart. They thought that, like most boys his age, Tom was navigating the typical ups and downs of adolescence. They tried to cheer him up when his spirits sagged, and to calm him when he was angry and upset. They were demonstrative in their praise for his achievements—notably his high grades and clarinet playing. But Tom's mother was growing more and more disturbed by his increasing hostility at home. She did not suspect anything radically wrong, however, until she walked into the kitchen and saw Tom standing over the family's pet poodle, which was sprawled on the floor in a pool of blood. Only after his shocked mother and father took their son to a psychiatrist did the truth emerge. Tom and his friends had gone on shoplifting binges and rampages of vandalism "just for kicks." While skipping classes, he had smoked marijuana and popped pills. Tom didn't tolerate disagreement. When he failed to get his way with his friends, he exploded with a string of obscenities and felt a pounding desire to beat them up, an urge to which he succumbed when he figured he'd come out on top. Finally, when the family pet destroyed the wiring on his stereo set, Tom decided he was not going to tolerate that, either. He grabbed a kitchen knife and thrust it into the animal again and again. After these revelations emerged during the consultation with Tom's psychiatrist, any illusions that his mother and father had about his being a normal teenager were shattered.

As a child, the criminal has contempt not only for his parents' advice and authority but for the way they live, no matter what their social and economic circumstances. To him, their lives are plodding, dull, and barren. If his parents are poor, he scorns their lack of success. If they are affluent, he scoffs at their achievements. If they do not work at all, they are bums. He does not fathom how toiling at a job can consume the bulk of his parents' working hours, especially when they have to work on someone else's terms. He cannot comprehend their placing obligations ahead of convenience or pleasure. To him, having a good time is what life is all about. Work and other duties have nothing to do with having a good time. "What is life for? You live it and die," said one delinquent from a middle-class family. He had decided that he would live as he saw fit, and not be a slave as his parents were. And that's what he did. "*They* decided to have *me*," he said. "It's not a free ride. If they don't like the way I act, tough." He was totally impervious to the fact that it was his parents' sense of obligation, their patience, their sense of purpose—the very qualities that he derided—that had provided him with the comfortable home that he assumed was his birthright.

Many a teenager adopts a critical, if not despairing, view of his parents' lifestyle. A developmental task of adolescence is to evaluate what one has been taught and subsequently internalized. The teenager may rebel during this period of intense questioning and doubt. Most of those who flirt with danger do not become outlaws; they discover that breaking away from legal and moral restraints to any great extent exacts too high a price. It jeopardizes their future and hurts people whom they value and who cherish them. Eventually it dawns on them that being responsible offers a wealth of possibilities from which one can carve out a life and still be his own person. Living outside the law drastically limits alternatives and thereby curtails one's freedom. For a criminal, it's just the opposite.

The child who becomes a criminal gradually slips beyond his parents' reach, becoming ever more secretive and defiant. The accumulation of minor irritants as well as major infractions is so debilitating to the parents that they frequently doubt they can stand another day under the same roof with him.

When there are other children in the family, they are victimized by their delinquent sibling, who bullies them, helps himself to their belongings, and pins the rap on them when any discipline is about to be meted out. This behavior is far more extreme than the rivalry that usually exists among siblings. Not only does the criminal youngster appropriate their toys, records, and clothes without permission, but he destroys or loses them. He also steals their money. Brothers and sisters, if younger or smaller, are cowed into submission. They are warned to keep their mouths shut about what they see, and are told that if they squeal they will regret it. Because they retain a sense of loyalty to their sibling, some suffer in silence. One such sibling told me that he believed that if he complained too much, his parents would send his brother away to a school for bad kids. No matter how badly he was mistreated, he didn't want to shoulder the guilt of causing that to happen.

As long as the delinquent is at home, his brothers and sisters know few peaceful moments and have virtually no privacy. The greatest tragedy is that, in a sense, their parents have been usurped. In a home simmering with dissension, mother and father have little time for them, their problems seem less urgent, and so they feel shortchanged. The family is not really a family. The moments they do have together are often conflict-ridden. Because the parents are worn out and on edge, they have less of themselves to share. It is amazing to see how some extremely disturbed families are instantly at peace once the criminal member leaves home.

I had just concluded a lecture to an undergraduate psychology class. A young woman stayed behind to speak with me. She said that she was one of the "good kids," an honor-roll student who helped at home and never got into trouble. She was ignored while her brother received constant attention for all the bad things he did. Now that she was older, she said, she understood why her parents had behaved as they had, and she was no longer resentful. Her mom and dad had little choice but to deal with the unending series of crises her brother created. She urged me to advise counselors and parents not to shortchange the child who is behaving responsibly.

Even though the delinquent makes life miserable for his brothers and sisters, he sometimes acts as their keeper. No matter how shabbily he treats them, he will not permit anyone else to inflict harm on them, and is quick to rally to their defense—with violence if he deems it necessary to protect them. On the one hand, he belittles them for being "goody-goodies," yet he rebuffs them for wrongdoing and threatens to tell on them. If a sibling who has been a good kid grows curious and wants to accompany him on some of his clandestine missions, he discourages it. He doesn't want anyone tagging along, being a nuisance. In addition, he wants to keep his brother or sister out of harm's way. On the other hand, if there is a sibling who shares his lust for adventure, he welcomes him as a companion and accomplice.

When an older brother precedes a younger sibling in taking a delinquent path, it is often assumed that the younger has identified with and been corrupted by the older. A psychological report on one fourteen-year-old marijuana smoker and thief cited his older brother's unwholesome example as having had a critically detrimental influence on him. This interpretation is based on psychiatric theories of role modeling and identification. Deviance is often attributed to identification with a deviant sibling or parent. In this situation, extensive clinical interviewing revealed that the younger boy considered himself a guy with his own mind. He *chose* to emulate his brother rather than emulate the other male in the family—his father—who was responsible. He was suggestible only to whatever appeared exciting at the moment, but he was not receptive to the predominant influences in his environment—parents, neighbors, teachers—that encouraged him to follow a more constructive path.

Identification theory fails to account for the process of choice in the lives of the delinquent youngster. A teenager wrote to Dr. Robert Wallace, an advice-giving columnist, recounting his horror when he discovered his father smoking marijuana.[2] When he confronted him, the father told the youth to live his life his way, and he and the boy's mother would live life their way. The columnist advised the adolescent, "Do as your father said. Lead your life as an example for your parents to follow. It's sad that you must learn right from wrong by not doing what your parents do." Had the teenager been smoking marijuana, a counselor undoubtedly would have concluded that it was because he had such poor role models. Many psychiatrists, psychologists, and social workers seem to ignore the individual's power to choose. Children do not inevitably pattern themselves after the qualities of their parents. Responsible role models may have an irresponsible child and vice versa. Children decide who they want to be like, and in what ways.

There is a theory that some children become antisocial because they failed during infancy to attach themselves to a parent or other primary care giver. They do not develop empathy, intimacy, or trust later in life because of an "attachment disorder" suffered during their formative years. Parents of some delinquents have found this not to have been the case with their children. They describe their offspring as cuddly, affectionate, and bonding with others. Only later did the trouble come. With regard to boys and girls who never seemed to have attached to others, what is it about these youngsters that was different from their siblings who formed strong bonds with their parents and later with others? "Attachment disorder" seems, then, to be a descriptive term, but not one that is particularly helpful in cogently explaining or correcting antisocial behavior.

As the personality of the criminally inclined child unfolds, his parents are gripped by a gnawing fear that something terrible is going to happen. Their nerves are constantly frazzled. Every time the phone rings, their hearts sink. What is it this time—a distraught neighbor, a teacher reporting a fight, the police, or, worst of all, a hospital informing them that their child is injured or dead?

As their concerns mount, parents try new ways to cope with the youngster's misbehavior. They more closely restrict his movement and privileges, but end up suffering more than the child, who sneakily circumvents the restrictions or blatantly flouts them. In fact, it is a relief to the parents when they can bring themselves to lift the restrictions. Then there are fewer battles.

In many of these families, corporal punishment is an unpalatable solution because the parents prefer reasoning. They find that resorting to violence is no solution at all. Whacking their offspring has virtually no long-range positive effect. The child absorbs the physical punishment and shows he can take it. He still does as he chooses.

Sometimes even the parent who intends never to strike his child finds his patience depleted and lashes out in frustration, only to feel intense guilt later. These are not instances of child abuse, although the youngster may find an ear sympathetic to trumping up such a case. One fourteen-year-old was totally incorrigible. He did exactly what he wanted, listening to no authority and screaming at his parents to "fuck off" when they tried to control him. On one occasion he met with his school counselor, who wanted to discuss the boy's repeated unexcused absences. The youth shifted the subject and complained about his home life, asserting that his father was violent and that he was subjected to repeated beatings. The shocked and sympathetic counselor referred the matter to protective services, and a caseworker contacted the parents. The boy's mother and father were mortified. The only particle of truth to their son's allegation was that several times, after repeated provocation, his father had slapped him. That was the extent of the "child abuse." The family underwent a humiliating investigation that eventually resulted in the case being closed with no charges brought. Meanwhile, the youth was delighted at what he construed as his parents being called on the carpet. He now had a new weapon: "If you touch me, I'll report you."

An antisocial child can intimidate parents, teachers, and others by threatening to report them to authorities for abusing him when no abuse occurred. One teenager started yelling and cursing at her dad when he asked her to empty the dishwasher. Having been subjected to her nastiness repeatedly, her frustrated father raised his voice, then shoved her out of the way. She ran to her school counselor claiming that her father had abused her, whereupon the counselor called child protective services. The authorities launched an investigation that at one point jeopardized this father's sensitive job. I talked at length with the investigator about the situation, which I knew well because I was counseling the family. The father was wrong to push his daughter. But the push offered no evidence of a single episode, much less a pattern, of parental abuse. Rather, it was the child who was continually abusing her parents, opposing their simplest request and turning life at home into a battleground. The investigation was terminated with the conclusion that no abuse had occurred.

Family profiles of some delinquents indicate that they truly were victims of child abuse. One psychiatric theory posits that they identified with the parent who was the aggressor, and therefore became violent themselves. Another conclusion is that severe early punishment resulted in their becoming so submissive that they were rendered vulnerable to the influence of those who would lead them into crime. One boy was punished as a child by being locked in the bathroom, tied up in the basement, and beaten with a strap. He was the only one of six children who enraged his parents to the point that they meted out such brutal punishment. This is not to condone his parents' methods of dealing with him. The point is that children like him, by their unrelenting provocation, may elicit a violent reaction even from a parent with a normally placid disposition. Rarely does that part of the story come out. A psychiatric school consultant, evaluating a thirteen-year-old delinquent boy, understood how a parent could be driven to extreme measures. He wrote in the youngster's clinical record, "This is a child who relates to adults in a manner that could easily move the adult to be physically abusive." There are no clinical studies that conclusively reveal why many, perhaps most, children who truly are victims of child abuse do not become criminals. In fact, researchers have pointed out that having abusive parents is "among the poorest predictors" of violence for children ages six to fourteen.[3]

Some mental health professionals assert that administering any form of corporal punishment teaches a child that violence is acceptable, thereby making a youngster more inclined to resort to violence when he is angry or unhappy. The *Washington Post* reported a study in which investigators found that "antisocial behavior is increased" in children who are spanked.[4] The American Psychological Association's publication, *Monitor*, stated that children who are corporally punished "are more prone to violence, sexual misconduct, and crime."[5] But the experts are clearly not all of one mind. *USA Today* cited various research findings indicating that the effects of spanking can be beneficial, not detrimental.[6]

After years of assault upon their own values, some parents gradually embrace what earlier seemed to them to be radical ideas. For example, a mother who had regarded any illegal drug use with abhorrence became an advocate of legalizing marijuana after realizing that she was helpless to prevent her child from using it and after being convinced by him that everyone else was using it. Such shifts in attitude are a consequence of a parent's desperation to draw closer to a child who appears completely alienated. In a calculating manner, the youngster callously exploits his parent's desire to strengthen their bond. He believes that rather than risk a setback in the relationship, this parent will cave in on other issues. If the less susceptible parent continues to withstand such attempts at psychological blackmail, a major rift in the marital relationship may develop. In the long run, the parent being exploited realizes that he has been played for a sucker and that he has been won over by the child into a destructive alliance against his spouse.

No matter how much upheaval in the family, and no matter how serious the wayward child's offenses, his parents believe for a long time that he is basically good. They witness incidents of their offspring's unacceptable behavior from the time he is little. (Research indicates that 10 to 15 percent of preschoolers demonstrate behavior problems serious enough to warrant treatment even at this early point in their lives.[7]) No matter how destructive, the parents regard their youngster's misconduct as indicative of immaturity—isolated events, not a pattern. In the short term, denial proves to be an effective defense against facing a very disturbing reality.

As the child enters adolescence, his parents become alarmed at the increase in occurrence and seriousness of the misbehavior. (Still, they are aware of only a fraction of his delinquent activities, as he is very clever in covering his tracks.) To cling to a benign view of their offspring in the face of his mounting difficulties becomes increasingly problematic, then impossible. One mother in this quandary said, "At first, we felt that he would just naturally grow out of this disruptive behavior, but as time went on and things began to escalate, it became obvious that there was something else wrong." She had seen his traits as a young child—his daring, his sense of adventure, his cunning and persistent way of pursuing what he wanted, his occasional tantrums—give way to incessant lying, belligerence, defiance, and destructiveness. "The cute," she said, "gave way to the unbelievable." It is conceivable that parents might regard their own child as emotionally disturbed, but it is unlikely that they'd consider him an antisocial person or a criminal. Even parents of adult criminals who are behind bars generally don't think in such terms.

Few parents remain indifferent or give up. They do what they can—spend more time with the child, enroll him in a different school, support his joining organized sports and clubs, send him to a counselor, seek counseling themselves. In grasping at solutions, the soul-searching goes on. Mothers and fathers blame themselves, each other, and people and events outside the family. Those who are psychologically oriented devour books and then fault themselves for causing their child's delinquency. Some parents seek therapy. I have received calls from parents throughout the United States who have told me of the unfortunate outcome of that decision. Having already been completely devastated by their child's destructive behavior, they find that therapy has created more misery, saddling them with more inner conflict and a huge dose of guilt.

There comes a time when parents of such a child have to face the fact that they are powerless to change the course of events. "I'm learning to let go," said one father. "I don't want to tie my life to this problem. It's like a very ill relative. You prepare yourself for the death of that person." Still the daily pain is great, and commonplace events become sources of humiliation. What can the parents tell Grandma when she asks how her grandson is doing? What reassurances can parents offer to the neighbor whose little boy is in tears after being tormented by their son? It is mortifying to admit to a school counselor that they cannot control their child at home, much less what he does in school. Each incident serves as a powerful reminder to them that they have failed at what they consider perhaps the most important experience in life—raising a child. Through it all, the youngster has not a shred of comprehension or concern about his parents' agony. In his opinion, it is they who have inflicted the wounds on themselves by demanding that he be something he has no interest in being. He thinks their worry is needless; he is fine the way he is. When asked how he felt about his parents' distress, one boy responded coldly, "It's like an operation. They have to live with the pain. It's their problem."

The criminal child knows that one way to be free of hassles is to strike out on his own. However, such children usually think things through enough to realize that if they run away, their parents will summon the police and they will be caught and brought back, only to have more restrictions piled on. Besides, most have no place to go. They prefer that their parents leave. But no matter how unsatisfactory life is at home, it is still home, a familiar base of operation. One fifteen-year-old boy said, "All I want is three hots and a cot, nothin' more." And so these youngsters stick around, continuing to victimize those who care about them the most.

Parents often wish they could let their child leave and live on his own. But when he is under seventeen, the legal responsibility is theirs. Boarding school is usually an untenable alternative because of expense and the probability that the youngster won't stay. In families with a delinquent child, a major disagreement may arise when the youngster does become old enough to live independently. At issue is whether his mother and father have a right to their own lives after years of turmoil. When he is legally of age to be emancipated, some parents say goodbye. For most, it still is an agonizing experience. One mother wrote her friend, "Probably the most difficult step we *ever* had to take was finally to follow the advice of a respected judge, a doctor, and Art's psychiatrist. We were to let Art take off as he wished before finishing high school, and later we were told to stop bailing him out of trouble every time he called collect. Our sending money didn't help make him responsible for his many debts. We still run into people to whom he owes money."

A situation in which the youth refuses to leave is no easier to face. The parents are often terrified of forcing their son into doing something drastic if they try to push him out. One mother said, "We've been through a flaky suicide attempt. He slashed his arms close to the wrist. Believe me, I hope I never have to go through anything like that again. I can handle emergencies—but all that blood! My intense feelings of dislike after he was in the hospital scared me. Sometimes I think I need an analyst. These kids don't realize what they do to their parents."

Parents turn to me for advice about whether to compel their adult offspring to leave home. Since everything they have tried to help their son or daughter has failed, I tell them that now they must look out for their own welfare. If having their child leave will cause them more misery than having him stay, then they should let him remain under their roof, then try to back off and go about their own lives. This does not mean they should endure the mistreatment that he dishes out. I have instructed parents of both minor and adult children to press charges if their son or daughter commits a crime on their property (brings drugs in, assaults a family member, destroys property, or steals). Short of that, they should specify their expectations, preferably in writing, while recognizing that even these written expectations are likely to be ignored. When life with their offspring becomes intolerable, then it is time to let him or her go.

A final break rarely occurs. No matter how tenuous, a tie is maintained between parents and their very difficult child. One mother said, "While our boy was in prison, we sent food packages, art supplies, a radio, an electric fan, and some money, but he *demanded* more. We continued to write in spite of his stealing from us by ordering stereo equipment on our credit card. Again, he lied about doing it and then about being sorry. As usual, he promised to change. We did not feel we could afford to send him all the things he demanded. Therefore he angrily told us off and said he never wanted to hear from us again."

Some parents finally conclude that confinement of their child is necessary both to bring him to grips with reality and to protect innocent people. One mother said, "It's the most horrible thing in the world to say—I am afraid of my own son. I'm afraid I'll go to bed some night and never wake up in the morning." The parents of one eighteen-year-old had done all in their power to help him, including shelling out thousands of dollars for his psychiatric treatment at a prestigious inpatient center. Not long after his release from the hospital, he was apprehended for the abduction of two girls and was sentenced to a long prison term. All that his father could say was, "Justice has been served."

Any parent who has read this chapter may be alarmed if he has a child who is showing any of the behavior just described. But before concluding that he has a budding criminal in the family, he should ask himself whether his youngster is showing isolated instances of the behavior or evidencing patterns over time that are expanding and intensifying. Every child who swipes a few coins from a cookie jar or steals a candy bar from a store does not become a criminal. In a classic textbook on child development, psychology professors L. Joseph Stone and Joseph Church cite "normal or casual delinquent behavior" that "will usually be outgrown without any special measures" because children who show such behavior "develop their own inhibitions and controls without any action by authorities."[8] This chapter documents patterns in a minority of children who eventually inflict enormous damage upon society no matter what their parents or others do to deter them.

Psychologists and other professionals have longed blamed parents for nearly all the problems of their offspring. The assumption has been that if you have a delinquent child, there must be something wrong with you! Whatever your shortcomings, your youngster starts making choices very early in life that determine the sort of person he wants to become and the kind of life he wants to lead.

The reader may conclude that I have let all parents off the hook, no matter what their inadequacies. This is not so. Parents who are abusive, neglectful, inconsistent, and psychologically disturbed are likely to have an adverse impact on their offspring. This is not to say, however, that they will invariably produce criminals. Fortunately for society, most youngsters who suffer neglect or abuse do not become criminals. Furthermore, it is striking to observe that some criminals are the sons and daughters of parents who are devoted, stable, and responsible. Unfortunately, the best efforts of parents to help and correct this kind of child can and usually do fail. As it turns out, the parents are usually the victims, the child the victimizer, not the other way around.

3

PEER PRESSURE:

NO EXCUSE FOR CRIME

IF PARENTS OF CRIMINALS were asked what went wrong in their children's lives, many would reply, "My child ran with the wrong crowd." They would maintain that their son was a good boy at heart, but that he was corrupted by others. The belief is widespread that youngsters turn to crime, alcohol, and drugs because they succumb to the pressures of their peer group.

Peer pressure is a force that we all have to contend with from the time we are in nursery school until we die. But we choose which peer group or groups to belong to. As is the case with nearly all children, the criminal as a child chooses his friends. No criminal I have evaluated or counseled was forced into crime. He chose to associate with risk-taking youngsters who were doing what was forbidden. Once he worked his way into their confidence, he gained increasing recognition, which meant more to him than acceptance anywhere else. His parents, teachers, and numerous others tried to persuade or compel him to associate with responsible youngsters, but they were rebuffed. The delinquent youngster scorns his contemporaries who are "straight," and sticks with his own kind. Sometimes alone, but more often with youngsters like himself, he commits more and more crimes, bolstering his self-image in the process and finding that no one can do anything for very long to bring a halt to his spiraling criminality. Certainly there is no incentive to break away from those who share his interests and are very much like him.

It doesn't take a sociologist to point out that youngsters are influenced by their peers, that they want to be in step and belong to the crowd. But some sociologists and mental health professionals regard the child as a hapless victim who is contaminated by pernicious influences. They believe people contract criminality through exposure, much in the way they pick up a contagious disease.[1] Yet one must ask why, if this is true, so many children in high-crime areas, including the criminal's own brothers and sisters, do not become criminals.

A somewhat different perspective on delinquency is that boys are "driven" into deviant behavior because they fail to achieve status in society. This is seen as one motive for joining a gang. Through criminal behavior, the individual gains recognition and a sense of belonging that he did not achieve in mainstream endeavors.

The view that a youngster is *led* or *driven* into crime to gain status ignores the role of personal choice. It also ignores the question of what group an individual wants to belong to, and what sort of recognition he seeks. From the time he was little, the delinquent has chosen the company he keeps and has determined what kind of status he wants. Only when he was held accountable for his actions did he resort to blaming others, claiming that "some kids got me into shoplifting" or "the kids I hung with all did it."

A young woman whom I interviewed in the adult detention center told me that when she was a little girl, her mother wondered why she didn't play with others her age. This inmate remarked that her contemporaries at the time were playing hopscotch, jumping rope, and playing with dolls. "I wanted something more!" she exclaimed. The "something more" involved activities far more exciting than hopscotch. She started hanging around older kids who were doing things on a dare, engaging in petty shoplifting and hanging around places she wasn't supposed to go. She wasn't "driven" to do anything. She went in search of excitement, and she found it.

Whether the delinquent is from a poor family or a wealthy one, whatever his neighborhood is like, he shares much in common with a boy like Tim, the fourth-born in a lower-middle-class Catholic family of six boys and one girl. His sister and brothers were, for the most part, obedient and conforming. Not Tim. His parents date the beginning of his criminal career to age four. The family next door had driven off for a picnic and left the front door of their home ajar. Tim walked in and cleaned out as many toys as he could stuff into his arms.

Stocky and strong for his age, he established a reputation as the neighborhood terror, a thief and a bully who would take on anyone in a fight. At six, he left the neighborhood and roamed across the boulevard, where he was forbidden to go because of the rough area and heavy traffic. There he was attracted to an older bunch of toughs who hung out on streetcorners and who were far more fascinating to him than the "goody-goodies" on his block. A favorite activity of this group was to enter a store and, while one boy diverted the owner's attention, make off with as much as they could carry. Tim started drinking with these boys when he was ten, often supplying them with beer stolen from his parents' refrigerator. Tim's pilfering escalated during early adolescence to breaking and entering and stealing cars.

But Tim was not a total outlaw. He surprised people by participating in conventional activities, such as church functions, which he attended with his family. An excellent swimmer, he aspired to be an Olympic participant. In high school he joined a local swim team, which at the time was having a losing season. Even in a legitimate enterprise, he was determined to do things his way. Because he was so highly valued, Tim got away with infractions for which his teammates would have been severely reprimanded or suspended. The only member with stringy long hair, a mustache, and a headband, Tim sauntered in for practice whenever he felt like it, which was rarely. Tim recalled showing up for swimming meets "reeking from pot" or "half-crocked on booze," but then executing a perfect dive. As long as he remained on the team, it compiled a winning record. He thrived on being a prima donna, but spewed contempt for the suckers who showed up for practice regularly.

Everywhere he went, Tim gravitated to those who offered him opportunities for excitement. While in the army, he became friendly with an alcoholic priest whom he assisted in serving mass. The priest took a liking to Tim, and invited him to imbibe wine after services. The priest used his influence to obtain extended passes for Tim, who would stagger back to his army post roaring drunk. One night some of the men in Tim's unit who were fed up with his belligerence threw a "blanket party." After he fell asleep, they tossed a blanket over him and started pounding away at him through the blanket. His reaction: "I went insane." He broke free, determined to kill the sergeant. It took several soldiers to restrain him. After one month, the army discharged him. Again, Tim had rejected living within a social unit.

When Tim grew tired of being home, he violated probation by taking off for his brother's home in St. Louis. His parents were hopeful that, away from his old associates, he might make a fresh start and find more respectable friends. Asking for the court's indulgence and consideration, Tim's father wrote the judge, "We believe that Tim's full recovery could be enhanced under the influence of his older brother, whose opinions he respects." Despite a change in environment, Tim chose to travel a familiar path. He found friends cut from the same cloth as himself, returned to drugs and drink, and then began stealing from his brother, the very person who was providing a roof over his head. Eventually he was sent to jail, convicted of assault and battery.

In the preschool years, neither Tim nor others like him divide the world into good kids and bad kids. But such a child realizes that some children are adventurous while others are not. Like a magnet, he is drawn to those who are daring and disobedient.

In inner-city and suburban areas throughout America, youngsters flock to organized activities practically from the time they are of age to toddle around in neighborhood play groups. As they meet new people and discover new interests, they become involved in sports, church groups, scouting, community service, and school clubs. A process of socialization occurs as these children learn about cooperation, competition, sharing, and self-control.

What offers opportunity for fun and personal growth to the responsible child leaves the delinquent with little but gnawing restlessness and mounting boredom. Some delinquents steadfastly refuse to participate in any organized activities. Some responsible youngsters do the same, but for different reasons. The delinquent refuses to subordinate himself to anyone else's authority. Invariably he regards a coach or other leader as knowing less than he. Contemptuous of the activity, its organizer, and the other participants, he chooses instead to engage in something more exciting, often illicit. The responsible youngster, on the other hand, may reject organized activities because he feels inferior in a group or simply because he prefers to do other things that he finds more enjoyable. The delinquent rejects the organized activity for an irresponsible alternative, while other youngsters usually do so for one that is responsible.

Some delinquents are attracted to competition, where they are determined to outshine everyone else. Then their entire self-image is on the line, and they resort to any tactic that they can think of in order to win. To achieve a personal victory, they strive to impose their will and either con or force others to operate by their rules. If they even begin to sense that they will not come out on top, they cheat, fight, or quit. They are impossibly arrogant winners or else revenge-seeking losers.

Eventually such a child grows contemptuous of his contemporaries who live an ordinary existence at home, in the neighborhood, and at school. To be part of that life is, as one twelve-year-old said, "like being put on a leash." Dissatisfied with his age, the delinquent seeks out the more adventuresome, usually older youngsters, whom he regards as having all the fun. One young teenager told a counselor, "I've always wanted to grow up fast. I don't get along with anyone my age. I get mad because they act too immature." At fourteen he was hanging around with a partying crowd of eighteen- to twenty-five-year-olds who were neither working nor in school.

Every secondary school has groups with different names—preppies, jocks, nerds, freaks, and so forth. Snarled one fourteen-year-old, "Preppies, I hate 'em. They think they're so cool." He chose to associate with the "freaks," who skipped school, used drugs, and went on shoplifting binges. One father said of his son, "If Guy saw a group of neatly dressed students holding their books and talking about girls, cars, and sports, and he saw a scraggly bunch of boys swaggering around, drinking and cursing, he would always choose the second group."

Far from being enticed into crime, the criminal as a child admires and cultivates those who are in the action. In fact, to gain their acceptance, he must prove himself by demonstrating that he is tough and, even more important, that he can be trusted. He dresses as they do, apes their language, follows them wherever they go, and does whatever they ask. In time he is no longer viewed as a tag-along, but as one of the crowd. He may feel used during his period of initiation, but he overlooks this because he values just being with them and will continue to associate with them even at the risk of violating probation and being confined.

Donald's probation officer forbade him from having any contact with Pete, his drug-pushing buddy. Donald flagrantly violated this prohibition, correctly calculating that his probation officer would not find out and that even if he did, he wouldn't lock him up. Some of these youths form a loose-knit alliance, while others belong to an organized group or gang. (Some don't mix much with anyone.) In the city, delinquent youngsters congregate on street corners. In the suburbs they flock to shopping malls, fast-food outlets, game arcades, skateboard parks, or wherever else kids gather just to see what's happening.

Responsible youngsters also hang out at some of the same places. But if one were to view a videotape of the conversation and activities of the two groups, striking differences would be observable. It is a matter not only of where teenagers congregate, but of what they do once they get there. At the shopping mall, the more conventional kids might be spending their allowance or job earnings, engaging in window shopping, or standing around conversing about who is going with whom or discussing what went on in school. The delinquent youngsters would be wandering through stores, casing out merchandise, considering how to abscond with whatever seems appealing at the moment. Or they might stir up excitement by picking fights, making unsolicited, provocative comments to shoppers, drinking, and becoming rowdy. For delinquent kids, a favorite hangout because of its privacy is the home of someone whose parents are at work all day. If his neighborhood is dead, the child travels to where the action is, even if it requires boarding a bus or hitchhiking across town.

The parents of these children rarely know where their offspring are. Contrary to what many counselors and court workers believe, usually this is due not to negligence but to the youngster's ingenuity at concealing his activities. He may check in with his parents to satisfy them that he is visiting a friend, but he fails to disclose where he will be heading later. He often says he is going one place, but goes another. Not only do the parents not know where their child is, but often they are in the dark as to who his friends are because he refuses to bring them home to introduce them.

If the child is home alone because his parents work, the so-called latchkey kid has ample opportunities to get into trouble. But only if he has the inclination to seek out trouble. A lot can happen between the afternoon close of school and the time a parent arrives home. Most latchkey children come home, do homework, watch television, and play in the neighborhood, but some children exploit a lack of parental supervision. I know of one family where a single mother worked at two jobs to make ends meet. She told her sons to go next door after school, where a parent was home, to call her at work, then play with kids in the neighborhood. If either boy wanted to do something out of the ordinary, he was to call his mom at work for permission. One child lived within those restraints. The other wandered out of the immediate neighborhood and attached himself to a group of older youths who were smoking, stealing, and vandalizing property. He was finally caught leaving a store with concealed stolen merchandise. It might be tempting to ascribe the one youngster's delinquency to his mother's absence and the pressure of peers around him filling the vacuum. But that would not fit with the facts. It was the same mother, the same set of restrictions, and the same neighborhood. Living under identical conditions, the two boys made different choices.

If the family ends up in counseling sessions, the counselor is likely to be critical of the parents for failing to make their home a place where their child's friends feel welcome, thereby leaving the youngster more vulnerable to pressures of the streets. But the fact is that the youngster does not want his parents to know who his friends are. "My parents don't know half my friends," said one fifteen-year-old. "If they got a look at most of them, they'd give me a rough time." He knew that his mother and father did not approve of his hanging around with a hard-drinking, school-skipping gang, some of whom had been in trouble with the police. Even suspecting the worst, many parents still prefer that the youngster bring his friends home instead of roaming the streets. "I've tried so hard to make our home a pleasant place for my son to bring his friends," said one such mother. "But he always goes out. They never come here." Her son knew that his buddies would be bored to tears at his house if his parents were lurking nearby. What could they do, sit around and drink Cokes and watch television?

The delinquent youngster is intent on conveying an image of himself as unflappable and invincible. As each youth is attempting to prove himself to other kids, he is also struggling to overcome intense and carefully concealed fears. Fears of the dark, heights, water, and lightning persist into adolescence, sometimes into adulthood. These youngsters are also fear-ridden about their bodies. They exaggerate the significance of each ache, often to get out of fulfilling an obligation. However, their physical distress does not motivate them to consult a doctor, because they fear that even greater pain will be inflicted. Consequently a minor ailment that is neglected may develop into an infection or a real illness. These youngsters fret over their height, weight, strength, and physical attractiveness. Some worry so much about their penis being undersized that they refuse to attend physical education classes in order to avoid undressing. When one fifteen-year-old shared a cabin with a group of boys on an overnight outing, he neither took a shower nor changed clothes. Despite the fact that he was well endowed, he did not want others to see his genitals. He was at ease in a group shower only when he was among much younger boys. In private, he tried to overcome his perceived inadequacy by tying a brick to his erect penis to stretch it.

Because the delinquent youngster is always striving to impress his peers, to have others sense that he is afraid is just about the most humiliating thing that can happen. To avoid embarrassment, he may shun any potentially anxiety-arousing situation. Or he may try to push fears aside and fly in the face of them. Some delinquents cope with apprehensions about physical weakness by lifting weights, taking up boxing, or acquiring training in martial arts. Obsessed with a desire to display bulging biceps, one thirteen-year-old lifted weights for two hours a day until he was able to lift 250 pounds. He was determined to be able to stand up to any threat. In addition, he thought that rippling biceps would impress girls.

Responsible youngsters have some of the same fears. They too may be afraid of the dark, experience dizziness in high places, and be preoccupied with their bodies. Many a teenage boy has dreaded undressing in front of others who have more pubic hair and larger genitals. But the responsible person handles both his neurotic and reality-based fears differently from the delinquent. He accepts fear as part of life and tries to overcome it. Fearing failure at school, he studies harder. Fearing disapproval from the coach, he gives his all at each practice. Neurotic fears may be embarrassing and, if intense enough, they may disrupt his life to the point that he becomes phobic, in which case he lives disabled or is driven to seek help. The delinquent fears fear because it demolishes his superman stance, leaving him feeling weak, exposed, and vulnerable. He copes with fear by denying it or lashing out at whatever he identifies as the source of the fear, or at any other convenient target.

Reputation is all-important. These youths build and maintain a "rep" for themselves through the way they talk, their style of dress, and the type of activities in which they engage. The profanity and street slang lacing the language of the middle-class delinquent is indistinguishable from that of his inner-city counterpart. Even as a small child, the delinquent accepts dares from others to show that he is not "chicken." These youngsters prove their mettle by jumping from high places, careening down steep hills on skateboards, riding the scariest roller coaster, racing a bike through someone's flower bed, competing to see who can swipe the most candy from a store. They play rough and take unfair advantage both in organized sports and in their own sandlot games. They prove to one another that they are physically tough by deliberately inflicting pain on themselves—holding their breath, sticking pins in their arms, burning themselves with cigarettes. No tears at any time; they show that they can take it, whatever the source of the pain. One boy cracked several ribs during a playground accident. He did not shed a tear or even wince as the ribs were taped. Later that day, to prove that he was invincible, he carried several packages out of a store without so much as a grimace. As teenagers, these youths demonstrate their daring by racing each other in cars, guzzling liquor, experimenting with drugs, and engaging in high-risk crimes.

"People aren't going to fuck with me" is the youth's stance toward his parents, teachers, other kids, the police, and the world in general. The smallest slight to his self-image, the least hint of interference with his plans, may trigger a violent reaction. One sixteen-year-old said tersely, "If anyone aggravates me, I'm ready to kill him." He then added, "I just like to fight, to feel skin against my knuckles, to feel noses break. I always win, except when it's four against one." This same youth thought of lashing to a tree a boy against whom he had a grudge and turning dogs loose to tear him to shreds. In such a boy's view, anyone who backs away from a fight is a punk or sissy.

At fourteen, Milt was bigger than most kids. He used his size to intimidate others. Whenever Milt had a bad day, defined by him as "when everybody gets on my nerves," others had better watch out. On such a day, Milt took offense because he overheard a classmate making a nasty comment about him. He confronted the boy, and they exchanged insults. Milt took things a step further by pushing the youngster, and was shoved in return. The other boy attempted to back off, ready to let things ride. Not Milt! He slammed his fist into the other boy's stomach and kept pummeling him until a teacher arrived on the scene. To an administrator, Milt explained, "No one gets by saying anything about me." When Milt heard that the boy's parents had pressed charges, he commented that he didn't know what the big deal was: "I didn't make him bleed." During a counseling session, Milt declared, "I like to fight. You really get to see how tough people are. Sissies get their butt beat easily." Milt hung out with others like himself, youths whom others didn't mess with unless they were spoiling for a fight.

Many children get into scrapes, and some go through a phase of fighting. But they eventually respond to socializing influences and learn that compromise, tact, and persuasion are more effective than fists. The delinquent's attitude of "no one messes with me" persists into adulthood. A thirty-eight-year-old criminal expressed it thus: "If you do me wrong, then you got to whup me."

Not all delinquents are tough guys. Some are terrified of physical injury and, transforming this fear into a virtue, they look down on those who are violent as crude, lacking class. Said one teenager with disdain, "I never hung around with rednecks. I wasn't violent." Such youngsters build their reputation by outsmarting or verbally intimidating others. A sixteen-year-old confessed, "I've got a fearless image on the outside, but inside I'm a scared guy. Fighting wasn't my thing. I don't have the weight." But he bragged that he didn't have to use his fists because "I can talk a good fight." What he meant was that intimidation was sufficient to accomplish his objective.

Whether or not he is a fighter, the delinquent takes but rarely gives. He does not know what friendship is because trust, loyalty, and sharing are incompatible with his way of life. The delinquent does not know how to hold a discussion, for he has little regard for anyone else's point of view. He says his piece and ignores or shouts down those who disagree. He engages in a fiercely competitive one-upmanship, building himself up by bragging about his exploits, usually with plenty of exaggeration. He diminishes others at every chance through unrelenting goading, teasing, and deception. Even his best buddy is not immune to being conned or made to look the fool. If a youth can get a good chuckle at this fellow's expense, it's another victory notched in his belt. The youngster finds humor in the misfortune of others. He delights in mocking, mimicking, and in other ways of making fun of people, his closest associates included. He guffaws whenever someone is off guard and surprised or humiliated. Even an accident, such as someone toppling down a flight of stairs, produces a laugh. What is predictable is that nearly all his friends will be the same way.

In the last few years, a handful of American schools have been devastated by student shootings, several of which resulted in the death of fellow classmates and teachers. Attempts to make sense of what motivated two boys to massacre their peers at Columbine High School in Colorado centered around a theory that the assailants were goaded into lethally assaulting their classmates because they had been ostracized. Critiques of the peer culture and of the school's social environment ran rampant through the media. However, those who engaged in such social criticism appeared to invert cause and effect. They surmised that the killers became angry and sought retaliation because they had been rejected by the mainstream. Largely ignored was the fact that these two youngsters did not behave as though they wanted to be part of the mainstream. They were known to have dressed strangely, behaved oddly, bullied others, and displayed an intense dislike for entire groups of students. A national magazine characterized them as having compiled "an inventory of their ecumenical hatred: all 'niggers, spics, Jews, gays, f—— whites.' " They especially disparaged athletes. The students who committed the atrocious crimes were in fact the very ones who had engaged in much of the ostracizing, setting themselves apart from others and priding themselves on doing so, on being different from those they scorned.[2]

An eerily similar situation occurred several years later in New Jersey, when a Columbine-like plot failed. Three teenagers set out on a murder spree with 2,000 rounds of ammunition. The plot was frustrated when the youths bungled a carjacking. Many in their community stated that these youths had been teased and bullied by their peers. However, they had called attention to themselves by wearing dark clothes, isolating themselves from their peers, and banding together as "Warriors of Freedom." The question again is whether the boys were ostracized unfairly, or whether they deliberately set themselves apart by their odd dress and behavior.[3]

The teenage delinquent's crimes become more frequent, daring, and serious. He is neither corrupted by others nor dependent on them for ideas. A torrent of schemes cascades through his mind, and he enacts those that are most exciting and feasible. The youth has his own tastes and preferences in crime, and looks down on kids who take what he considers foolhardy risks. One fifteen-year-old sneered, "I don't break into houses. It's too easy to get caught. These people don't think about the chances they take." Some youths operate as loners, others in groups, and some both ways. They detect frailty and vulnerability in people, and proceed to stalk their prey. Some operate by stealth and run a string of con games. Others operate by force and rob newspaper deliverers, snatch women's purses, roll drunks, and mug the weak and unsuspecting. Some youngsters have had a long-standing fascination with weapons and become knowledgeable about them. In their fantasies, they have shot, bludgeoned, clubbed, and blown to bits any number of people. Eventually the fantasies are transformed into reality. A thirteen-year-old boasted, "I have a nice arsenal." With a sadistic smile, he went on to enumerate his switchblades, chains, knives, and clubs. Virtually any convenient object can be used as a weapon. A stick becomes a club, a letter opener a knife. A stone can hit a windshield with the impact of a bullet when it is dropped from a bridge high overhead.

If a youth wants to obtain a firearm, he figures out how to get it. If adults in the family own firearms, the child knows where they are kept and figures out how to gain access to them. Otherwise, he finds sources on the street. Once a gun is procured, altercations that might have been settled with fists or nonlethal weapons or even verbally may result in tragic outcomes.

The central issue here is not the peer culture or the ease of finding a gun or even the current state of our gun laws. It is all about the mentality of the individual. If a gun were lying on a table in a school cafeteria, a crowd of students might gather out of curiosity. Most boys and girls would be frightened and immediately inform an adult. A few might stare at the gun, even handle it. Most likely, no one would seriously think of firing it unless it was a guy like Milt, mentioned above, having what he considers a "bad day." The criminality resides within the individual, not in his peers, and not in the gun. One could rightfully argue that a murder or serious injury could not occur if the gun were not present in the first place. The point remains that most students would not entertain the thought for a second of using the weapon even if it were within arm's reach. They would be horrified by its presence and probably act to have it removed safely and immediately by an adult.

Many things can be turned into weapons by children who are intentionally destructive. The automobile broadens opportunities for all youngsters, and there may be a new set of pressures from peers. Responsible teenagers regard "having wheels" as lessening dependence on their parents to take them places. They may drive in a reckless manner to impress their friends. And some take advantage of their new freedom and misuse the automobile by going places that their parents would highly disapprove of. A preoccupation with cars is typical of many adolescents, but what delinquents do with a car far exceeds the norm and has nothing to do with pressure from peers. Impatient to drive, many a delinquent is behind the wheel before he is licensed. Their buddies allow them to do this, or they "borrow" the family car. The automobile is unleashed as a weapon, and the youth drives as though he owns the road. Roaring about at raceway speeds, these teenagers terrify and aggravate motorists by cutting in, tailgating, screaming obscenities, and hurling objects out windows. In a car, more territory is accessible for criminal activity. The city kid can hit the more affluent areas, and the suburban kid can make contacts in the inner city.

In his book *Wiseguy: Life in a Mafia Family,* Nicholas Peleggi cites a criminal's statement attesting to the critical role of choice in determining his path in life: "At the age of twelve my ambition was to be a gangster. To be a wiseguy. To me being a wiseguy was better than being president of the United States. . . . To be a wiseguy was to own the world. I dreamed about being a wiseguy the way other kids dreamed about being doctors or movie stars or firemen or ballplayers."[4] If becoming a member of the mob seems to be extreme, consider a middle-class teenager who announced in no uncertain terms what sort of life she wanted. She spoke of her self-imposed separation from responsible peers, for whom she expressed the utmost contempt. She remarked, "What straight people do for fun, I'll never know. What do they do? If they started partying, they'd freak out." She remarked that she had nothing to talk about with straight people, and affirmed that the kids she wanted to be with were people like herself—those who lived in what she characterized as "life's fast lane."

All sorts of temptations exist for any youngster—an expensive jacket hanging in an open school locker, keys dangling in the ignition of an unlocked sports car, an expensive racing bike left unattended resting against a tree, alcoholic beverages lying within arm's reach in his parents' home. It is not such temptations or pressure from peers that compel a youth to commit a crime. Responsible boys and girls will leave alone what does not belong to them. They distance themselves from peers who steal, fight, lie, and are irresponsible in other ways. Pressured to do something contrary to their own ideas of right and wrong, they choose not to participate. If, by chance, an otherwise responsible youngster errs in judgment and succumbs to temptation, he is overcome by remorse when he is apprehended, or sometimes even if not found out, and is unlikely to repeat the behavior. In contrast, the developing criminal becomes emboldened, determined not to get caught the next time. He seeks out others like himself, is receptive to their schemes, and initiates plenty of his own.

4

"THE HELL WITH SCHOOL"

SCHOOLS HAVE SHORTCOMINGS, and valid criticisms can be made of them. Incompetent teachers, overcrowded classrooms, an antiquated physical plant, an unimaginative or rigid curriculum, and lack of discipline all have an adverse impact on learning. But only a minority of students exposed to any or all such adverse conditions are criminals.

For decades, schools have been accused of spawning criminals by failing to meet their needs when they are young and shutting them out of the social mainstream. Such charges ignore the fact that criminals reject school long before it rejects them. As a child, the criminal is bored by school, and his objectives have little to do with academic learning. Instead he exploits the school, using it as an arena for crime or else as a cover for it. Like his parents, the school is unsuccessful in socializing and educating the criminal. Even special education programs and counseling often fail to diagnose accurately the criminal pupil, much less change him.

The criminal as a child increasingly sets himself apart from those who take school seriously, and refers to them in disparaging ways. The "puny, cross-eyed bookworms" bear the brunt of the delinquent's teasing and bullying, especially those whom he labels teacher's pet. The youngster unmercifully preys upon any inadequacy or insecurity in his classmates, and loves to embarrass and terrorize them. A child who is visibly afraid of him becomes a repeated target of harassment all year. He is called names, cursed, mocked, threatened, punched, and made a scapegoat.

Although the delinquent picks on the serious students, he makes trouble mostly with kids like himself. He provokes them with an obscene sign, a hurled object, or a menacing gesture so that the recipient rises to the bait and gets into trouble, while he, the instigator, goes scot-free. A child mutters an obscenity to another boy, who responds by throwing a pencil. The teacher sees the flying pencil, but then is confronted with each child blaming the other: "He called me a name"; "He threw a pencil at me." A favorite occupation is the cutdown battle, in which boys compete to see who can be the most vicious in verbally tearing one another apart. When such incidents erupt regularly, the teacher is like a firefighter who is summoned to extinguish several blazes simultaneously.

All this troublemaking is an antidote to the boredom that the delinquent experiences in the classroom while his fellow students are engaged in learning. What others find tolerable or even fascinating, he disdains. He stirs up excitement through a series of power plays designed not only to relieve tedium but to call attention to himself and establish a reputation. What others consider getting in trouble he perceives as a boost to his self-image.

If the youngster is doing little or no work, his teacher and school administrators wonder whether he is intellectually deficient, emotionally disturbed, inherently lazy, or a combination of these.

When a delinquent is failing academically, his ability may be questioned. Results of intelligence testing may support a belief that he is just not very bright. Unfortunately, IQ tests are not always valid indicators of ability in such youngsters, because the scores are partially dependent on knowledge acquired in school. Low scores result not only because of a lack of information, but also because these youngsters have not acquired skills vital to success even on tests that do not require mastery of specific academic subjects. To perform well on puzzles and mazes requires concentration, persistence, and thinking things through. A child may be bright, but this may not be evident because his impatience, distractibility, and lack of interest lower his scores.

Rarely is the problem a lack of intelligence. Rather, the child refuses to absorb academic offerings much in the same manner that he balks at learning what his parents try to teach him. He rejects that which is meaningless to him, and consequently does not acquire basic information. A shocking example is that of a fourteen-year-old boy who could not write his complete address. An observer might have concluded that he was mentally retarded. But as a con artist he could run circles around his teacher, and was a genius at ferreting out weaknesses in people and exploiting them. His illiteracy was not a consequence of mental deficiency but of an attitude toward classroom learning described by one instructor as "I dare you to teach me something."

The high rate of illiteracy among juvenile delinquents and adult criminals is often attributed to a learning disability, an organically based condition alleged to account for both their academic and behavioral difficulties in the following fashion: Because the child is learning disabled, he fails and grows frustrated, and his self-esteem plummets. It is thought that because he cannot achieve academic recognition, he seeks it through antisocial behavior. Perhaps a tiny minority of delinquent children are truly learning disabled, but it has not been conclusively shown that there is a causal connection between learning disabilities and delinquency. An assumption that a delinquent youngster can't read because of a learning disability is usually unwarranted. The reason most delinquent youngsters are illiterate is that they refuse to learn to read. Think about what reading requires—concentration, drill, sticking with a task that may become tedious or difficult. Actually, the child is certain that he is smarter than others. Typical is the statement of one boy who claimed, "I could get all As if I wanted to, but school sucks." The youngster thinks it is not incumbent on him to exert effort except on his own terms. The idea is to do the minimum and get the work over with. He doesn't care about the product. He sets the standard for what is acceptable. So if he does homework, it is in an erratic, disorganized way. Some delinquents decide not even to go through the motions, and do no work. One teenager said, "I didn't see the need for homework and told the teacher I wasn't going to do it."

The criminal child appears to have a short attention span for most classroom assignments. If he is diagnosed with an attention deficit disorder, it is as though that explains and excuses everything, including criminality.

Sixteen-year-old Andy was referred to me for a consultation after he had fractured a classmate's skull during a locker-room brawl. Andy's mother came prepared with a stack of papers, including reports of educational and psychological evaluations. The reports were replete with references to her son's recently diagnosed attention deficit hyperactivity disorder (ADHD). Practically every difficulty this teenager had was attributed to ADHD, including low grades, emotional volatility, poor problem solving, impulsivity, avoidance of challenges, and a negative self-image.

How ADHD explained why Andy would threaten to attack a boy and then deliver on that threat more than an hour later, I haven't a clue. ADHD also seemed irrelevant to the criminality that Andy revealed to me, which included other fights, dozens of shoplifting episodes, vandalism, theft from his parents, truancy, anonymous phone calls, driving without a license, guzzling beer, and smoking marijuana. Excusing this boy's behavior because of his diagnosis did nothing to help him improve his conduct, nor did it make his victims feel any better. Besides, once Andy reaches adulthood, a judge won't accept ADHD as a reason not to throw him in jail if he is convicted of a crime.

Educators and mental health professionals frequently latch on to a diagnosis and cite it when discussing almost any aspect of an individual's personality. Yet with Andy and others like him, the diagnosis may be in error to begin with.[1]

Even though he performed poorly academically, Andy showed exemplary classroom behavior. His teachers reported that he was "wonderful" to have in class. At the very least, this meant he could sit still, which many children with ADHD cannot do without great difficulty. In fact, his mother remarked that if Andy wanted to do something, that activity could engage his attention for a very long time. And one of his teachers commented that in photography, about the only subject Andy liked, he was highly motivated and diligent. This reminds me of another teenager whose parents related to me that their son, also diagnosed ADHD, spent two days assembling a model airplane that required meticulously following complex instructions. In school, which he despised, he showed no ability to focus. Clearly his difficulty stemmed not from a biological inability to concentrate, but from an unwillingness to concentrate on anything not of interest to him.

But even if Andy's diagnosis were correct, ADHD does not preclude academic achievement. Many boys and girls who have difficulty paying attention desire to succeed academically. These are responsible children who show no signs of antisocial behavior. They will do anything to improve upon their school performance, including work extra hours with a tutor, or they may work to compensate by excelling in areas other than academic endeavors, such as athletics, mechanical skills, or the arts. Some benefit from medication.

Teachers often observe that the criminal child's lethargy is transformed into a burst of concentrated activity once he finds an interest. An observation not elaborated on in one of the reports about Andy was that he "does not think school is useful." Clearly the boy's interests lay elsewhere, and it was no wonder that he appeared unfocused and lethargic. Commenting about another delinquent youngster, a surprised teacher commented, "Roland can be very interested in a project if it is something that attracts his attention." Roland had the capability! However, very little that the school offered engaged Roland's attention. One teenager recalled that whatever independent academic interests he had vanished as soon as someone provided direction, tested his knowledge, or imposed a deadline. He said, "The interest would turn into a conflict when something had to be produced like a paper or test." His "conflict" was that he objected to anyone telling him what to do, whether at school or anywhere else. Furthermore, he refused to tolerate others evaluating him. He reflected, "Grading systems always bothered me, because I just disagree with them totally. If there's anything I'm interested in, I can do it."

An examination of the transcripts of such youngsters is likely to show spotty performance. When allowed to plan their own schedules, such youngsters choose the easiest subjects, and in these they may receive high grades. In areas where they naturally excel, they will also perform well because no real effort is required. These youngsters detest courses demanding the drudgery of drill, memorization, and step-by-step reasoning, notably mathematics, science, and foreign languages.

They often miss the main point of a story or of an episode in history because their focus is so narrow. Challenged one boy, "Why study history? It's all in the past." Unless the subject matter excites them, they do little work. Aspects of the curriculum that do interest them tend to appeal to their sense of adventure and thirst for excitement, such as a detailed account of a bloody battle or a dramatic science experiment.

In any group project, such a youngster expects to take charge and receive credit for the final product. He has no sense of teamwork. He *is* the enterprise, whereas others are merely lackeys to carry out his wishes. If they prove not so amenable, he quits, dismissing the activity as silly and boring. If he is not permitted to withdraw, he demeans the efforts of others, insisting all the while that things should be done his way. If he is allowed to take over, he is certain that he has more expertise than anyone else and operates as a dictator. When problems arise and he is unsure how to proceed, he is like a captain of a ship who is aware that he has lost his bearings but doesn't want to admit it to himself or to others and instead stubbornly plows ahead, insisting he is on course. For such a youngster, to seek help is to acknowledge that he does not know all there is to know. Like the proud captain, he'd rather run his boat aground than admit ignorance.

Academically, most delinquent children function far below their potential. But because of strong social pressure and school attendance laws, they remain in school long enough to avoid hassles with parents, teachers, truant officers, and the courts. When they reach an age when the law says they don't have to be in school, many leave. A minority stay and do well in school. If they earn good grades, others are likely to think well of them. As and Bs provide a cover for crime.

Evan was an honor-roll student and president of his high school's student council. People who regarded him as a model student and leader did not suspect that he was leading a double life. Outside school and away from his neighborhood, Evan was hanging around with a fast crowd that was drinking, using drugs, and stealing. He became increasingly involved in serious criminal activity, but was not caught. Because of his accomplishments at school, he was beyond suspicion. For years he had maintained the façade of the all-American boy, and so it was a shocked community that learned of his arrest for rape.

Some delinquents delight in raising hell in the classroom. If this starts in the primary grades, it is rarely regarded as a serious problem at the time. One teacher observed of a restless, pugnacious seven-year-old, "He has something cooking all the time." She sympathetically conceived of him as the class clown who was starved for attention. Parents and teachers strive to help such children through what is thought to be a period of adjustment. The problem is that the period never ends. The adjustment is never made, and the teacher's kindness is exploited as a sign of weakness.

Some delinquents go on a rampage of theft and destruction during school hours. If they want something that another pupil has, they snatch it when it is unguarded. Belongings vanish from desks, coats, and lockers, and items disappear from the teachers' lounge, from musical and athletic supplies, and from the cafeteria. Youths with stolen goods line up customers to take hot merchandise off their hands. The parking lot is a potential treasure trove for loot from unlocked cars. Drug sales to an eager clientele flourish. Vandalism takes an enormous toll as desks are carved, walls defaced by graffiti, books marked up, windows shattered, and furniture broken.

Instead of being centers of learning, schools can become battlegrounds as delinquents stake out their territory and establish supremacy. According to a survey quoted in a national publication, more than half of the students responding feared for their safety while attending school.[2] It is extremely difficult for a child to concentrate on the morning's math lesson after he has just been shaken down for his lunch money and warned that he'd better return with more cash the next day. Studying is next to impossible when a pupil has been told that unless he regularly hands over money for "protection," he will be beaten to a pulp. Some children will do anything to avoid using school bathrooms out of fear of being victimized in these unsupervised places. The school building may be a refuge, but once the child leaves, he faces the prospect of being terrorized on the playground, on the school bus, and on the street. Fear stalks the corridors of some schools, where fistfights occur daily and youths brandish weapons, although "zero tolerance" policies are helping diminish the incidence of violence.

If enough delinquent youngsters are concentrated in one place, the school is affected as though it were under siege. Students, teachers, and administrators are hostage to youths who create a climate of fear and paralyze the learning process.

Teachers who run afoul of antisocial youngsters find themselves accused of abuse. Capitalizing on what is a veritable national hysteria over abuse, all a boy or girl has to do is claim a teacher shoved, pushed, hit, or in any other manner physically maltreated him. Teachers are called on the carpet, virtually deemed guilty until they prove their innocence, which sometimes proves impossible. Their reputations and jobs are on the line. Confronted with an abuse claim by a child and his outraged parent, a school administrator is likely to come down on the side of the child at least to the extent that he or she launches an investigation, which at the same time serves to make a public statement that other children will be protected. Teachers are often so intimidated by anti-abuse policies that they fear even to pat a child on the back to offer reassurance or to put an arm around a student who injures himself on the playground. Teachers who instruct delinquent children in special schools must be super-cautious never to react physically.

School personnel perennially walk a tightrope in managing disruptive students. For example, if they restrain or isolate a violent child, they may be berated by administrators or parents, dragged into court, or assaulted by other students. Each time the school cracks down, it has not only unruly students to cope with, but also their parents and often the community. But they can get into deep trouble if they take no action and a child is harmed. Suspension of an unruly youngster provides temporary relief, but rarely can the permanent expulsion of a disruptive student be justified. To do so, administrators need a truly airtight case. Expulsion is rarely a solution. An attempt to transfer such a child to a special program or facility meets with cries that he is being stigmatized, deprived of opportunities, and dumped.

In some troubled institutions, instruction is usurped by the necessity of devising survival strategies. The problem of unteachable students is not confined to the United States. An article in a British daily newspaper stated that teachers had "blacklisted seventy-eight of the country's most violent and disruptive pupils."[3] Educators and students had been injured so severely in some instances that they required hospitalization. However, the expulsion of these "unteachables" did not last long, for they were returned to the classroom by governing bodies or independent appeals panels. The lack of support given educators was said not only to expose teachers and students to further danger, but also to affect adversely efforts to recruit and retain teachers.

A school must choose which among a staggering array of problems merits concentration of precious resources. Behavior that is not terribly disruptive or long-standing may be temporarily overlooked. Nonattendance is one area in which many schools are lax in imposing penalties, at least until it becomes a frequent pattern. When the school does take action, the child may deny having been absent, compose his own excused absence notes and forge a parent's signature, or destroy notices the school sends home before his parents see them. Thus parents may have no idea that their offspring has skipped school, or any awareness of their child's behavior and activities during those missed classroom hours.

Schools and teachers are evaluated by the criminal youngster much in the same way as are parents, relatives, and friends. The delinquent praises virtually anyone who lets him do what he wants, and reviles anyone who imposes limits. A group of adult inmates in a Minnesota prison brainstormed seventy-seven ideas in response to being questioned about how schools could help eliminate crime.[4] Their suggestions revealed a perspective unchanged from childhood, namely that school should cater to them rather than that they should fulfill the requirements of the school. Among the inmates' suggestions were "more spontaneity," "dump dress codes," "more rap sessions," "supervise kids and not teach them," "let kids teach some classes," "let students choose teachers." Additional proposals were offered, but most were directed toward allowing students free rein while requiring little personal responsibility.

To the delinquent youngster, a "good teacher" assigns little work, takes the class on field trips, and generally is lenient. Teachers who make students toe the line are to be outwitted and made fools of, just like other strict adults. When a teacher reprimands them, these youngsters are likely to go on the offensive, first charging that the teacher was wrong in giving them a bum rap and then proceeding to curse, mock, and threaten the teacher. The incidence of assaults on teachers in American schools has skyrocketed. The school will summon the police when serious offenses occur on school grounds. Because drugs have become so widely available at some schools, undercover police have been hired whose purpose is not so much to arrest the occasional marijuana user as to detect sources of supply and stem the flow of drug traffic. The delinquent who uses drugs regularly not only finds out about the hiring of police, but seeks to penetrate their anonymity. One boy was certain that in his school with its staff of black janitors, the new white janitor just had to be the "narc." He scoffed, "They have a secret cop, but that's so stupid. We all know he's a cop, but he doesn't know that we know. White janitors are a giveaway." Knowledge that an undercover policeman is around may deter some delinquent youngsters from involvement with drugs on school grounds. But others are incited to outwit police surveillance and conduct business as usual. A "drug bust" may drive the trafficking from the school premises, but it returns as soon as things have cooled off.

As delinquents know, schools often fail to report crimes to the police. They prefer to handle it internally and not call attention to the problem. One reason is that administrators do not consider the behavior at issue to be a crime. A second reason is that reporting crimes brings in outsiders who want to conduct their own investigations, which can be disruptive. A third is that it makes the school look bad and, by implication, the administration as well.

Administrators and faculty generally have broad discretion as to what penalty to impose internally for most disciplinary infractions. Some offenses are so egregious, however, that a firm stand must be taken in all such incidents, including mandatory notification of an outside authority. For example, the "Parent Handbook" for Montgomery Blair High School in Montgomery County, Maryland, lists as "non-discretionary expellable offenses," for which police are to be notified, "bomb or bomb threats, distribution of intoxicants, firearms, violent physical attack on a staff member, and weapons used to cause bodily injury."[5]

When matters are handled internally, each disciplinary step taken by the school poses an exciting challenge to the youngster, who wears his bad reputation like a Boy Scout merit badge. Often, too, the child's parents prove challenging to administrators. When notified by the school, some parents respond immediately by laying down the law to their child. Others are not so receptive. They find school conferences threatening because they hear the school asserting that if they were only better parents they would have better-behaved children. Failing to recognize the seriousness of the problem, some mothers and fathers defend their child. Then there are the parents who are virtually impossible to involve. They see their child's acting up as a school matter only, and shrug off responsibility for taking any action, often because they are as powerless as the school.

Some parents believe that their offspring would be less troublesome if he were away from his friends and under closer supervision. A decision to enroll him in a different school is agonizingly reached because the parents know that he will be up in arms at the idea of leaving his friends and will recoil at the prospect of unknown authorities exercising greater power over him.

Many private schools will not accept a child who has a history of causing turmoil in the classroom. Those that agree to enroll him usually have many others just like him. If the change of school is made, from the first day the child sizes up the teachers and other pupils. What appears to his parents to be a new attitude is simply the child's early decision to lie low until he figures out the new situation. Eventually he discovers that the school is not the prison he imagined. After a few weeks he gravitates to other students like himself. A change of school has not resulted in a change in the child. His parents' flicker of hope again dies out. Only now they are spending a lot of money (in the case of a private school), and in some cases they have changed their daily schedule in order to drive their son to a school distant from their home. Some settings offer such close supervision that the child realizes he can't get away with much. If that is so, he is superficially compliant. Then his parents may preserve the illusion that he has reformed, which lasts until the first phone call from an angry neighbor or the police.

Educators everywhere understandably want to give a child the benefit of the doubt. They want to do everything possible to help a youngster learn. When the school places the child in a special class for pupils who have learning deficiencies, he finds that less is expected. It's easier to satisfy the teacher and get away with more on the side. Many educators consider keeping such a youngster back a year, but usually conclude that it will be of little value. The child will simply be one year older, one year bigger, and one year angrier. So he moves on to become another teacher's problem.

Even though these youngsters have been regarded as unmotivated, inattentive, passive, negative, sad, hostile, and withdrawn, teachers are sympathetic and usually find something favorable to say. For the most part, they continue to believe that such pupils are emotionally disturbed and victims of forces beyond their control. Their classroom strategy is to foster whatever strengths they can find and to nurture a positive self-concept. They encourage the delinquent in what he can do well, and downplay his academic weaknesses and unruly behavior. The child is lauded for his talent in art or music and for his prowess in athletics. Whatever good work he does is held up as an example to others. A teacher may go out of his way to establish a positive emotional relationship by finding an area of common interest, no matter how unrelated it is to academic matters. Such an approach is calculated to provide the child with success experiences and to reduce his antagonism toward the teacher as an authority figure. The child laps up the praise and is inwardly triumphant when pressure to make him shape up is relaxed. With the teacher no longer on his back, he may settle down for a while. It appears that a constructive cycle is in motion. As his teacher accentuates the positive, he behaves even better, and the teacher has more to praise. Eventually the youngster has the teacher where he wants him. Enthusiastically, the pupil expounds to his teacher on sports, cars, or video games, but assiduously avoids percentages, punctuation, and spelling. He figures that the instructor won't push him because he'll want to keep the peace. As soon as the teacher applies pressure for him to perform academically, the close-knit relationship unravels and the youngster acts as though an ally has betrayed him. Faulting the teacher, he once again presents himself as a victim of injustice.

The delinquent also takes advantage of a sympathetic school counselor who regards him as emotionally disturbed. One fourteen-year-old boy regaled his counselor with a long, sad, and false story of how his parents didn't understand or trust him. The counselor urged his teachers to go easy on him because of the terrible problems he was having at home. The boy's mother, knowing her son very well, later reflected, "He used the counselor as a cushion. She was eating out of his hand after he convinced her that my husband and I were to blame for his problems." Some counselors are not so gullible. They designate such a child as emotionally disturbed, not out of sympathy but because it is the most expedient way to remove a disruptive influence from the classroom and place him elsewhere.

In many school systems throughout America, no special services exist for such a child. As long as he is designated "socially maladjusted," he disrupts every classroom he enters and remains a thorn in the side of classroom teachers for years until he becomes so bored and fed up that he just quits. If educators fudge a bit, however, there is an out. Because the criteria for designating a youngster "seriously emotionally disturbed" are so broad, school evaluators can apply this terminology to the delinquent so that he then falls into the even broader category of "handicapped children." Under state and federal law, if the public schools cannot educate a handicapped youngster, then he becomes eligible for special services, which may include placement in a private residential school, the high cost of which is borne by the taxpayers. Thus a youngster who is antisocial and who deliberately rejects all that any school offers may be placed in a setting with children who are genuinely emotionally disturbed and who suffer from depression, severe anxiety, crippling neurosis, or even psychosis. Once an antisocial boy or girl is designated handicapped, it becomes even harder for a teacher to manage that individual because of restrictions placed on disciplining pupils with a "disability." Placed in classes for the handicapped, the antisocial youngster's reactions are mixed. Usually, the work is easier and less is demanded. On the other hand, he may resent going to school with kids whom he tags as "dumb," "weird," or "crazy."

In some school systems, segregation into behavior modification programs is one means of managing these children. The objective is to equip them with skills so that they can return to their regular classrooms. Behavior modification entails systematically rewarding desired behavior and ignoring or penalizing undesirable behavior. Such an approach has proved effective in many skill development and training programs as well as in treating some problems in psychotherapy. When used with delinquents and criminals, it may evoke short-term compliance. But there is no evidence that it promotes long-term changes in personality, or that it produces sustained responsible behavior.

The delinquent eventually regards behavior modification as a game. He is presented with a system of earning points and fulfilling contracts to accomplish what some educators describe as getting the child to "buy into the system." At first such a child opposes any program that removes him from his friends and imposes more-stringent controls on his behavior. Consequently, during stormy confrontations he may be sent to cool off in a "quiet room." The scenario is very much like that of prison, where the recalcitrant inmate is sent to the "hole" and the cooperative prisoner earns time off his sentence. The youngster wants the "good time," but despises earning it on others' terms. Eventually he realizes that his stubbornness only prolongs his stay in the special program. Even though others have established the rules, behavior modification becomes a worthwhile game to play. If he goes along with the program or "buys into the system," he works his way back to his friends. His basic stance toward school is likely to remain as it was, but his conduct may become more civilized, at least temporarily. Some pupils steadfastly refuse to cooperate with any program and are not in the least frightened by the prospect of expulsion or some other consequence.

By age twelve, many of these children have been through the evaluation and diagnosis mill repeatedly. Still they remain an enigma, and their problems become increasingly grave.

Delinquents who find school intolerable just don't attend. If they are old enough, they find work or else just roam the streets. A minority follow a different path. Educators are most baffled when a youngster has done well academically and then his grades take a nosedive. Thirteen-year-old Rob had been in a program for the gifted and talented, but he was failing eighth grade. Seeing that he was having problems, the school tried to accommodate the youth by allowing him to take less rigorous courses. A social worker wrote in her evaluation of the boy, "School personnel have been creative in attempting to modify their regular program to help his adjustment, but have not yet been able to satisfy him." Rob's family was stable, and the social worker simply could not fathom the drastic change in Rob's school performance. She finally concluded, "It is assumed that the stress of adolescence and the combination of hormonal changes with prescribed and illicit drug use is responsible for much of his difficulty." When I evaluated Rob, I found a simpler explanation. Through the sixth grade, he had received honor-roll grades without ever working hard. However, in junior high school, he was no longer able to slide by when he had to meet stiffer requirements of quizzes, exams, papers, and projects required by not one but several teachers. Rob's refusal to apply himself was an old pattern, but the consequences were evident for the first time, and seemingly overnight, once he entered junior high.

Delinquent youngsters who are bright enough to earn above-average grades, usually with little effort, can gain admission to college. There they continue to be dissatisfied with teachers, courses, requirements, and the routine. Their complaints about college are often echoed by other students who are not involved in crime. The serious students continue with their education despite their dissatisfaction; they have long-range goals in mind. Some who are not so persistent drop out, but find other, responsible areas of endeavor. The criminal uses the college campus as an arena for his excitement-seeking. He may get fed up and leave. Or he may stick it out because he finds the life soft—"a four-year paid vacation," according to one sophomore who was knee-deep in crime. Those who remain in school emerge as criminals with degrees rather than as criminals without degrees. Their education serves them by helping them gain entrée for their criminal operations into sophisticated, affluent circles.

The psychiatrist Samuel Yochelson used to quip that the school could engage the delinquent and hold his interest if it offered courses in lock-picking, safecracking, and arson. However, even this seems dubious because if such subjects were *legitimate* offerings, the delinquent probably would reject these also. Even the achievement of honor-roll grades does not signify that he values an education. Reflecting a lifelong attitude, one twenty-year-old criminal who maintained a B average in college commented, "School was so meaningless for me that it's hard to imagine someone getting something out of it."

For the criminal child, school is mainly a place to hang out with friends. For a while he may satisfy academic requirements because he is bright enough to get by with minimal effort. As the work becomes more difficult, his grades fall except in subjects he finds easy or intriguing. As he becomes disenchanted with school, he interferes with his classmates who want to learn. Though the faculty tries to accommodate him with special classes and programs, he rejects their efforts and eventually drops out.

Then there are those who take a different approach. They excel academically, advancing to college and beyond. What a shock it is when it's discovered that for these accomplished men and women, their education facilitated their involvement in new arenas for criminal activity, or that their academic and social success provided a cover that allowed them to get away with crimes outside of school and later outside of their work environment.

5

WORK AND THE CRIMINAL

THE CRIMINAL'S IRRESPONSIBILITY occurs as a *pattern* through-out his life. His deviousness and exploitation of people at work and his self-serving utilization of a job reflect how he treats the world. He scorns hard workers with modest aspirations. For him it is far more gratifying to steal electronic equipment than to earn and save enough money to buy it.

Tanya was an intelligent, capable young woman. She could have excelled in any number of legitimate occupations, but instead chose employment of a different sort. Daily she set out for shopping malls, much like an employee going to a regular job. Tanya became such a skilled shoplifter that thievery became her "career." Acting like a personal shopper, she would take orders from friends for items they would like her to bring them, only she intended to steal rather than purchase the merchandise. Her shoplifting career occasionally got interrupted by an arrest. Then she was back at it. Finally she exhausted all options of the local criminal justice system, including probation, counseling, and local jail time, and was sentenced to a Colorado prison for women on grand larceny charges and violations of an earlier probation.

Earning money is not a criminal's chief inducement to work, because he may net far more from a single crime than from weeks of employment. *The criminal's most pressing business is crime,* not his job. The criminal who holds a job may have the intelligence and skill to acquire substantial money and power through legitimate means. However, even enormous wealth and power, if honestly earned, would count for little. If something is legitimate, to him it is hardly worthwhile. Corporate officers who are criminals enrich themselves at the expense of their faithful employees, who eventually lose their jobs when the company folds, and of the company's stockholders, who find their shares worthless. Their interest is not chiefly in money, of which they have plenty, but in proving they are savvy enough to outmaneuver and outsmart others. The mentality is no different from that of an offender who breaks into and robs an electronics store.

Criminals are at heart antiwork. Some work rarely, if at all. Others intermittently hold jobs to appear respectable, meanwhile committing crimes under the nose of their employer. These individuals stick with a job until they become bored or until they suspect that the authorities are hot on their trail. Others hold a job for a long time and perform well. Securing a good reputation makes it easier for them to indulge in illicit activities without being suspected.

Unemployment and crime have long been linked. Almost any sociology textbook will assert that people turn to crime because they have been frustrated by a society that denies them opportunities to earn a living. Being unemployed is devastating for most people. During recessions, millions of Americans have been laid off temporarily or lost their jobs permanently. But people have reacted differently to this crisis. Some have taken any job, no matter how much of a step down it seemed. Others have received unemployment benefits while continuing to search for work. Some have become despondent and stopped looking for jobs. Although the unemployed and their families have suffered terribly, most of them have not become criminals. Economics writer Robert J. Samuelson stated that a 1982 drop in crime during a period of rising unemployment constituted "one of those massive, unexpected assaults on conventional wisdom that prompts a reconsideration of how society functions."[1] The *causal connection* between unemployment and crime is weak. What one must look at is the personality of the individual and how he reacts to adversity, whether it is unemployment or anything else.

Criminals have been regarded as particularly disadvantaged because of their lack of job skills, their low self-esteem, and their stigmatizing criminal records. What frequently is not taken into account, however, is that many criminals were antiwork long before ever being incarcerated. If a criminal lacks vocational skills, it is not, in most cases, because he was denied a chance to acquire them. Agencies assist offenders in numerous aspects of preparing for and obtaining employment.[2] They help write résumés, compose letters, prepare for interviews, and provide information about job openings. If a criminal lacks job skills, employment counselors will refer him for vocational training. Opportunities exist; it is a matter of what the individual does with them.

For many criminals, work means to sell one's soul, to be a slave. Small wonder that they refuse to equip themselves for that. Yet, with few marketable skills, they refuse to assume the only positions for which they are qualified, often involving routine and menial work. Rather than scrub floors, pick up trash, or carry luggage, they prefer to remain unemployed. Such labor is not at all in line with their inflated notion of their deserved station in life. Rejecting a janitorial job at a restaurant, one young man told his job counselor, "I ain't no peon." Another criminal, after being dismissed from his tenth job in one year, admitted, "If the job meant something, I would have been there."

When unemployed, the criminal's most frequent excuse is that no jobs are available. Probation officers and counselors constantly hear this refrain when the truth often is that the criminal neither made an inquiry nor submitted an application. He may claim that a job is too far away or that he lacks transportation. Yet, if there were a female of interest even father away, he'd manage to see her anytime he wanted.

Offenders may acknowledge that while jobs are available, none fits their requirements. A job that they deem acceptable makes few demands but still offers power, prestige, and a high salary. When questioned about whether this attitude is realistic, they respond indignantly, "Well, you like your job, don't you?" They do not consider that the person with whom they are speaking has devoted years to preparing for his current position. Ignoring this reality, the criminal thinks he is inherently more capable than others and equipped to do a top-notch job; it is not incumbent upon him to obtain the requisite education, training, and experience. Consequently, no job is acceptable. He regards himself as above entry-level jobs, but he is not qualified for a job that would be to his liking. So he continues not to work, and offers excuses when held accountable.

Twenty-two-year-old Brad had training and experience in small-engine repair. He said that he didn't like that type of work, and it didn't pay enough. Moreover, he had quit a job in that area because he could not tolerate working with people who, in his opinion, didn't do their job as they should. Brad decried the fact that no one recognized his exceptional talents and skills. In his notes, Brad's counselor reported, "He says that he is a very creative and emotional person and is right-brained. He says he quit school to preserve his creativity because school causes you to think only left-brained. He says that he has knowledge but no one will listen to him. He plans to move to Europe because they will understand him there."

The criminal's fantasy has long been that, were he to deign to work, he would stride through the door, snow the interviewer, and land a high-paying job. He assumes that he will be a resounding success at anything if others will only recognize his talents and surrender the reins of authority to him. He readily envisions himself the manager of a department store, but never would he conceive of himself sweeping the floor of that very store. With some education and experience, he may present himself so impressively that he persuades a company executive to offer him a position carrying considerable responsibility.

Having refused for months to look for work, twenty-eight-year-old Mike finally changed his tune after his wife threatened to take their two children and leave. Dressed in a chocolate brown pin-striped suit with a tan vest, a subdued striped tie, and shined cordovan shoes, he strode into a bank and asked to see the manager. His immaculate appearance and air of confidence had an immediate impact. Ushered into the manager's office, Mike seemed so knowledgeable about public relations and customer service that the manager hired him on the spot, even though there had been no vacant position. In addition, he offered Mike a choice of working hours. As part of a training program, Mike had to begin as a teller, but he was assured that he'd move up the ladder into the ranks of management. After just three months of cashing checks, logging deposits, and updating passbooks, Mike became impatient. He saw no further need for training, resented not gaining a promotion, and decided he'd had enough. Again, he was unemployed by his own choice, but in talking to others he blamed his boss.

Even getting locked up does not jolt the criminal into examining, much less modifying, his pretensions. An eighteen-year-old awaiting trial for murdering a drug dealer told me that he expected to make "a whole bunch of money" both as a rock star and as an investor in the stock market. This man with a tenth-grade education and no job skills envisioned owning a home in the Caribbean, a yacht, and a Mercedes. In a similar vein, a defendant awaiting trial for capital murder declared that his ambition was to be "a businessman, have a desk and a computer, and own my own stocks. I'm trying to get my life on track so I can be the biggest businessman there is." This individual had never held a full-time job of any kind. A sixteen-year-old in detention said that he wanted "a normal life without any major tragedies." In the next breath, he made it clear that work was not to be part of that existence. "I just want to stay alive and have fun. Somebody put me here, but not to work."

When doors do not open immediately to a criminal who has actually decided to seek employment, he complains about lack of opportunity or discrimination. One criminal revealed the basic antiwork attitude usually underlying such gripes when he confided to his rehabilitation counselor, "People like me don't like hard work, and we're not going to work. It's like trying to make a respectable butcher out of Jack the Ripper." One twenty-five-year-old criminal hardly knew what work was, but conditions of his parole from prison mandated that he find out. Formally uneducated, but having a sharp intellect and a persuasive tongue, he turned to sales. In two months he became a top department store salesperson, for which management recognized him with a badge and a salary raise. But still he had little zest for the work. By noon of each day, he felt sapped of energy, despite getting twice as much sleep at night as he did when he was unemployed and carousing until all hours. Selling shirts, slacks, coats, and sweaters day after day was insufferable. After quitting, he told others his boss was a tyrant and that no one appreciated his efforts.

Sometimes a criminal stays on the job for a while because he is placed in charge of something. For example, while sitting atop a gigantic crane and operating it in the construction of a twenty-story building, one man felt extremely powerful. Had he been shifted to collating papers at a desk in the firm's office, he would have resigned. For such a criminal, even the acceptable becomes unacceptable, and within a short time he demands a change or resigns. Eventually the crane operator grew bored and quit, even though he had no other job awaiting him.

Some criminals are relatively steady jobholders because they realize that employment is their badge of respectability. If the criminal works, others ask fewer questions about how he spends his time. (Often parents, spouses, and counselors think a criminal is mending his ways just because he holds a job.) When he chooses to put forth effort at a job, he learns quickly and is a fireball of energy. His employer values him, and he earns promotions. At least for a while, he basks in the recognition because it conveys publicly what inwardly he has been certain of all along—that he is a cut above the ordinary. But that is about all it means, for he still does not think of himself as a regular workingman like his co-workers, and more than likely he has contempt for the job and for the very people who promoted him. Nevertheless, he knows that just as good grades at school helped him or his buddies get away with things on the side, so can an impressive job history.

Status and authority are far more important to the criminal than the quality of the work he does. To rise meteorically to the summit is his due, just because he is who he is. On the job, he maintains that his way is the only way. He gives unsolicited advice and imposes his opinions. A ruthless critic of others, he bristles at anyone who offers even a minor suggestion to him. Co-workers resent his dogmatism, inflexibility, and closed mind. He locks horns frequently over trivial issues with fellow employees, subordinates, and supervisors. He abuses authority that he holds legitimately rather than exercising it in ways beneficial to the company. As an executive, he reaches his decisions in isolation rather than through consultation. Opinions and conclusions are stated as decrees. In the short term, the employee's self-confidence and certainty may be so highly valued by his supervisor that his shortcomings are overlooked. His executive style creates a convincing front until it becomes evident that he is not only antagonizing people, but also has no in-depth knowledge of the business.

Some criminals are smooth rather than contentious, ingratiating rather than surly, devious rather than intimidating. They pretend to be interested in what others say. Appearing to invite suggestions, they inwardly dismiss each idea without considering its merits. They seem to take criticism in stride, but actually ignore it and spitefully make a mental note of who the critic was. They misuse authority and betray trust, but are not blatant about doing so. With the criminal at the helm, employee morale deteriorates. His method of operation sooner or later discourages others from proposing innovative ideas and developing creative solutions.

For the sake of perspective, it is important to acknowledge that people who are not criminals have some of the same personality flaws. It is a matter of degree. Some executives would be far more effective were they less dogmatic, more self-critical, and generally more sensitive to the needs of others. Still, they value their jobs, loyally give their best to the firm, and do not intentionally exploit their co-workers. A criminal values his job mainly as an arena for power-seeking. He attains power at the expense of others, sometimes quite ruthlessly, and exercises it to further his own objectives.

It is the routine of a job that gets to many criminals, who seem allergic to routine anywhere in life. In order to overcome the tedium, some use drugs while at work. When the criminal is high, his day is bearable, for drugs help his mind soar from the mundane to the exciting. In addition, there is the intrigue of finding out which fellow workers are users, identifying new sources for buying drugs, or discovering markets in which to make sales. Because he performs satisfactorily at his job, the criminal's drug use is unlikely to be noticed by management. If he becomes lackadaisical or careless, his employer reprimands him and perhaps assumes that something is temporarily troubling him. If the poor performance persists, the criminal may be fired, but without his boss ever suspecting his involvement with drugs. In the unlikely event that the criminal is caught red-handed using drugs, his boss may advise him to seek treatment, perhaps at company expense. Some employers even shoulder part of the blame. Rather than penalize the user, they assume that unsatisfactory conditions at work drove him to drugs. The worst that is likely to happen is that the criminal loses his job, which to him may not be a particularly severe penalty.

Criminals utilize jobs directly for crime. Businesses suffer more from inside theft than from pilferage by customers. Employees abscond with millions of dollars' worth of merchandise and embezzle substantial amounts of cash. The stealing may be as brazen as an employee's backing up a truck to the loading dock and hauling away a computer, or it may occur on the sly from behind a desk as a company executive alters books, takes kickbacks, and sells confidential information.

Criminals set up their own businesses in which they purport to provide services or deliver products and then do neither. The home-repair business is one of many that are plagued by fly-by-night operators. A contractor drives around a neighborhood, offers homeowners a good price for driveway resurfacing, pockets a deposit, and is never seen again. If a criminal has merchandise to sell, he misrepresents its quality. One man bought cheap foreign watches at $4.25 each. He slipped each one into a burgundy-and-gold velvet case and advertised it as a seventy-dollar timepiece marked down to thirty-five dollars. Customers snapped them up, certain that they had a bargain. The purveyor of this merchandise had a whole string of confidence games running by which he extracted money from trusting people. He was not above swindling widows on fixed retirement incomes out of their meager savings.

Even if the criminal does not actually engage in crime at the work site, he may learn skills on the job that are eventually useful in crime, such as those of a locksmith. In the course of his duties, he gains entrée to the homes and businesses of the affluent, who later become his victims.

Frank, an air-conditioning repairman, regularly cased out homes during customer service calls. During a casual conversation with the owner, he gathered information about the habits of the family, often succeeding in getting a customer to reveal specific times when no one was home. Frank gained the confidence of his customers because he appeared thorough in his service. By taking a long time to check out equipment, he had ample opportunity to scrutinize the premises closely. Examining air ducts throughout the house and tinkering with one mechanism and then another, he gained access to every room. When he inspected the outside condenser, he looked around for the best route to make a fast entrance and an immediate getaway. He might notice that the condenser next door was running and, in the future, rely on its incessant drone on a sweltering day to conceal the sound of his footsteps.

Criminality in corporations burst into the news during the steep stock market decline between 2000 and 2003. A front-page article in the *Washington Post* cited corporate events that continued to rattle markets and drastically affect millions of individuals: "A major accounting firm convicted of obstructing justice. A leading brokerage caught misleading its clients. Imperious chief executives falling like flies. Huge corporations tumbling into bankruptcy. Business pages that read like crime blotters."[3] The ripple effect was widespread. Loyal employees lost jobs. Those who invested a significant portion of their pension funds in company stock found their savings wiped out. The criminality of a relative few inflicted massive damage as distrust and cynicism reverberated through the entire economy. This was succinctly summarized in *The Economist* of June 8, 2002: "[Investors] have . . . lost confidence in Wall Street's ability to act as an honest broker between them, the providers of capital, and the corporate users of it."[4]

The mentality of the executive who misuses corporate funds is the same as that of the armed bank robber; for neither individual is a desperate need for money the paramount motive. The amount of money gained in the crime is just an index of how skillful the person is. The bank robber extracts money by force. The corporate executive does the same through sophisticated and wily schemes and deceptive maneuvers. Both know right from wrong, but shut such considerations out of their thinking. Both calculate how to avoid detection, and revel in their success at pulling off the job. And neither cares about the impact of their conduct on others.

The mental makeup of professionals who commit crimes is no different from that of other criminals. Because of their accomplishments and esteemed position, they are beyond suspicion. Victims are reluctant to come forward because they know it is their word against that of a highly regarded professional. The criminal counts on the victim remaining silent. In the event that his wrongdoing comes to light, he mounts an attack on his accuser's credibility.

There is a conventional wisdom with respect to the contribution of environmental factors to corporate crime. It is basically the same as explanations that are offered for many other types of offenses. The thinking is that if temptation is dangled in front of an ambitious individual, greed may override integrity and sound judgment. In a university magazine article, the observation is made that "executives are sometimes tempted to slip into the criminal realm."[5] Great risk-takers are considered especially vulnerable.

To assert that elaborate corporate swindles result from a "slip" into crime is absurd. Business executives do their homework, some more carefully than others. They know the legal from the illegal and have the resources to consult others if there is any question. It is one thing to miscalculate—businesses do fail—but it is another to brazenly disregard possible consequences, which greedy individuals do when they pursue power and seek to enrich themselves at the expense of others.

The claim also has been made that illegal activities are more likely to occur when oversight is less. Less regulation does provide more opportunity for dishonest men and women to exploit situations for their own aggrandizement. However, it is the individual who decides how to function, whatever the environmental conditions are.

Why would a person successful in his profession take such risks? It goes back to the criminal's basic view of work as being for slaves and suckers. Reaching the highest rung on the corporate ladder is not enough. Holding a trusted, esteemed position as a teacher, counselor, or clergyman is not enough. Whatever legitimate rewards his job offers, they do not satisfy him. The criminal never has enough power, control, and excitement, which are the oxygen of his life. Over and over, he must prove that he is more clever, more capable, more ingenious than others and can get away with crossing boundaries, violating policies, breaking rules, defying laws, and manipulating others into serving his own objectives.

Criminals in positions of power have few scruples about taking advantage of the vulnerable. During 2001 and 2002, revelations of child sexual abuse and its cover-up by members of the clergy rocked the

Catholic church. Moreover, the misconduct was not a single occurrence, but a pattern repeated in some cases over a period of many years.

Freddy's mother, a single parent, was a devout Catholic. Father Anthony became a trusted confidant of his mom, while Freddy looked up to the priest as being godlike. He could hardly believe it when Father Anthony first visited his home, the purpose ostensibly being to urge his mother to encourage Freddy to become more involved in church activities. The result was that the boy spent more time around the priest. Freddy told me that when he was eleven, he was startled and confused when Father Anthony started rubbing his buttocks. "I ignored it, figured it was my imagination," Freddy told me during a counseling session. Then the priest began hugging and kissing him on the lips. Freddy dared not tell his mother what was happening, although he wanted to. He knew that she practically worshiped Father Anthony, and thought she'd only be angry and not believe him. The situation worsened as Father Anthony unzipped the boy's fly, fondled him, performed oral sex on him, and asked Freddy to watch him masturbate. When Freddy finally summoned the nerve to disclose to his mother some of what was going on, she reacted as he'd feared. She became enraged and punished him for accusing Father Anthony of such horrendous things. "I just gave up hope," Freddy recalled. The contact finally ended when Freddy and his mother moved. As an adult, Freddy has no interest in any organized religion. Moreover, he has no contact with his mother.

It is a shock to discover that a person like Father Anthony has victimized the children he has been entrusted with teaching and protecting. Teachers, coaches, youth group leaders, clergymen, and others who care for children are often regarded as role models and certainly beyond suspicion of any sort of criminal conduct. It is the investment of absolute trust that makes it feasible for unscrupulous individuals to utilize their positions for their own purposes. When allegations of wrongdoing surface, members of the community leap to their defense. Those who raise the allegations may become the targets of angry adults who remain incredulous.

Because of his integrity, achievement, and service to the community, Lewis appeared to set a wonderful example for young people. A college-educated man, he had been a teacher and scoutmaster. Scrutiny of his résumé, however, revealed that he had changed jobs frequently. His passion for twelve- to fourteen-year-old boys landed him in trouble. Lewis was asked to resign in several situations when his sexual involvement with minors came to light. Finally the police were called by parents who learned of his ongoing sexual relationship with their son, who was a member of Lewis's scout troop. It turned out that sexual episodes had occurred close to twenty times on camping trips and at the boy's home.

Lewis was proud of the many good things he had done for youngsters. "I came to know youngsters and really understand them," he said. He helped more than one boy achieve the rank of Eagle Scout. Lewis endeared himself to the scouts' parents. He recalled one mother expressing her gratitude by saying, "Jesus Christ sent you to us." Tearfully, he acknowledged, "When I crossed over the line, all the good I did was destroyed." Regarding the particular case when he was criminally charged, Lewis reflected, "It didn't feel inappropriate at the time of the act." In fact, he commented, "I was teaching him about himself. I had a warm feeling of being helpful." Asked whether he thought he had harmed the child in any way, Lewis replied that the publicity had been devastating, but he could think of no other adverse outcome. "I'm not the monster I'm accused of being," he said. After receiving a thirty-year prison sentence, Lewis told me he felt "abused and used by the system." He remarked, "Everything I did was out of love."

I am not saying that every person who succumbs to temptation one time is a career criminal. In moments of weakness, people do things they shouldn't. Either because they were caught and suffered the consequences or because of their own remorse, they do not repeat that behavior.

Professionals in many fields held in high regard by the public have exploited their positions and abused the trust vested in them. A teacher is an accomplice to students' cheating on standardized tests. She cares far less about her pupils than she does about looking good when the scores are published. A police officer promises to tear up a traffic ticket if the female driver has sex with him. An executive of a charitable organization skims money from contributions for his own personal luxuries.

No matter how accomplished they are, criminals lack a work ethic.

Some refuse to work at all unless an authority such as a probation offi-cer is breathing down their neck. Some utilize the job as an arena for committing crimes—stealing, establishing contacts for drugs, embez-zling funds. Others, by excelling in a profession or business, acquire excellent reputations so they are able to get away with crimes both out-side and within the workplace. Their talents and accomplishments enable them to victimize trusting colleagues, loyal subordinates, clients, and an admiring public.

6

PEOPLE AS PAWNS

THE CRIMINAL VALUES PEOPLE only insofar as they bend to his will or can be coerced or manipulated into doing what he wants. He has been this way since childhood, and by the time he is an adult he has a worldview in which he believes that he is entitled to whatever he wants. Constantly he is sizing up his prospects for exploiting people and situations. To him the world is a chessboard, with other people serving as pawns to gratify his desires. His actions express this view of life, and it also pervades his fantasies.

The criminal conjures up visions of himself as a super-criminal, dramatically pulling off big scores that outdo the exploits of the most legendary figures. Typical of his fantasies are masterminding a worldwide diamond-smuggling operation, working for a syndicate as a hit man, and living lavishly from the proceeds of multimillion-dollar heists. By no means limiting his fantasies to crime, the criminal fancies himself at the top of the heap in any undertaking. He is the Medal of Honor combat hero, the secret agent, or the sleuth who cracks a murder case that has stymied an entire police department. He also envisions himself as the self-made millionaire luxuriating in a palatial seaside home, with his Rolls-Royce, harem of women, retinue of servants, private jet, and yacht.

I have asked many men behind bars what kind of work they wanted to do when they got out. Many have responded that they wanted to run their own business. One can hardly fault them for aspiring to achieve what, for many people, is the American dream. When asked what being an entrepreneur involves, most haven't a clue. Dwelling in the world of their pretensions, they envision themselves barking orders while others scurry to do their bidding. Rather than anticipating the endless problems that plague people as they build and operate a business day to day, criminals focus on the enormous wealth that they are certain will be theirs. It is the "big score" notion all over again—a huge bonanza obtained easily.

Many people might imagine themselves as heroes and multimillionaires. Such idle thoughts flash into their minds and either self-destruct automatically or are consciously pushed aside. Some fantasies recur and spur people to take creative initiatives and work hard to achieve what they want. But the criminal believes that he is *entitled* to whatever he desires, and he will pursue it ruthlessly. Every day, illicit schemes cascade through his mind like a waterfall. Said one professional holdup man, "Every minute of my life I scheme." Many of the criminal's fantasies range beyond what is feasible, but once he comes up with an idea that seems plausible, he nourishes it until he is positive that he can enact it without a hitch.

Wherever the criminal is—sauntering down the street, buying groceries at the supermarket, driving in rush-hour traffic, riding the elevator to his apartment—he visualizes people and property as opportunities for conquest. The sports car parked by the curb with the keys in the ignition could be his for the taking. The purse dangling from the supermarket cart is a tempting target. The bank he passes looks like an easy hit. And he is certain that the blonde on the elevator would find him irresistible. Put a criminal and a responsible person in the same store, and ask each as he comes out to recount his thoughts while there. The responsible person comments on the attractiveness, quality, and price of the merchandise, and perhaps on the efficiency of the service. In addition, he may describe a pretty salesperson or customer and recount a conversation overheard. The criminal notices little of this. He determines the best means to gain access to the merchandise as well as to customers' purses, wallets, and other personal belongings. He also notices the location of the cash register, cases out the security arrangements, and locates the nearest exit. In addition, he regards any attractive woman as his for the taking.

The criminal's attitude toward people is mercurial, dependent on whether they serve him. One day he may regard a person as his bosom pal and the next as his mortal enemy. Even his appraisal of his mother vacillates from saintly to satanic, depending on how readily she does his bidding. The transformation in his view of her is especially striking when he is confined. So what if he has caused her years of heartache; he still expects her unswerving loyalty and devotion. She is to visit, write, and mail or bring whatever he tells her he needs. However, if she fails to comply with his demands, she is reviled. An inmate affectionately closed one letter, "I love you, lady, and I hope you're taking good care of yourself." Not long afterward, this same young man cruelly berated his mother for unknowingly visiting him on the same day he expected his wife, thereby using up his quota of one visit per day. On the heels of that incident, he penned a letter riddled with sarcasm, saying, "I am quite sorry that you were so greatly inconvenienced by my stupidities while I was out, and I am truly sorry that I have been such a poor son to you. I hope that you can find it in your heart to forgive me for my transgressions. At least I hurt you without malice. I try each day to convince myself that your hurting me here has no malice. Happy Birthday." A continuing expectation on the part of this inmate and others like him is that his mother will galvanize forces to turn the wheels of justice in his behalf. After this fellow wished his mother a happy birthday, he added a postscript instructing her to call the judge's clerk and maneuver to have another charge dropped that was still pending.

Criminals proclaim that they value their family, that they want to be fully accepted, no matter what they do. Yet they treat family members like personal possessions. Over and over, they demand, intimidate, threaten, betray, disappoint, and exhaust their families. When the criminal's parents don't do what he wants, he tries to make them feel guilty. Writing a progress report, a counselor described how exploitative a young offender was toward his family who had given unstintingly of their emotional support as well as financial backing to help him become a responsible person: "When [Dana's] family refuses to compromise their values and expectations for him, his complaint is that no one understands him. When his parents disapprove the choices and decisions he has made, [Dana's] response is to accuse them of attempting to control his life. It is as though [Dana] wants to solicit support from his family to allow him the opportunity to engage in self-destructive behaviors."

The criminal expects to prevail in every situation. He considers himself the hub of the wheel, never one of the spokes. Reflected one man, "I made myself a little god at every turn." Another recalled, "I always wanted to feel like a king." The pursuit of power per se is by no means exclusively a criminal characteristic. Power can be sought responsibly and utilized to benefit others as well as oneself. It is critical to achieving success in many walks of life, and is wielded to some degree by everyone from a parent to the president. The issue is how a person pursues power and how he uses it once he acquires it. People rise to positions of power through besting the competition by being smarter, more skillful, more creative, or more interpersonally astute. They may also do it through intimidation and deception and by preying ruthlessly on others' weaknesses. When people are in a position of power, they may use it responsibly or irresponsibly. For example, a policeman may have to use force as a last resort in making an arrest, or he may get a kick out of brutally subduing someone when force is not necessary. Criminals crave power for its own sake, and they will do virtually anything to acquire it. Insatiable in their thirst for power and unprincipled in their exercise of it, they care very little whom they injure or destroy.

A criminal does not regard himself as obligated to anyone, and rarely justifies his actions to himself. The justifications come later, and only when he has to defend himself to others. Just the fact that *he* has decided on a course of action legitimizes it. One man who had committed scores of burglaries said, "I turn people on or off as I want. My idea in life is to satisfy myself to the extreme. I don't need to defend my behavior. My thing is my thing. I don't feel I am obligated to the world or to nobody." Other people and their property exist for his benefit. One criminal reflected that whatever his brother owned belonged to him also: "I just saw his money as being mine. I was just reveling in what I would do with 'my money.'" One man said of patrons at a neighborhood bar where he mixed drinks, "All the people there were pawns or checkers waiting for me to deal with them as I wished and to sacrifice any I wished." They were potential victims for burglaries and rapes.

The criminal strives to gain the upper hand, but not through fair competition. Instead he operates by stealth, loading things in his favor. His secrecy offers him great advantage and provides him with a sense of power. Others are unaware of the sinister intentions that lurk behind an often benign façade. Only he knows when and where he will strike. Assuming that everyone plots and conspires as he does, he enjoys "playing games with people's minds" and catching them off guard.

Intimidation is the criminal's other great weapon. His domineering manner may be so menacing that he need never utter a threat, raise his voice, or clench his fist. People cower in fear of the criminal's tearing into them, revealing their inadequacies, and making fools of them. There are times when a display of anger accomplishes his purpose. This may occur in a carefully orchestrated, dramatic manner to make a point, or he may simply fly off the handle. In either case the result is the same. Snarled one man, "My girlfriend has seen my anger. She is afraid of me and will do as I say." Getting one's way may be accomplished through raw violence; this will be discussed in the next chapter.

Even after he has been apprehended for a crime, the criminal continues to show the world that "people don't fuck with me and get away with it." He harasses the victim and the victim's family as well as witnesses. He badgers his own lawyer and anyone else who might help his cause. Before the case is concluded, he may have successfully intimidated the plaintiff, who then drops charges, or he browbeats witnesses, who then bow out of testifying.

The criminal demonstrates his power even over other people toward whom he bears no malice. A high school student spotted his math teacher's green automobile with its black vinyl roof. When the school bell rang, he bounded out of the building to the parking lot. He delighted in the hissing sound as he released air from two tires and gleefully watched them go flat. When he later saw the teacher gazing helplessly at the car, he strolled over and eagerly offered assistance. This boy was not rebelling against authority or retaliating for any alleged injustice. In fact he rather liked the teacher. But he had scored a double triumph, first by deflating the tires without being detected and then by appearing innocently on the scene and posing as rescuer of a lady in distress. To him the teacher was just another person on his chessboard.

Contrary to popular image, the criminal is not anti-authority. He recognizes the need for someone to establish and enforce rules, maintain order, and impose consequences on violators. He not only expects a teacher to teach, a parent to restrain, and a policeman to arrest, but he supports such people in the exercise of their authority. Even the most hardened criminals who spout anti-police rhetoric to one another recognize society's need for police. Some have thought about being policemen themselves. The only time a criminal opposes authority is when that authority stands in his way. His parents, teachers, and the police are fine people until they interfere with his plans or later hold him accountable.

From early in the day until bedtime, everything must suit the criminal. His wife is to have his shirts pressed, his clothes laid out, and his breakfast on the table. His ride to work must be prompt. His boss must meet with him when he is ready. Service at the lunch counter must be immediate. At whatever hour he walks in the door, dinner must be waiting and hot. Although there is an urgency to his every demand, he is none too quick to comply with requests made by others. Despite their prodding, he puts things off, eventually defaults altogether, then offers excuses when in fact he had no intention of doing what they asked.

This description may appear to characterize many men who are domineering but not criminals. Tyrants though they sometimes are, most such individuals do not commit crimes, nor are they necessarily unprincipled. Because they attempt to control people close to them, their relationships are rocky. The criminal, on the other hand, tries to dominate in every situation and resorts to any tactic to get his way. Anyone who evades his control reduces him in stature and thus is seen as a danger. Whenever others fail to do his bidding, the criminal's entire self-image is at stake. An individual who thinks in extremes, he regards himself as either number one or a zero. One offender acknowledged thinking of himself either as a "tough guy" who could take on anyone or as a person whom others "walk on." There was no in-between.

Criticism or interference with the criminal's plans constitutes a monumental threat because it signifies to him that he is not the omnipotent person he thinks he is. Instead of modifying his expectations and changing his behavior, he insists that it is others who err, not he. His pride is such that he adamantly refuses to acknowledge his own fallibility. Unyielding, uncompromising, and unforgiving, his attitude is "I'm going to hold my ground if it costs me everything," no matter how trivial the matter at hand.

Whether pride is a virtue or a flaw depends on its basis and on how it is manifested. Pride is an inner sense of satisfaction experienced when a person accomplishes something positive. A coach takes pride in his team's championship, or a student takes pride in completing his thesis. This is different from the criminal who is pretentious and whose pride is expressed in an attitude of superiority, in a refusal to yield to another's authority, in an unwillingness to compromise, and in a refusal even to listen to a different point of view. The criminal's gloating over triumphs and conquests is a far cry from the inner pride of quiet satisfaction that others experience when they responsibly achieve a goal.

Because the criminal's inflated view of himself is imperiled so many times in a single day, those who live and work with him are afraid, for they never know what might set him off. When he angrily explodes, he is in effect announcing that he is somebody to be reckoned with. His anger may be thinly disguised in sullenness, silence, or feigned indifference. It may spurt forth in ridicule and sarcasm, or erupt into screaming and cursing. Its most devastating form is raw physical violence.

Criminals are often portrayed as having unusually strong sex drives. However, it is the excitement of making a conquest, not a biological urge that provides the impetus for sexual activity. Often the criminal does not even conceive of his partner as a person, and so he has sex with a pair of breasts, buttocks, and a vagina. He brandishes his penis as a weapon before which others will succumb. Anyone may be vanquished, from the tramp in the bar to the wife of his best friend. A virgin is a special challenge.

Criminals find little satisfying in a consenting sexual relationship. Sex is mainly an assertion of their own power, and as a result they usually give little thought to the feelings of their partners. Criminals often pursue their conquests through deception (sometimes by means of force) and with the intention of exploiting their partners.

Jake, a thirty-one-year-old lifelong criminal, boasted that he would bed down on the first date "whoever I can get my hands on." This was true enough, given the sleazy women he knew. But Lisa proved to be a stubborn exception. That she would only kiss and hug made her all the more tantalizing and Jake all the more determined. As he dated her, he persuaded Lisa that he was in love. In fact, Jake half managed to convince himself that he might enjoy marrying and settling down. Once he proposed marriage, Lisa's resistance to intercourse melted. Having scored sexually, Jake began to feel restless, then trapped by the impending marriage. Several weeks before the wedding, Jake vanished, never to be heard from by Lisa again. He had achieved all he had wanted.

No matter who the partner is, the process of winning her over is far more exciting than the sexual act. One criminal recalled that, as a young man, his penis led him to church. "I would go out looking for women to con. I felt that there were a lot of women in church, and I was right. They were dying to be loved." His approach was to offer to walk an unmarried congregant home from church, all the while conniving how to approach her sexually. Usually he was invited to stay for refreshments. The woman would excuse herself and go into the bedroom to change, and he would carry out the following scenario:

"I sat there about two minutes, and I got up and went to her bedroom. I walked up behind her and kissed her on the neck. She turned around and said, 'I'm surprised at you.' The way she said that made me know she went in for more. So I sat down on her bed and pushed her back and kissed her. Then I ran my hand up her leg. At first, she was just lying there limp. She put both arms around me and she started kissing me back. Afterward, I made love to her. I don't have to tell you where I went to put the make on other women. I found other women who could give me money. Then I'd drop them and find others who could give me more."

Another criminal recalled how he had wooed a young widow by endearing himself to her little daughter. Charlie had totally charmed Vera's three-year-old daughter by buying her candy and ice cream and taking her to the zoo. He continued to shower her with attention.

Charlie was genuinely fond of the child, but what he had in mind was marrying her mother, who was left financially well fixed when her husband was crushed to death in a head-on automobile collision. Charlie intended to help himself to Vera's money, significantly enhanced by the life insurance payment, then extract additional funds from her wealthy father. He figured that once the marriage got to be a drag, he'd take off.

The criminal believes that others find him singularly appealing as a potential sex partner. If a woman fails to confirm this assumption, she poses a challenge. He pursues his conquest through a soft sell of flattery and conning, or he employs force.

Criminals misuse anyone or anything for their own purposes and constantly search out arenas in which to operate. The Internet has extended enormously the arena in which the criminal pursues power and control. By contacting people anywhere in the world, he can pull a variety of scams. He dupes the unsuspecting into disclosing personal financial information that allows him to assume their identity and steal from them. He induces them to send money to order nonexistent products or purchase items of inferior quality. He has an arena in which to operate globally and with total anonymity, greatly reducing his chances of being caught.

The computer is also a means for identifying and then casing out potential sex partners. The criminal may find excitement seekers like himself, or latch on to the innocent and vulnerable. Gradually he makes the acquaintance of total strangers, seeking to entice them into an intimate relationship.

Seventeen-year-old Arlene had the emotional maturity of a ten-year-old, but she had the body of a young woman. Grossly overweight, failing in school, and dependent upon her parents for virtually everything, Arlene had almost no social life. One outlet she did have was whiling away time in Internet chat rooms. Inclined to fall in love with anyone who professed interest in her, Arlene instantly developed a crush on Joe, a fellow in his forties pretending to be a teenager. Prowling the Internet in search of a vulnerable female, Joe had found his prey. Arlene confided in Joe, responding to his most personal questions. Eager to meet him, Arlene told Joe where she went to school, and he arranged to pick her up on a particular afternoon. They met, drove to a secluded spot, and engaged in sex. The experience was far from the thrilling, romantic rendezvous that Arlene anticipated. Although Joe had other ideas, Arlene became apprehensive and was able to persuade him to drop her off near her home. She was so frightened and confused by the encounter that she confided in a relative what she had done. The relative promptly informed her parents, who had been conscientious about supervising her, but had never dreamed that their daughter was doing anything more on the computer than e-mailing a friend at college. Arlene's mom and dad locked the computer away and talked with her about the risks that she had taken—the possibilities of becoming pregnant, contracting a disease, getting abducted, or worse. Fortunately, Joe did not pursue Arlene, and she had supportive family members to help protect her from falling victim in the same way again. Others who become enmeshed in Internet relationships are less fortunate. What begins with verbal bantering and flirtation can and has led to tragedy.

Some male criminals exploit men sexually. Those who engage in homosexual acts are likely to be bisexual and even to prefer heterosexual activity. Homosexual prostitution can be highly remunerative, but neither money nor sex is the main motive for the criminal. Rather, it is the charge that he gets from seducing, conning, or intimidating another human being into doing exactly what he wants. The criminal may indulge in a string of one-night stands, or he may latch on to one partner, quite possibly an older, lonely, well-to-do man. In such liaisons, the criminal may appear to be the passive, parasitic member. Actually, he is aggressively staking out his quarry and plotting to reap a host of benefits. In return for sex, he may be supported in high style and gain entrée in the homosexual community to a new circle of potential victims. Blackmail is an extremely effective weapon for extracting just what he wants, especially if his partner has a respectable standing in the community. When the criminal tires of the relationship, he leaves, taking his benefactor's money and belongings, sometimes by force.

The criminal views people only in terms of their use to him. They are like property. From adolescence, when the criminal refers to "my girl," he really is asserting that she belongs to him, but he considers her as disposable as an old tattered shirt. Rarely does he speak of love, nor does he have a concept of what a love relationship entails. He may be charming, but rarely tender or considerate. He insists that a woman change to suit him, but he requires that she accept him just the way he is. He demands that *his* girl be totally faithful, while he has sex with whomever he pleases. Once a woman presses a criminal for a commitment, she risks being discarded. Snapped one criminal, "This is a man's world. I don't want a bitch telling me what to do. Because she has a pussy, that doesn't mean she can control me."

The criminal may have his eye on a girl who is young and virtuous, but naïve. During his early infatuation, he may treat her like a queen. This was true of Ted, twenty-four, who courted Gwen, a twenty-two-year-old teacher who was a minister's daughter. Romantic and affectionate, Ted was always full of surprises. On a beautiful spring day, he picked her up for a date and told her he was going to blindfold her and drive her to someplace fun. When they got out of the car, he led her into a lush evergreen forest in the mountains and removed the blindfold. Then he took out the picnic basket and jug of wine. Gwen was his in every way, except that she still chose to remain a virgin. The luster of their relationship began to tarnish as her suitor seemed to turn into an egomaniac. An early sign was Ted's talk about outfitting himself to take her camping. This idea appealed to Gwen until she found out that Ted would be satisfied with only the best equipment on the market. No pup tent and sleeping bag on the ground for him. "He went on a spending spree like I never saw," she recalls. His purchase of three expensive tents and two backpacks was only the first sign of his extravagance. He also insisted on designer-label clothes, trendy restaurants, topflight stereo equipment, and the best of everything else. Believing that everyone has faults, Gwen was tolerant and patient. But it was hard to discuss much with Ted, because he stated an opinion and that was it. His utterances were like decrees, not meant to be challenged. Eager to please, Gwen stifled her discontent. But gnawing at her were his lavish expenditures of sums of money that she knew he had not earned as a carpenter. Hesitantly she wondered aloud several times whether he wasn't going overboard. Once when she summoned the courage to ask him directly where he was getting the money, he shot back, "Don't ask me any questions, and I won't tell any lies."

Reluctantly she acquiesced. One night Gwen got the shock of her life when the phone rang. It was Ted, calling from the police station to inform her that he had been charged with a string of robberies. At first she thought he was playing a practical joke, but she knew differently when his voice cracked. She was incredulous. How could her Ted have it within him to rob a store or a home? He made a decent living. Rather than condemn him, she concluded that she must be to blame. Somehow she had failed and, in doing so, had driven him to desperation. With Ted in prison, she remained faithful, writing, visiting, and vowing to be more understanding when they were reunited permanently. It was harrowing for Gwen to live in a small town, where she was sure that everyone was gossiping about why she never went out. Gwen feared that if her narrow-minded supervisors discovered that she was planning to marry a convict, they would find cause to fire her. This preacher's daughter found herself living a lie, trying to conceal all clues of her romantic association with a convict. Awaiting his release, Gwen still blamed herself and remained determined not to fail Ted again.

Inexperienced or unsophisticated women like Gwen are vulnerable to the Teds of this world, who will zero in, lavish them with attention, then try to own them. If a female resists any request, a guy like Ted will do his utmost to make her feel at fault and guilty. Pressure to surrender to sexual demands is one example. Gwen was determined to remain a virgin until marriage. But how could she refuse to be physically intimate with this man who had been so extraordinarily kind and devoted? Her resolve crumbled, and she had sex.

When a partner finds herself under pressure to go against her better judgment or to violate long-held values, a red flag should go up immediately. The individual should start questioning the viability of the entire relationship. A person who truly cares for another will not attempt repeatedly to browbeat a person into doing something against her will.

Some criminals do marry. In some cases the wife is as irresponsible as her husband. (Said one criminal, "Us kinds are attracted to each other.") Such a woman would find life with a responsible man intolerably boring. Marriages of people who are both irresponsible are highly volatile, as each struggles to control the other. Often they terminate in divorce when husband and wife seek what each expects will be greener pastures. Other marriages resemble the relationship between Ted and Gwen, the spouse being responsible but naïve. Then there is the woman who doubts that any man will find her suitable and so she latches on to any matrimonial prospect. Unaware of her future husband's criminality, she finds him bright, charming, and promising the security she craves. Hardly have the marriage vows been exchanged when serious problems arise. But, much like Gwen, the responsible partner is inclined to fault herself long before she blames her husband. One young lady married to a criminal sought my advice because she was sure it was she who needed the help. Tearfully she poured out her story and said, "If he doesn't get better, staying with him will destroy me." But then she continued, "I'm sitting here with a black eye from when he hit me. I wonder at times whether I am like I am because my father used to beat me when I was little and that I want to prove to myself that men who beat me still can love me. I need his love, but it's making me unhappy and him too. If you think I should see a therapist with my personal problems, please tell me. I am not unwilling."

When the criminal's wife discovers what he is really like, she is likely to minimize and deny the seriousness of his irresponsibility. Rather than seek a way out of the marriage, she becomes a reformer, confident that if she tries hard enough, she can have a steadying influence on her husband. As the magnitude of the problem strikes her, she may conclude that he has emotional difficulties and needs outside help. By no means does she regard him as malicious or any sort of criminal. Not wanting her marriage to fail and frightened to face life alone, she hangs on. This is especially true of women who lack self-confidence. They would rather stay with the known than be alone and have to start all over. Nurtured by any crumb of kindness thrown her way, such a woman assures herself that her spouse still cares. She attaches inordinate significance to any good deed, praying that it indicates he is mending his ways. After his wife's nervous breakdown, one criminal reflected, "She had been living on hope, just purely the hope that I would change."

The criminal expects family members to anticipate his desires and account to him for whatever they do. His conduct is not to be questioned, however. If he stays out until the wee hours of the morning, his wife has no right even to ask where he has been. If he spends money, she dares not request an accounting. In making purchases, only his preference counts. If his spouse argues, she risks being harangued, harassed, and assaulted. Repeated self-doubt, depression, and anger that follow in the wake of vicious arguments persuade her that few issues are worth pressing. In fact, even a seemingly minor disagreement may ignite a massive anger reaction or an assault. The criminal is the ultimate male chauvinist. His wife is an object, not a partner.

When the criminal's wife has had enough and decides to separate, he is surprised and angrily blames her for the collapse of the marriage. He is at a loss to understand her dissatisfaction and believes that if she would shape up and adopt a better attitude, there would be no discord. Marcie became fed up after enduring years of Neil's emotional and physical abuse. She realized that keeping the marriage together for the sake of the children was harming them. Abandoning hope that Neil would change, Marcie summoned the courage to take their two daughters and leave. Neil was furious and decided to fight her for custody of the children. In one of many vituperative letters, he wrote, "You broke my heart and destroyed my life and my relationship with my girls. You alone are responsible for the family split." On the memo line of his child-support checks, he scrawled derogatory comments such as "for the crazy woman." Another man seeking custody of his son wrote letters that he personally delivered to offices of his wife's company in different cities, denigrating her character and falsely accusing her of being an addict.

The criminal's appetite for conquests is temporarily appeased but never satisfied. No sooner has he achieved one triumph than he pursues the next. Rarely does the career criminal stick to one type of crime.[1]

A criminal becomes known to the police, the court, and the community for the immediate crime that resulted in his arrest. Little do others realize that a runaway youngster, classified simply as a "status offender," may also be a thief, vandal, and drug pusher. Nor can others know that a man arrested for the first time and charged with disorderly conduct may have committed scores of felonies.

Clearly, for our system of justice to work, there must be a presumption of innocence. However, people who conduct background investigations and make evaluations of offenders should be aware that an arrest may represent only a fraction of crimes committed, and there should be at least an attempt to determine how extensive the prior criminality has been. This would have some relevance to sentencing decisions, for judges are permitted to consider prior convictions in sentencing.

Arthur is a classic case of the successful career criminal. He was a one-man walking crime wave. His stealing began at five, when he swiped toy cars and soldiers, crayons, and books from neighborhood playmates. His thefts grew in variety and number as he became sneakier and more imaginative. At nine, he gathered together a small gang of children who raided stores almost daily. At twelve, he helped defraud customers at a carnival booth. As a teenager, he terrorized small boys until they emptied their pockets and surrendered every last penny. At school, teachers were forever pulling him away from fights. His specialty was breaking into neighbors' homes while they were away, often leaving the premises in shambles. As a young adult, Arthur still had a violent streak and was a party to several assaults, including one in which he vindictively mowed a person down with his sports car.

As he grew older, Arthur preferred conning to violence, and fronted a host of fraudulent enterprises. One after the other folded, but only after he had raked off his "profits." When he worked for others, he arranged kickbacks and embezzled funds. While employed by a department store, a job he couldn't stand, he livened things up by stealing $4,000 worth of merchandise and embezzling $3,000 in cash in eighteen days. Over a three-year period, Arthur illegally wrote and cashed checks ranging from $75 to $100 per day, amounting to approximately $30,000 per year. Arthur swindled a bank out of $30,000 by borrowing against fraudulent securities. He stole close to $4,000 worth of securities and turned them in to another bank as collateral for a loan. Impersonating a physician, he wrote prescriptions for drugs, which he sold or used himself. Subsequently he became involved extensively in the marketing of illegal drugs.

Arthur had a fixation on pubescent girls. When he was selling cosmetics and soap, he always hired teenage girls, to whom he would pay extra commissions for sex. Before his marriage, Arthur established liaisons with women ostensibly for romantic purposes, whereas his real objectives were sex and money. He succeeded in obtaining both, the latter by conning women into giving him cash to invest. They never were quite sure what they were investing in, but Arthur seemed so honest and knowledgeable that they were certain he was looking out for their interests. Of course, he was looking out only for himself and absconded with their funds. His wife's money was no safer because, without her knowledge, he had written overdrafts on her checking account.

If one were to count every arrestable act during Arthur's forty years of life—each theft, each assault, each bad check, each misrepresentation and embezzlement, each sex offense, each drug offense—the toll would climb into the tens of thousands of crimes. (Sometimes there were a dozen thefts or several bad checks in a single day, as well as other crimes.) Yet this man served only one short prison term for drug offenses. He beat a few other charges through brief hospitalizations for mental illness, which was considered the underlying cause of his criminal behavior. The rest of the time he was on the streets.

Arthur was a "player," ready for just about anything at any time. But some career criminals are more selective. They may reject crimes that they consider "chickenshit" or too petty. And if a criminal thinks a crime is too risky, he rules it out. Criminals who are terrified of physical injury shy away from situations where force may be necessary. Even the most daring and versatile refrain from specific acts that they find personally repugnant. Some are disgusted just at the thought of molesting a child sexually or of mugging an elderly woman.

Although criminals differ in the crimes they find acceptable, they are carbon copies of one another in their view of themselves and the world. All are liars and hide behind a mask of secrecy. They have an inflated self-image in which they regard themselves as special and superior, and they assume that people will do their bidding. Contemptuous of the world of law-abiding people, they share the view that the responsible world is a barren wasteland.

In nearly all his operations, the criminal has the advantage. He has an eye trained to spot vulnerable targets, and capitalizes on opportunities. Also working in his behalf is the fact that many of the crimes he commits are never reported to police. According to Department of Justice estimates, in 1999 rape and attempted rape went unreported by 67 percent of victims, robbery by 38 percent, aggravated assault by 42 percent, and property crimes by 65 percent.[2]

Many reasons underlie the nonreporting of crime. Some citizens do not call police because they think the crime is not serious enough. Then there are people too embarrassed to admit that they were gullible, greedy, or careless. Some commercial establishments find that they save money by not reporting crimes. To report thefts embroils them in time-consuming procedures with the police and may ultimately result in higher insurance premiums. Furthermore, since a sizable proportion of theft is likely to be by a firm's own employees, it is better for the company's image to handle such matters internally.

Witnesses may not report a crime because they do not want to spend hours and perhaps days talking to police and appearing in court. They also fear becoming known to the offender and suffering reprisal. A victim may not report a crime even when he knows who did it because he fears retaliation. The impact of terror at the prospect of being victimized again cannot be overestimated in accounting for either nonreporting or the dropping of charges. Unless the crime is serious and the evidence conclusive, the offender may get off scot-free or else be confined only briefly. As long as the criminal is on the streets, his victim lives in fear. Even if the criminal is confined, there is the haunting fear that the criminal might retaliate once he is released, or that he might contact someone to seek revenge on his behalf. Such apprehension may be well-founded. Some victims receive threatening letters if not directly from the criminal, then from his friends or family. Even if there is no explicit threat, just their vivid recall of what they experienced at the hands of the criminal is enough to terrify them when they think about his being free in society.

In 1982, as a member of the President's Task Force on Victims of Crime, I witnessed firsthand a crisis of confidence in the criminal justice system.[3] Although sensitivity to victims has increased, more can be done. Victims still are neglected or mistreated from the time police arrive until after the case is finally disposed of in court. They miss days of work to come to court, only to have trials or hearings postponed. Victims of sex crimes may have to endure humiliating investigative procedures followed by the trauma of a public trial. In the course of a trial, personal information about the victim may be made public. In short, a crime victim may feel victimized twice, once by the criminal and then again by the system. All of this has some bearing on the reluctance of citizens to report crimes.

The criminal's skill in avoiding apprehension and the nonreporting of more than half the crimes that are committed account for a high percentage of crimes that are never solved. The Department of Justice reported that in 1999 just twenty-one percent of offenses known to the police were cleared.[4] (Clearing a crime means identifying the offender, charging him, and taking him into custody.)

It is no wonder, then, that the criminal's sense of invincibility mounts. The simple fact is that he is unlikely to be caught, much less confined. Some criminals grow so cocky that, although they execute a crime flawlessly, they betray themselves by carelessness, such as parking a getaway car in a loading zone, where police immediately spot it. On drugs, they may be especially brazen and reckless. But generally the criminal is a pro at what he does. In crime after crime he asserts who he is—a singularly special and powerful person with whom the world must reckon.

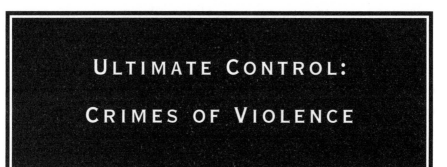

7

ULTIMATE CONTROL:
CRIMES OF VIOLENCE

CRIMINALS INTEND TO PREVAIL in every situation, whether by stealth, intimidation, or brute force. Although perhaps disdaining violence outwardly, even the smoothest con man is not beyond resorting to violence when he feels thwarted and powerless. I have encountered many such men who appear highly respectable because they are educated, socially sophisticated, and hold positions of considerable responsibility. But ask their wives about the bruises, black eyes, and other injuries. Inquire about the holes in the wall or the door that was torn off its hinges.

Violence is the criminal's extreme response to a put-down, his perception that his entire self-worth is on the line. He takes the slightest threat to his sense of control as a personal affront. A "put-down," or diminishing of an individual's self-worth, occurs only in a person's mind. If we are recipients of criticism, no matter how harsh, one of two things is true. If the criticism has merit, we can benefit. If it is without merit, we can disregard it. Our entire self-image is not on the line unless we interpret the remark and then react to it in a highly personal way. The same with a gratuitous insult. Consider the source! For example, a driver suddenly cuts in front of us—no signal given. We have a choice as to how to react. A responsible, safe driver will drop back and keep his distance, perhaps muttering under his breath. The criminal takes the situation as a personal affront. Determined to even the score, he'll show he's someone not to be messed with. He retaliates by pursuing, screaming, cutting in front of the offending driver, or forcing him off the road entirely.

The responsible person recognizes that there is a lot he cannot control. He adjusts his expectations accordingly and grows accustomed to coping with "Murphy's Law"—if anything can go wrong, it will. In the life of a criminal, there is no room for Murphy. And so he is perpetually angry at a world that does not give him what he thinks he is due. Although the criminal's anger cannot be seen on the outside, it simmers internally, then boils over when he encounters the one thing too many that eludes his control. Like a cancer, anger festers inside, then metastasizes so that anyone or anything in his path can become a target.

The criminal has a thin skin. He will dish it out, but he won't take it. His insistence upon "respect" is another indicator of just how different the criminal's mentality is from that of an individual who is basically responsible. Most individuals know that respect is earned, not demanded on a whim. A person gains respect through achievement or by a good deed. The criminal demands what he terms respect as recognition of his power and as confirmation that he is in control. When "disrespected," he will do whatever he thinks it takes to show that no one can push him around. Put-downs occur in a flash, so quickly that it may be impossible for an observer to pinpoint precisely what precipitated the violence. A criminal can be saving a seat for a buddy, but someone else occupies the chair. The other person sitting on "his" chair punctures his inflated ego, and so he seeks to reinflate it by violently challenging the new occupant's right to sit there. The same dynamic occurs when someone looks at him in what he deems an objectionable manner. Taking offense, he flies into a fury and lands a punch.

Criminals experience what some have called an "adrenaline rush" by fantasizing about violence, talking about violence, and behaving violently. A sixteen-year-old stated bluntly, "I like to bash faces in. Killing is on my mind." Those who tangled with him wound up with fractures, sprains, dislocations, concussions, and lacerations. This youth felt no remorse after hurling a brick at a person and leaving him sprawled unconscious in an alley.

Sixteen-year-old Phil told me about how he would experience "this buildup of rage and explode." He proceeded to relate that he would erupt even when little things got on his nerves. When his five-year-old nephew, whom he was baby-sitting, started whining, Phil slammed his own fist into a wall and bloodied his knuckles. At school he became enraged at a teacher, kept his mouth shut, then dashed into another room and hit a wall. Later that day a friend referred to him with an ethnic slur. "I grabbed him and threw him against the wall. I slammed him into the counter. Blood was spraying. I kept killing his face. I asked how he'd like me to slit his fucking throat. Then I slapped him across the face. I told him 'If I see you outside school, you're dead.' " Phil told me that this episode ended only when four guys pulled him off. This is how Phil went through life. He said that his anger would emerge from nowhere: "I'd just kind of lose it. When I start, I don't stop. I just react." He recalled an argument with his best friend: "I opened the door, ripped him out of the car, threw him on the ground. I could have killed him." Speaking without remorse, he assured me he was "a genuinely nice guy" and dismissed his violence as "just being a teenager."

Others do not often suspect that the thinking behind the placid exterior of an acquaintance may be shockingly sadistic. One man was enraged at a co-worker who criticized his printing layout. He pictured himself tying up this person, yanking his pants off him, then slicing off his testicles, tying them around the victim's neck, and stabbing him to death. But, figuring that this man was "scum" and that it wasn't worth the risk, the would-be assailant did nothing. Thus none of his colleagues had the slightest awareness of the anger seething inside him. Deferring immediate action, the criminal may conceive of a scheme in which he will get even later. He retaliates at a time least expected and in a manner totally unanticipated.

Then there are individuals like Clark, whose identity rests largely on making others afraid. Clark had been expelled from school for severely injuring another student during a fight. This strapping varsity football player was barely passing academically. Other than latching on to a girl whom he struggled to control, he had few close friends and no outside interests. Allowed to return to school in September because he was in counseling, Clark was eager to play football, and hoped to graduate with his class. Six months into counseling, he told me had been taunting a guy who he heard had a crush on his girlfriend. "He's a doofus!" Clark exclaimed, and declared that his adversary was too much of a punk to fight him. Clark had an audience to play to, buddies who egged him on, excited by the prospect of a fight. "I got in his face and dared him," Clark told me. When I asked him to consider the consequences to him of a fight, he acknowledged that these were possible but irrelevant. "It's a pride thing; that's how I've been," he explained. He emphasized how others would think he was a sissy if he didn't goad the boy into a fight. When I commented that our next meeting could well be in a detention center, Clark laughed and nodded in agreement. As if to remind me who I was talking to, he said, "I'm the guy; you don't mess with me." I inquired, "Is that all you are—a tough guy?" Clark dropped his head and somberly replied, "I don't have anything else." He said this had always been how he won recognition. "Fighting was the big thing. Even in elementary school, I beat up kids. I did it in middle school. I did it in high school. You don't mess with Clark!"

Clark was no dummy. He had a certain charm, spoke well, could describe how he felt about things, and was known to be easygoing unless challenged. However, he was without drive or goals and had let opportunities pass him by. He really didn't even care about playing college or professional ball. High school football was just a way to fortify his reputaton as a big guy on campus. The tragedy was that he was in his senior year, barely passing academically, and he had done nothing toward planning his future. He was starting to realize he was lost. As June approached, his classmates would go on with their lives, and all he would have left was his high school tough-guy reputation.

Maudlin sentiment and savage brutality can reside within the same individual. A prison inmate became attached to a little kitten that managed to find its way into the jail. He cuddled it, spoke to it tenderly in baby talk, then asked the deputy whether he could keep it. When the deputy explained that the cat would have to go because of health and sanitary regulations, the inmate became so enraged that he grabbed the kitten and hurled it against a wall, killing it instantly.

When violence occurs during a crime, it may not have been part of the original plan. A burglar, surprised in the act, may gun down a returning homeowner in order to eliminate a witness. The criminal targeted the home for a break-in, not for a murder. But he came armed, prepared to do whatever he thought necessary if he encountered opposition. When a victim retaliates, the criminal may flee. More often, such a challenge fans the flame of the criminal's determination to win out, and he resorts to more dire means than he anticipated. Victims are hurt when they do something that catches the criminal off guard, such as physically resist or make a sudden move leading him to think that they have a gun. Said one holdup man, "When you go to rob a liquor store, you never know when the guy might pull a gun. So it's a calculated risk. You never know who is going to stop you or mess around with you. Of course," he added, "we don't go out with the intention of hurtin' somebody. We are always prepared to hurt somebody in self-defense."

If the criminal is later held accountable, he blames the victim for the violence because he interfered in the successful execution of the crime. Exclaimed one man who shot his victim during a street robbery, "That man must have been nuts! It wasn't my fault that he was crazy enough to risk his life over the fifty bucks in his wallet." Remorse for the victim, if existent, is short-lived.

Because he will employ any means to achieve his objective, violence is acceptable in the pursuit of anything the criminal wants, including sex. Dr. Ann Burgess, a pioneer in research on rape victimization, pointed out that rape is "an act of aggression and violence, motivated primarily by power or anger, rather than by sexuality."[1] It is an attempt to subjugate another human being and offers a challenge to get away with the forbidden. The rapist does not necessarily hate women, nor is he sexually deprived. In fact, he may regularly have sex with a girlfriend or spouse and still rape.

People who rape are irresponsible in other ways and are likely to have committed other kinds of crimes, violent and nonviolent, even though they may not have been apprehended for them. Rape is just one expression of their attempt to dominate others, to seek excitement in the forbidden, and to build themselves up. There is no attempt to punish women, nor does the offender believe that a nice woman wouldn't have sex with him. In fact, he believes that he is irresistible to all women. At stake in a rape is the criminal's affirmation of his image of himself as powerful and desirable. The assailant believes that his victim already wants him, or will want him once she gives him a chance. Her attempts to ward him off only heighten his excitement. Then he tries to reduce her to a quivering, pleading speck of humanity and helps himself to what he believes was rightfully his from the start. Brute force is rarely necessary because intimidation works.

As he rode the bus, Carl eyed an ample-breasted, middle-aged woman wearing a sheer white blouse through which he could see her bra and bare skin. He observed that she wore no ring and concluded that she was single. Alighting at her stop, he walked behind her at a safe distance and noted where she lived. That night he returned, climbed up the fire escape, and jimmied open her apartment window. Removing his shoes, he slipped into her living room and tiptoed into the bedroom. After gingerly drawing back the bedclothes, he cupped his hands around her breasts and fondled them. The woman awakened, sat bolt upright, and was about to scream when Carl clamped his hand over her mouth and warned her to shut up. He unzipped his fly and jammed his erect penis into her mouth. Hearing her gurgle as though she were about to choke, Carl withdrew from her mouth, then commanded her to lie back and spread her legs. Yanking up her nightgown, he directed her to guide his penis into her vagina. When she meekly complied, he concluded that she was discovering that he was quite the stud and enjoying him.

Sex crimes may grow increasingly bizarre as the criminal searches for more and more excitement. Even rapes can grow routine to a man who has committed scores of them. Such a person may become bolder and more sadistic, as in the case of a young man who abducted a woman at knifepoint and dragged her off to an apartment where he tore off her clothes, lashed her to a bed, paraded around naked, leering and cursing, masturbated until he ejaculated all over her, terrorized her for another hour, and finally thrust himself upon her for intercourse. Does such a person hate his victim? Often he does not even know her. Is he acting out of an unconscious, long-smoldering hatred against some other woman in his life, perhaps his mother? One could always speculate that this is the case. But then what of the thousands of people who suffered rejecting and inconsistent mothers, crueler than his, but who resolved their resentments differently?

The rape starts in a fantasy about totally controlling a person through sexual contact. The control may not be limited to people. More than one criminal has confessed to having had sex with a family pet or farm animal when he was a youngster. During "phone sex," Cecil paid women to engage in sexual conversations. When the phone bills got too high (he spent hours in this pursuit), he turned to the computer and viewed videos where he could direct computer-generated images of females to do exactly what he wanted. He masturbated as he watched these and "rape videos" that he later discovered. A skilled computer operator at his job, Cecil found it easy to break into pay sites, so access to pornography cost him nothing. Cecil reflected, "I was a different person behind the computer. I was in control, and what I told the computer to do, it did. And I didn't have to worry about the computer falling in love with somebody else or cheating on me or hurting me. The computer would always love me. Before the rape fantasies, I used to fantasize that I had special powers and that I could make any girl I wanted have sex with me. Sometimes this would include the power to stop time, or maybe a form of hypnotizing them." Cecil recalled, "I would start actually believing that the computer-generated girls were real and that I was really having sex with them."

Cecil was a voyeur, hiding outside women's windows late at night, masturbating while he watched them undress. He recalled this being "the first step" to envisioning himself committing a rape. Cecil said, "It got so bad that I would get up before school while it was still dark and go looking in people's windows." Finally it happened. Cecil broke into a neighbor's home at night and jumped on her as she slept. However, he grew frightened and fled. Years after this happened, I interviewed Cecil in jail. He had been arrested for striking a girl with a brick, knocking her to the ground, then attempting to rape her.

People find it puzzling, as well as repulsive, that elderly women become rape victims. Why, they wonder, does a rapist not prey upon an attractive younger person? It is the conquest that is of primary importance. Since the criminal selects an available and vulnerable target, who fits that description better than a frail, elderly person?

The criminal refuses to take no for an answer. In fact, a rejection may incite him to pursue unrelentingly whatever he wants, terrorizing the person who is his target. Stalking is defined as "the willful or intentional commission of a series of acts that would cause a reasonable person to fear death or serious bodily injury."[2] States began enacting statutes against stalking during the 1990s. According to a study by the U.S. Department of Justice and the Centers for Disease Control and Prevention, "one in twelve women and one in forty-five men have been stalked during their lifetime."[3] The person who is stalked is usually someone with whom the criminal has had a relationship. However, the criminal may stalk someone he has never met, such as a celebrity or a stranger to whom he or she is attracted. Both men and women engage in stalking behavior.

After a stormy eight-year relationship with Graham, Trudy decided she'd had enough. When she announced she was moving out, Graham flew into a panic and begged her to stay. Leaving did not liberate Trudy as she had expected. Although Trudy did not inform Graham where she was moving, he tracked her down. Graham repeatedly phoned her, showed up uninvited at her new residence, sent gifts, threatened her and her housemates, then threatened to kill himself. Trudy lived in constant fear, paralyzed as to what to do. She did not want to offer Graham the slightest encouragement, yet she worried that a total lack of response might drive him to kill himself or harm her. Having taken out a restraining order against Graham, Trudy nevertheless occasionally accepted his calls. Shortly after he had sent her Christmas gifts, she allowed him into her home, where she implored him to go to Alcoholics Anonymous and to seek inpatient psychiatric treatment. She ceased responding to any further overtures, except for one call that got through from a psychiatric facility where Graham was a patient. Trudy grew terrified after hearing her former boyfriend declare that he was fed up and might kill her.

Graham was finally arrested when he was pulled over for a motor vehicle infraction and found to have a loaded gun. Interviewed in jail, he denied that he harbored any violent intentions toward Trudy, himself, or anyone else. In no sense did he see Trudy as a victim. He indicated that he perceived himself as the victim when he claimed, "I keep feeling beaten. She's using the law to beat me." Although incarcerated, an unrepetent Graham asserted, "I still care about her, even though she abused me." Continuing to protest his innocence of harmful or illegal actions, Graham said, "I didn't stalk her; I tried to reestablish a relationship." While spending time in jail, this man continued to think about Trudy, and ruminated over composing a letter asking her to specify conditions under which she would reconcile.

Some criminals won't permit their partners to leave, and restrain them through intimidation and violence. During the year 2000, according to U.S. Department of Justice statistics, 1,247 women and 440 men were killed "by an intimate partner."[4] Perpetrators of domestic violence are certain that they will not suffer major consequences for what they do. They are usually correct in this belief. A study of military families found that among 482 victims of domestic violence, most spouses desired to remain married.[5] Although these women wanted help, they were apprehensive about reporting the abuse to authorities. Their reticence was based on fear of further abuse, embarrassment, and loss of privacy, as well as fear that it could lead to the breakup of the family. The chief barrier to reporting was that their husbands' careers might suffer.

The criminal dominates his family as he attempts to dominate everyone else. Everything goes smoothly as long as his wife and children do not oppose him. Life is truly a "walking on eggshells" existence, with family members living in trepidation lest they upset the delicate equilibrium. Appeasing the criminal member of the family is uppermost in everyone's mind, for no one wants to incur his wrath. In such family situations, the memory of previous violence remains vivid, and the perpetual threat of more violence hangs in the air.

Cynthia had been through a lot in her six years with Johnny. He had thrown them into enormous debt, written bad checks, and forced her to sign checks that lacked the backup funds. Johnny allowed her to have no friends, and flew off the handle if she talked to anyone too long on the phone. He was so demanding of her total attention that one night he upbraided her for attending to their younger boy, who was suffering an allergy attack. Cynthia lived in terror of Johnny's temper, for he had broken down doors, smashed furniture, and beaten her. One time she decided to flee to her mother's, but Johnny came after her, blocked her car, and threatened her. Sex was a major battleground, because Johnny demanded it daily and on his terms. He would post a rating score on a calendar, and berate her when she didn't perform to his satisfaction. Even though Johnny constantly belittled her, he didn't leave and certainly didn't want her to leave. To a probation officer he remarked that Cynthia was like an old car; if he traded her in, he'd just get stuck with another model with a different set of defects. Finally, without Johnny knowing, Cynthia sought counseling. She began to think about establishing a life for herself and the children, but holding her back was her fear that Johnny would surely kill her if she left.

A criminal will use what he claims to cherish most, his own children, in an attempt to destroy his spouse. As a child custody evaluator, I have had a child snatched from my waiting room by a noncustodial parent and spirited to a hideaway. I have seen men and women who, fearing for their lives and their children's safety, turn to the courts for restraining orders and for the imposition of supervised visitation. Once in a great while a custody battle turns lethal for a parent, the children, or both.

The criminal's unpredictability makes him especially difficult to live with. His attitude toward his own children fluctuates wildly, determined more by whim than by anything the child does. He may pamper and dote upon a son or daughter. But then he is just as likely to ignore, neglect, or cruelly mistreat the very same youngster. The child is a burden not because of any misconduct, but simply because he is distracting his parent from pursuits far removed from even thinking about the youngster's needs. The child never knows what to expect. The same misbehavior may be overlooked one day but result in a beating the next. The U.S. Department of Justice reported that 71 percent of the homicides of children under five and 61 percent of children ages six to eleven are perpetrated primarily by family members.[6]

Judges refer some perpetrators of domestic violence to "anger management" classes. The notion that criminals should learn to manage their anger is tantamount to trying to catch a tidal wave with a bucket. The scope of the task is far greater than management; it is for the criminal to learn to handle life's difficulties better, so that he has less anger to manage. The criminal's anger stems from the fear of not being in total control, the fear that things will not go his way. Only if his thinking changes will he become more realistic in his expectations and thus less angry.

The last bastion of the scoundrel is to attack a person on the basis of race, ethnic origin, or sexual orientation. Striving to build himself up by putting others down, he injects these factors into situations where they have no relevance. The Federal Bureau of Investigation began compiling hate-crime statistics in 1990. The term *hate crime* refers to offenses that seem motivated by the offender's prejudice against a particular group. Sixty percent of the hate crimes reported between 1997 and 1999 involved violence. Arrests occurred in only 20 percent of hate-crime incidents.[7]

The criminal invokes race, ethnicity, or sexual orientation as a pretext for doing whatever he wants. He is no stranger to assault, robbery, or rape to begin with. Victimizing a person from a particular group that he professes to dislike heightens the excitement and increases the satisfaction. UCLA researcher Edward Dunbar found that 97 percent of the perpetrators of hate crimes had prior convictions for other types of crimes, 60 percent having committed violent offenses in the past.[8] An item appearing in the *New York Times* described a group attacking Jewish soccer players in France. It wasn't just a carefully planned assault upon Jews, for the perpetrators also stole from the victims' personal belongings anything of value. The mayor of the town where the incident occurred pointed out, "This was an anti-Semitic incident, but they were opportunists too. They took what they could."[9] There is nothing unique about the psychology of hate-crime perpetrators. They are criminals just like any other.[10]

8

"IT'S THUGS, NOT DRUGS;

IT'S THINKING, NOT DRINKING"

I FIRST ENCOUNTERED IVAN when he called for an appointment. With hesitation, he told me that a judge had ordered him to undergo a psychological evaluation, but on the phone he offered no reason why.

Ivan had worked for the federal government during his entire career. He and his wife lived in a Virginia suburb of Washington, D.C. Their son and daughter were grown and living independently. To all appearances, the couple's life had been conventional and law-abiding. At our first meeting, Ivan fessed up to drinking too much, then doing something he deeply regretted. This gentleman, whose only prior arrest had been for speeding, had beaten his wife so savagely that she required hospitalization. He asserted that if it weren't for his alcohol use, which clearly had gotten out of hand, and the judge's order, he would have had no reason to consult a mental health professional.

Many offenders identify their problem solely in terms of the mind-altering substance they used before their arrest. Numbers of incarcerated inmates who abuse drugs and alcohol run as high as 80 percent. It is not unusual for offenders, no matter what they were arrested for, to tell me that they would not be in their current predicament were it not for their drug or alcohol problem. (Of course, if they are arrested for actually possessing or distributing an illegal substance, their claim that

112

drug abuse is their immediate problem has some validity.) Otherwise, no matter how serious the crime they committed, they do not regard themselves as criminals. Like Ivan, they assert that their only "problem" is with alcohol or illegal drugs.

Criminality, however, does not reside in the bottle, the pill, the powder, or in any other substance. Drugs bring out and intensify only what already exists within a person; they do not transform a responsible person into a criminal. If ten men get drunk, all ten will not rape, rob, or kill. They may fall asleep, become boisterous, or grow argumentative. Their behavior depends on their personality before they took the first sip.

The man or woman with a criminal personality is likely to say that he or she uses drugs to escape. And plenty of professionals will agree with this explanation. Everything imaginable has been blamed for causing crime, and the same is true with respect to why people become drug users. Freudians conceive of drug use as part of regression to the oral stage, an attempt to recapture the infantile bliss experienced at the mother's breast. Sociologists characterize drug use as a normal response to bleak conditions—"a way to give purpose to an otherwise aimless and disorganized life."[1] Or they direct attention to a culture that values instant gratification and offers immediate relief from stress. Psychologists cite poor examples given by role models—the fact that Dad drinks or Mom takes pills to help her sleep. Bemoaning peer pressure, the user speaks of how his buddies turned him on to drugs. And social critics lament the glamorization of drugs in film and on television. The litany of reasons why people use drugs is endless. And these reasons are seized upon by users who have ample excuses of their own.

If you ask the user what he is escaping from, he may respond by complaining about the sordid circumstances in which he lives. Yet others, including friends and family, residing in the same environment do not use drugs. Steve traced his interest in drugs to "my peers who were doing it, not just the neighborhood I was in." His younger brother had no involvement with drugs, but enjoyed scouting, athletics, and community activities. If you press a guy like Steve on the escape theme, he may elaborate by describing distressing situations, some of which he created for himself by his own irresponsibility. He is out of work, bill collectors are closing in, he can't afford to get his car repaired, his wife is threatening to leave if he doesn't shape up. What it boils down to is that the drug-using criminal wants to avoid the mundane requirements that others impose on him to live responsibly. Far more important than escape is the excitement that drugs facilitate.

Many experts regard drug use as an adolescent rite of passage. The media bombard the public with reports dramatizing youthful drug use. But statistics are often misleading. It is true that curiosity prompts millions of people to experiment with drugs. Lumped together in the statistics, however, are individuals who experimented once or twice, then stopped, with the person who has been getting high daily for many years. In 2000, 34 percent of college students who responded to a survey acknowledged having used marijuana at some point during the preceding year. The percentage reporting daily usage of the substance dropped to 4.6 percent.[2] In 1997, one-third of all Americans had used marijuana at least once in their lives.[3] This means two-thirds had never used it. Of that one-third, only 9 percent had used the substance during the preceding year. We don't know how many of the 9 percent used it for the first and only time during that year. So the incidence of frequent marijuana users may be minuscule.

For most people, experimentation is short-lived. They don't like the effects. They know that drugs are physically harmful. And they don't want to subject themselves or their families to legal risks.

Contrast this with Alan, who began drinking at age ten. He and his buddies heisted beer and cheap wine from local stores. At sixteen he could pass for eighteen, and altered his driver's license so he could buy his own liquor. Concerned adults were positive Alan would be all right if he just left alcohol alone and associated with a different crowd. His mother observed, "When he didn't drink, he was a different person." But Alan told me that he used liquor to fulfill desires that he had when he was completely sober. "I'd go out and get drunk so I could commit the crimes I was thinking of," he said. "I controlled how much I wanted to drink and when I wanted to drink." In other words, neither alcohol nor his friends put ideas into his head; they were already there, waiting to be acted on. Even when he was plastered, he could exercise remarkable restraint if it was in his interest. When Alan was arrested for breaking and entering, he was remanded to an alcohol treatment program, not locked up in detention. This was because the judge regarded

Alan's alcoholism as the primary problem. While in treatment, Alan continued drinking and sought more kicks. "I wanted one continuous high all the time," he recalled. "I couldn't drink enough or do enough drugs. Anything or everything I could get my hands on would go in my mouth."

For a person like Alan with a criminal personality, involvement in drugs is another expression of the desire to do what is exciting and forbidden. He wants the drugs for their immediate effects, but, even more, he craves the excitement that the world of drugs offers. Criminals who are drug users love to talk with one another about the thrill of the deal. This involves searching out unsavory characters by venturing into dangerous areas to procure the best stuff at a good price. This excitement is in addition to the actual effects of the drug.

The young person who becomes involved with drugs may be apprehensive about getting caught. But outweighing that fear is the allure of the unknown and the forbidden. Initially, such youngsters new to the drug scene obtain drugs from friends. Pushers rarely foist drugs on the innocent, but instead protect themselves by selling almost exclusively to known users. As a youth becomes a regular consumer, he knows what he wants and finds out where and how to obtain it. This is a far cry from being a victim of peer pressure or unscrupulous pushers. The delinquent is open to anything new and exciting, and has chosen to associate with others who are willing to accommodate him.

The criminal who regularly abuses mind-altering substances is perpetually dissatisfied, restless, irritable, and bored. Before drugs came into the picture, he was a controller, a liar, a person who promoted himself at the expense of others. In every case that I have encountered, the criminal was immersed in crime *before* he smoked his first joint, popped his first pill, or first shot heroin.[4] Drugs knock out fears of getting caught and considerations of conscience. As a result, the criminal has the "heart" to do what previously he had only contemplated when sober.

Bob said he often fantasized about using a gun to rob a convenience store, but was "too chicken." With heroin coursing through his veins, he became emboldened, procured a pistol, and did just that. Heroin did not *cause* Bob to obtain the gun; use of the drug simply made it more feasible for him to eliminate fears for the time being in order to act upon what he had previously considered. "Drugs knock off my caution," acknowledged another user who took unusual risks breaking into houses in broad daylight, something he would have been too scared to do were he not on drugs.

Criminals want to be number one sexually, just as they do in other aspects of their lives. Drugs knock out fear of rejection, so they are more inclined to approach a partner. A man remarked, "Without drugs, I had a fifty-fifty chance with a woman, but on drugs she was a sure thing." He said that before he went on a date "it was essential to use—it was the only way to settle myself." By "settle," he meant eliminate his fears. Not only are criminals bolder in their advances when on drugs, but they may also become less choosy in selecting a partner. One man said that on drugs his criteria for a partner's desirability went by the boards. "All I wanted was a body," he acknowledged. Not only does the drug user have sex with people whom he might otherwise not even consider, but he also subjects himself to greater danger. Being robbed or assaulted, or contracting sexually transmitted diseases, are distinct possibilities.[5] Worries about inadequate sexual performance vanish under drugs, whether apprehension is over genital size, impotence, or premature ejaculation. The urgency for sexual pursuit varies with the particular choice and amount of the drug. Many boast of being sexual titans on heroin, but when their use of the drug escalated, they totally lost interest.

Some criminals wouldn't consider using drugs to commit crimes or pursue sexual conquests. They know that drugs will interfere with success by rendering them less vigilant. They use drugs while hanging out with their buddies. A criminal who may be socially reticent might transform himself into the life of the party. Ask a user what he means by "getting high." After expressing incredulity over your naïveté, he'll supply a vague response about feeling good, or perhaps say he becomes "euphoric." If you continue to probe, you will hear statements like "On drugs, I felt ten feet tall. On drugs, I felt I could do anything." The user is describing a heightened sense of being in control and an ability to surmount or totally eliminate any adversity.

Anthony described getting high on cocaine, then on LSD. On cocaine, he felt like a big shot, fearless, in complete control. "On cocaine, I'd feel like I was on top of the world. Everything was cool.

People gave me respect. I could go anywhere. I was like an idol to people. Without drugs, I was missing something. Cocaine made me feel more secure—confident—that I couldn't be stopped even if six guys jumped me." Anthony commented that "acid" provided a different sort of high. The central feature still was an inflated sense of his own importance: "Everything was a laugh. People were still coming to me. 'We can't have real good fun unless Anthony is with us.' I can get along with anybody. My friends can't even walk to the 7-Eleven. They have to come get me. They want me with them."

Anthony portrayed himself as a man of the world with a personal magnetism that drew people to him. However, in reality he was a man who ignored requirements imposed by others who implored him to be responsible. He left his parents' home, was fired from jobs, lied, fought, stole, and sold and used drugs.

If a criminal has been down in the dumps to the point of entertaining suicidal thoughts, drugs may intensify those ideas so that he harms himself. His despair is not about his own flaws. Rather, it arises from anger at a world that he finds disappointing and unacceptable. Making a suicidal gesture has an enormous impact whether the criminal is at home or incarcerated. With his judgment impaired by drugs, he may miscalculate and inadvertently kill himself through an overdose or infliction of a mortal wound. Or he may summon the determination to end it all, which he couldn't bring himself to do when sober.

Selection of a specific substance depends to a great extent on what is available. Any drug in sufficient dosage can give the criminal some sort of high. So when the supply of the drug of choice dries up, he turns to something else. The sophisticated user prefers particular drugs for specific purposes, and is well informed about the advantages and disadvantages of each. Amphetamines provide a quick infusion of energy but a severe letdown following cessation of use. Opiates knock out fear and sharpen thinking (given optimal dosage), but there is a risk of dependency. Barbiturates help the criminal to assume an "I don't care" attitude, but dosage is difficult to regulate, and risk of physical dependence is high. Marijuana is a desirable party drug, but not powerful enough to be of much assistance by itself if a user is looking to lessen his fear of committing high-risk crimes. And so on.

With respect to marijuana, the pendulum has swung from the

"reefer madness" scares in the first half of the twentieth century to a demand by reformers that marijuana be legalized. With marijuana widely available, penalties for its use and possession have been reduced. (In some states it has been legalized for legitimate medical purposes.)

The public is in danger of being fooled into thinking that marijuana is relatively harmless. This opinion is not shared by parents who have watched a child become a regular marijuana user, or by counselors or therapists who work with adolescent marijuana users. There is evidence that long-term heavy use of the drug results in damage to the lungs and reproductive system. But most frightening to witness is the psychological damage—the so-called amotivational syndrome—as the frequent user turns off and drops out, rejecting his family, school, and responsible peers.

Once he is associating almost exclusively with other drug users, the teenage marijuana user is exposed to other drugs. In such situations he may decide to try new substances just for kicks because marijuana has lost its allure. If one probes carefully, he will often discover that the youngster's dropping out and becoming irresponsible began *before* marijuana use, but was almost certainly accelerated by regular use of the drug.

Some drug users reach a point where being without drugs is unnatural for them. Then it takes progressively more of a particular substance to give the user the same impact he had experienced using less. This is called a "tolerance effect," and physical dependence may develop. His addiction, however, is not just to a particular substance, but to an entire way of life.

Consider Thomas, who spent a year in jail for a nonviolent crime. A judge suspended the remainder of his sentence and placed him in an intensive community corrections program where he was closely supervised. Thomas had a remunerative job with a growing customer base cleaning upholstery on furniture. He enjoyed good health, freedom from incarceration, the benefits of money legitimately earned, and a devoted girlfriend. One day he arrived at a counseling session seething with discontent and said to me, "I thought if I gave up drugs, I'd have no problems. Now I have more problems than ever." He complained, "My truck breaks down. My customers are a pain. Bills pour in. I have the hassle of all these meetings to go to—probation, Narcotics

Anonymous, counseling sessions. My girlfriend is on my case, wanting one thing or another. I have no time for myself. If this is life, it's a hell of a life." Thomas demanded, "What do you have that compares with cocaine?" To this stark challenge, I could only reply, "Nothing." I could not honestly assure Thomas that working, paying bills, and attending meetings could possibly match the excitement that he had experienced in the drug world.

Typical of the criminal who is a drug user, Thomas was a short-distance sprinter, not a long-distance runner. On numerous occasions we discussed benefits that eventually would accrue if he maintained a responsible course in life. He would not have to constantly look over his shoulder. He would not subject himself to physical danger, nor would he harm people who cared about him. By working hard, he would establish a base in life that would allow him to have respect for himself and earn the respect of others. But Thomas preferred the high voltage of the cocaine world, and back to that he went.

What was Thomas's addiction all about? Counting time served in jail, he had not had a drug in his body for a year and a half. (Random drug tests and reports by his girlfriend verified his abstinence.) He had no physical dependence on cocaine at the time he began using the substance again. Thomas made a series of choices as to how he wanted to live. His addiction was to an entire way of life, not just a substance.

Addiction has been characterized as a disease. Research indicates that a predisposition to mind-altering substances runs in families. A study of twins reported, "The heritability of alcoholism and drug abuse ranged from 60 percent to 80 percent."[6] But even with a genetic or biological aspect to addiction, people still are able to choose what they will or will not put in their bodies. If an individual is aware of a tendency toward addiction in his family, all the more reason to decide not to use mind-altering substances. An inmate who had a long criminal record told me emphatically that the one thing he did not do was drink or use drugs. This was because he had seen his father waste away and finally die at age forty of a condition directly attributable to alcoholism.

Addiction has been conceived of as a "brain disease."[7] Technology showing images of brain activity has revealed that heavy drug usage causes changes in the brain and nervous system. The course of this process can be affected by choices an addict makes. According to Dr.

David Deitch of the University of California San Diego, the brain alterations are reversible. As he put it, "A thought can change your chemistry."[8] In a monograph critiquing the brain disease model, two psychiatrists observe of addicts, "They are instigators of their own addiction, just as they are agents of their own recovery . . . or nonrecovery."[9]

Criminals are quick to pick up on the disease concept and invoke it as a convenient rationalization. Said one man, "I'm an explosive person. I may yell at you, but not hit you. It's part of my disease." Even the most heinous of crimes may be attributed to the "disease." A criminal told me that it was not he who killed a man, it was his disease.

Unlike a disease that a person contracts through no fault of his own, the criminal *chooses* to ingest, inject, or smoke certain substances. No one compels him to do so. Criminals regulate their selection and dosage of drugs. Contrary to what they tell a psychiatrist, psychologist, or drug counselor, they control their drug use; it does not control them. As a criminal seeks greater excitement, he may perpetuate a cycle of crime, more drugs, then more crime, until he is supporting an expensive drug "habit." Apprehended for a crime, the criminal is effective in convincing others that he got hooked and lost control. His stance is that he has been a victim of drugs and that, rather than suffer incarceration, he is *owed* an opportunity for treatment. The authorities do not realize that the offender cannot imagine living without drugs *and* crime, and that he has long known of treatment programs but would not avail himself of them. Or perhaps he went through treatment but resumed drug use later.

Criminals who become dependent upon drugs can overcome their addiction, if the motivation is strong enough.[10] Drug users have kicked their habits, some doing so entirely on their own. Their motives have not always been the purest. Aware that drugs interfere with their physical coordination and mental acuity, some have sought sobriety in order to become more proficient at committing crimes. Some have become abstinent to reinvigorate their sexual drive which had been diminished by drug use.

To return to Ivan, mentioned at the beginning of this chapter, the judge thought this man needed help because he was drinking to relieve depression, then behaved in an out-of-character fashion by assaulting his wife. I discovered something quite different! I interviewed not only Ivan but also his wife, Margaret, who was fortunate to survive the beating with no permanent physical injuries, and I had the opportunity to speak with one of Ivan's grown children. Margaret told me that, throughout their marriage, Ivan had abused her emotionally as well as physically. He was more belligerent when he drank. Neither friends nor family knew about her husband's tantrums, during which he yelled and cursed at her and belittled and berated her if she did not do what he asked or if she failed to anticipate his needs. Ivan had destroyed objects in their home, punched holes in walls, and hurled objects in Margaret's direction. During his rages he had grabbed, slapped, shoved, and shaken her. Afterward he would show contrition and apologize. Ivan's son told me that his dad was unpredictable. Ivan could be a softy or a tyrant depending on his mood, which changed with little warning. As soon as the children could support themselves, they were happy to leave. Ivan's primary problem was neither depression nor his intemperate use of alcohol.

A controlling, tyrannical bully, Ivan looked at life as a one-way street, expecting others to accommodate him. I learned that during ten years of employment by the same agency, he had not been promoted. Although I lacked access to his colleagues on the job, it was not hard to imagine that working with such an uncompromising individual would be no picnic. Until Ivan was arrested for felony assault, he had experienced no serious consequences for the many incidents of domestic violence. His expressions of remorse had been sufficient for his wife to forgive him and live in hope that he would reform. The remorse meant little because there was always a next time. This man had the personality of a criminal. The liquor he drank intensified his criminality; it was not the source of it.[11]

For Ivan and others like him, giving up the use of mind-altering substances, even if it is forever, does not eliminate the main problem—the uncompromising, controlling personality of a destructive individual. Reflecting on the devastation he and others had caused, one criminal commented that he realized, "It's thugs, not drugs; it's thinking, not drinking." Even if they become drug-free, Ivan and others like him have a lot more to change about themselves.

9

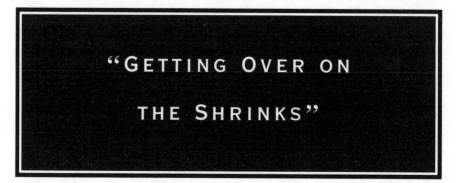

"GETTING OVER ON THE SHRINKS"

WHEN A PERSON COMMITS a crime that seems particularly bizarre or out of character, he may be referred for an evaluation to a psychiatrist or psychologist before the court pronounces sentence. The examining doctor is asked to explain *why* the defendant acted as he did. It is believed that an understanding of the motivation behind the crime will be helpful to a judge, jury, or other authority who must make a decision about the criminal.

Seldom does a criminal voluntarily seek the services of a psychiatrist or psychologist; rather, he is directed to see one by the court or perhaps by his lawyer. Since the criminal lies to his family and to others who know him well, it should come as no surprise that he will also deceive a person whose specific objective is to unmask him. As a result, erroneous conclusions are often drawn about his psychological makeup and motivation for committing a crime.

In this chapter the focus is on the frequent psychiatric misinterpretations of motives in five types of crimes: (1) the so-called crime of passion (or crime that is unplanned); (2) crimes that appear senseless and without discernible motives; (3) crimes that seem to arise out of a "disorder of impulse control" (with special reference to repetitive stealing, fire-setting, and gambling); (4) crimes committed because of insanity; and (5) crimes linked to mental retardation. Finally, I briefly address the perplexing issue of crimes that are committed by sufferers of types of "dementia" such as Alzheimer's disease.

CRIMES OF "PASSION"

Sometimes a person appears to lose control and commits an isolated, unplanned crime against someone he knows. Referred to as crimes of passion, these often occur within families, as when, in the heat of an argument, a husband grabs a meat cleaver and murders his wife. Such an individual has not been a killer in the past and, according to statistics, is unlikely to kill again. The perpetrator may have had a reputation as a loyal family man, a reliable provider, and a pillar of the community. But only immediate members of his household who intimately know this individual have experienced his dark side that lies behind the glossy public image.

Both the crime of passion and the calculated, cold-blooded murder by a criminal are products of a mentality with similar features. A close-up view of the enraged husband would reveal that he has much in common with the criminal in the way he views himself and deals with the world. Blustery, inflexible, and impatient, he demands that others do what he wants. He flares up whenever someone disparages him or disagrees with him. Instead of coping with unpleasant situations, he adds more problems by his manner of reacting. When frustrated or disappointed, he gets angry and is quick to blame others. While vowing to even the score, thoughts enter his mind of destroying the person who is thwarting him. The homicide that he commits may be preceded by a long series of threats or assaults that were hushed up within the family. Despite appearances, when the homicide is finally committed, it is by a man to whom violence was no stranger. The case of Stuart, who murdered his wife, illustrates this.

Stuart had been arrested for stabbing his wife, Angie, nine times in the parking lot of a government building. He had no prior criminal record and had been serving in the army for the previous four years. The court referred him to me for evaluation because it appeared to be a case of a stable man who had gone berserk and acted totally out of character. In fact, he had claimed that his mind snapped and that he didn't know what he was doing. My psychological study of Stuart revealed a different picture.

For ten years, dissension had plagued this man's marriage. Shortly after he married Angie, she began making derogatory remarks about his family. Stuart described to me his characteristic reaction when he became upset with her: "When I get frustrated, I hit the ceiling. Anything in front of me has to move." Husband and wife separated on several occasions, but reconciled each time. The arguments continued, and Stuart grew increasingly violent, threatening Angie numerous times, striking her on several occasions, and one time attempting to drown her in the bathtub.

Stuart asserted that to the outside world he presented a "perfect attitude," and this probably was not far from the truth, for he did not steal, cheat, or use drugs, and he appeared polite, educated, articulate, poised, and confident. Finally, after their last separation, Stuart set a luncheon date with Angie. When she didn't arrive and he couldn't reach her by phone, he became despondent and angry. He rushed home and, to his great consternation, discovered that most of the furniture had been removed. Determined to track her down, he combed the area for six days until he spotted their van. During this period, thoughts flashed through his mind of "burning her up," squeezing her to death, and other ways of getting rid of her.

Although he had discovered the location of her new residence, he took no immediate action. Several days later he drove to her neighborhood, followed her car to a subway stop, and parked where she did. Having no intention of harming her, he ran after her, pleading for an opportunity to talk and begging for reassurance that there was no other man in her life. Angie ignored him and got on a subway. In pursuit, Stuart jumped aboard and sat next to her. Still, she remained indifferent to his pleas and ignored his questions. When she got off he followed, now enraged. When they left the station and emerged into a parking lot, he continued to harangue her. Then from a brown bag he grabbed a pair of scissors and stabbed her repeatedly.

Stuart is similar to Ivan in chapter 8. As you may recall, Ivan attacked his wife during a drinking bout. She survived, but had he killed her, the homicide likely would have been regarded as a rash act committed in the heat of the moment. Alcohol would have been considered the agent facilitating the crime.

Because Stuart had been considered an upstanding citizen, his crime was widely regarded to be a result of a momentary lapse of control, a crime of passion. No one knew that Stuart had been violent before, and no one would have suspected that in his thoughts Stuart had many times murdered his wife.

This crime and others like it are not, in the strictest sense, premeditated. Stuart did not plan the date, time, place, or precise manner of the homicide. However, the act was not the product of a deranged mind, nor was it perpetrated by a man to whom violence was an alien impulse. The idea of ridding himself of his wife had occurred to him again and again. In that sense, he was programmed to murder his wife—programmed not by someone else, but by his own *habitual* patterns of responding to conflict. He was determined to control his wife, to have total power over her, no matter what it took. In evaluating such crimes, it is essential that the examiner probe *antecedent* patterns of thought and action. Almost invariably, what will emerge is that the crime at issue is merely one example of other offenses actually committed or else contemplated.

"Senseless" Crimes

Sometimes a crime is committed that seems to have no identifiable motive. A group of boys descend upon an old man sitting peaceably in the sun on a park bench. They drag him behind bushes, kick and beat him into unconsciousness, then leave him to die. Financial gain is not a motive, for this man is disheveled and shabbily dressed; he is not even wearing a watch. Revenge does not figure in the assault, for he is a total stranger. What the boys get out of the crime is kicks—just the thrill of doing something daring and vicious, and getting away with it in broad daylight.

A pair of bank robbers are nabbed red-handed by police. While checking the criminals' car, one of the officers discovers an attaché case containing $30,000 in cash garnered in an earlier robbery. When the astonished officer demands an explanation for holding up the bank when they already had so much money, one of the men replies blandly, "Well, ya got to do somethin'." What he means is that he and his companion were not satisfied with the earlier take and were after a larger haul. Yet they had given almost no consideration as to how they would spend the proceeds. Many a thief gives little thought as to how to dispose of the loot he steals. Criminals constantly complain about being broke. This is because they spend or give away the proceeds of a crime nearly as soon as they acquire them. It isn't the money itself that is important, but rather the excitement of knowing that they can pull off a really big score.

The common motive behind many crimes that appear senseless is kicks—the thrill of doing the forbidden. There is excitement in thinking about crime, bragging about crime, executing the crime, making the getaway, and celebrating the triumph. Even if the offender is caught, there is excitement in dealing with the police, in trying to beat the rap, in receiving notoriety, and, if it gets that far, in the trial proceedings.

THE "IMPULSE DISORDER" CRIME

To some observers, it appears that offenders repeatedly commit crimes because they are at the mercy of impulses over which they have no control. A child steals from home, from classmates, from neighbors, from stores, from construction sites. It seems that no matter where he goes, he returns with something that does not rightfully belong to him. He may be tagged a kleptomaniac, a psychiatric term for a person suffering from "an uncontrollable impulse to steal."[1] But behind the appearance of uncontrollable impulse lies the stark reality of the offender's *calculating* and proficient method of operating. Wherever he is, the thief habitually scans the environment to take advantage of opportunities. He does not have to develop an elaborate scheme for every single theft. He devotes about the same thought to some of his stealing as a person gives to driving. Both acts become matters of habit, and for each, vigilance is necessary.

What is habitual is not necessarily compulsive and beyond one's control. To say that a person has a habit of doing something does not mean he lacks responsibility for his actions. Just as a person can adapt his driving to icy pavements, so a thief adapts his pilfering to current conditions—what kind of surveillance he thinks there is, the accessibility of the merchandise, the location of exits, the number of people between him and the closest exit. This type of thinking is calculating, not compulsive. If the thief is apprehended, he may claim that he was compelled by an irresistible inner force to steal. By throwing the case into the bailiwick of the psychiatrist, he hopes to be evaluated as not responsible.

A person who frequently sets fires may be referred to as a pyromaniac, especially if readily understandable motives such as revenge or jealousy seem to be absent. Like kleptomania, pyromania refers to a condition in which there is a "recurrent failure to resist impulses" and an apparent "lack of motivation such as monetary gain."[2] But I have found that the pyromaniac, too, is a calculating person who is very much in control of his actions. He chooses the time and place to set a fire, and takes precautions to avoid detection. By setting fires, he wields a tremendous amount of power over human life and property. He can terrorize a community and inflict enormous devastation. Then he can enjoy his triumph as he smugly sits back, watches a building become engulfed in flames, observes the fire department struggle to contain the blaze, and all the while is reasonably certain that he will not be caught.

While some psychiatrists believe that kleptomania and pyromania are prompted by a search for excitement, they assert that this behavior is really motivated by unconscious and compulsive attempts to relieve sexual tensions. In other words, mention excitement, and a Freudian psychiatrist thinks of orgasm. Former Special FBI Agent Jim Reese has cited psychiatric literature which suggests that "the desire for thrill or orgasm is the sole reason for the fire."[3] Such reductionism leaves little room for free choice, despite the fact that the thief or fire-setter makes decisions as to whether or not to commit offenses depending upon his calculation of the risks involved. If the court regards the offender as a victim of his own ungovernable impulses, it may order him to seek treatment. Then the therapist may institute a treatment plan based on misconceptions while his patient continues to steal or set more fires.

From my clinical observations, I have concluded that "kleptomaniacs" and "pyromaniacs" are simply people who enjoy stealing or setting fires. They are as much in control of their behavior as the bank robber or offender who commits arson for profit. The fact that the stealing or fire-setting is repetitive only makes the issue *appear* more complex. Any criminal activity, repetitive or not, could be considered abnormal in that it is socially proscribed and most people do not engage in it. But this does not automatically make it a sign of illness or thereby exonerate the offender from responsibility. For behind such crimes is a person who deliberates and acts with the knowledge of possible consequences, information that he chooses to ignore in order to pursue his objective.

What of the man or woman who gambles so often that the activity invades work and family life and results in the amassing of huge debt? People who gamble to this extent claim that they are in the grip of a compulsion over which they have no control. Psychiatrists designate this behavior as an "impulse disorder" and have a diagnosis of "pathological gambling,"[4] citing its similarities to "substance dependence" in that both activities are self-destructive and persist despite adverse consequences to the individual who indulges. Psychiatrist Mark Potenza cites repeated and unsuccessful attempts on the part of "pathological" gamblers to quit or cut back.[5] He states there is evidence that "neural disturbances" including "changes in activity in multiple brain regions" may underlie this behavior.

If this is found to be the case, does it signify that gamblers are not responsible for their conduct? Let's look at the thought processes in "pathological gambling." The gambler has the expectation of making a

big score, receiving a large return with no effort and for little investment. It is one thing for a vacationer in a casino to gamble a modest
amount as a form of entertainment. Aware that the odds of winning are
low, he expends an affordable sum, then leaves. He does not recklessly
risk funds that he needs for daily living, nor does he endanger the
financial security of those who depend on him. For the frequent and
reckless gambler who deceives and injures others, the criminal thinking is there—the pursuit of excitement, the shutting off of consideration of consequences, the expectation of a bonanza without effort, and
the lying to others about his activities and the disappearing money.
Dissected, this so-called compulsion is the result of a series of choices
the person makes while eliminating deterrent considerations from his
thinking. The activity is under his conscious and willful control. His
absorption with what he wants and finds exciting is paramount and
overrides consideration of consequences.

Criminals exercise the greatest precautions to avoid being caught.
Usually they are successful, but sometimes even a pro can get overconfident so that it appears that impulsiveness got in the way of
judgment.

A young man strolled into a neighborhood grocery store late at
night. All the nearby shops were closed, and the cashier was on duty
alone. The customer looked around, picked up a six-pack of beer, and
took it to the cashier. He dug into his pants pocket, took out his wallet, and reached into it as though he were about to pay. Some papers
fell out, whereupon he quickly scooped them up and stuffed them with
the wallet into his hip pocket. As the cash register drawer opened, his
hand darted into his jacket pocket and whipped out a handgun. He
ordered the startled cashier to remove the money, and dropped it into
a small insulated ice cream bag. Yanking the phone cord out of the
socket, he ran out the door and took off in his car. The next day he was
apprehended by the police. In his haste to pick up the papers he
dropped from his wallet, he'd left behind a dry-cleaning ticket that bore
his name.

When an offender makes such an obvious gaffe, a psychiatrist or psychologist may believe that the perpetrator of the crime really wanted

to get caught. The basis for such a conclusion is in Freud's writings on unconscious guilt. In 1915, Freud stated that we all experience guilt, which is a remnant from the time in our lives when we had erotic feelings toward the parent of the opposite sex (the oedipal period).[6] He contended that children often misbehaved in order to be punished, which served to relieve that guilt. In "The Ego and the Id," Freud wrote, "It was a surprise to find that an increase in this unconscious sense of guilt can turn people into criminals."[7] Freud and his disciples extrapolated from findings on neurotics and applied them to criminals, even though they rarely treated criminals as patients. Present-day psychiatrists and psychologists do the same. Instead of seeing the offender as a person who is overconfident, they read into his motivation that he wanted to get caught, or may even go a step further and claim that his behavior represented a cry for help.

INSANITY

On a warm June Saturday night, nineteen-year-old Ralph was the only family member at home. His parents and brother were out of town, but he did not accompany them because he was scheduled to work on Sunday. Having just completed his freshman year at college, Ralph was glad to be out of the dormitory and welcomed having time to himself. He had grown up in a middle-class suburban household—no divorce, alcoholism, abuse, or other noteworthy problem. He had enjoyed high school popularity as a football player and claimed that his classmates knew him as a "nice, sweet guy." No one could have anticipated the tragedies that would unfold late that spring evening, forcing some in a shocked community to doubt this young man's sanity.

After dark, Ralph drove to a downtown area notorious for pornography, prostitution, strip joints, and drugs. He picked up a prostitute and took her to his home, where he had sex with her, then killed her. After he had disposed of her body, he returned to the same location, solicited the services of another young woman, brought her home, had sex, killed her, and disposed of her body. By daybreak, three young women had been slaughtered. How did this nice, sweet guy turn into a serial killer?

Ralph informed the psychologist chosen by his attorney that he heard voices directing him to kill. Specifically, the defense psychologist asserted that Ralph suffered from a mental disease and had an irresistible impulse to obey hallucinations that commanded him to do what he did. In court, his attorney entered a plea of not guilty by reason of insanity.

Appointed by the prosecution, I was to evaluate Ralph's mental state at the time of the crime. Ralph had no history of mental illness, nor had he so much as consulted a counselor. In reviewing the transcript of his confession to police, I saw no mention of hearing voices. The commanding voices surfaced only *after* the defense psychologist interviewed him.

I focused on three issues. Did Ralph truly hear voices, and what was their nature? Was he really a stranger to violence prior to the homicides? Was he as law-abiding as his reputation and lack of a criminal record suggested?

Ralph was inconsistent in his account of whether there was one voice or several. He described the voice or voices as harsh, but also as soothing and soft. Asked if he ever heard voices before the deaths of the three young women, Ralph replied that he had. However, he maintained that he could control the voices; they did not control him. He could drown them out by turning up the volume of the radio. Despite hearing them, he asserted he could ignore the voices and decide to disobey what they directed him to do. (If these voices ever existed, he certainly did not disregard them the night of the homicides.) The Monday after the murders, Ralph had planned to have lunch with a former girlfriend, hoping to rekindle their romance. Asked if he had been worried that the voice (or voices) might appear and order him to harm her, Ralph replied that it was possible, but he'd decided to take that chance. He added that he had forewarned the voice "to leave her out of it."

Interestingly, when Ralph was in jail, he claimed to hear the voice, but only under circumstances when he was being taken to task for a violation. For example, he became angry at a deputy and overturned a table, then explained that the voice had directed him to do this.

It is highly unlikely that Ralph had ever heard a voice. Rather, it seemed an after-the-fact phenomenon invented to provide a psychological defense for killing.

I learned that behind Ralph's calm congeniality there was a strong-willed individual who, even as a child, had forcefully and sometimes violently pursued what he wanted. Violence permeated his thinking, and he erupted into tantrums and attacks when he felt put down, frustrated, or disappointed. When his temper flared, he'd struck a boy with a hammer, dumped another headfirst into a trash can, and beaten another youth so severely that it took several boys to stop him. Ralph enjoyed terrorizing others, as evidenced by his joining a group whose mission was to intimidate certain students to the point that they'd want to leave the school.

This young man was never apprehended for other crimes he committed before that Saturday night. He stole money or merchandise from every job he held. He regularly entered laundromats and absconded with women's underwear, bringing it home and using it to masturbate. He pilfered items from his parents, feigned ignorance about their disappearance, then suddenly found and returned them, winning his parents' gratitude. Other antisocial behavior included speeding, destruction of property, and heavy use of alcohol.

If the above were not enough to indicate that Ralph was willful and deliberate in his conduct, the details of the commission of the homicides also provided evidence of his rationality: the selection of a site to dump the bodies, changing his blood-spattered clothes, depositing money stolen from the victims into his own bank account, and quickly resuming his daily routine, including arriving at work on time.

Ralph's insanity plea did not sit well with members of the jury after they heard all the evidence. His insanity defense failed, and Ralph was convicted on three counts of first-degree murder.

A notorious and still-unresolved crime occurred back in 1982. Seven people in the Chicago area died after they had innocently purchased and ingested Extra-Strength Tylenol capsules laced with cyanide. Before strong leads surfaced, people were saying that the mind of the perpetrator must be deranged. In an editorial, Denver's *Rocky Mountain News* termed the act psychotic and went on to comment, "Almost every time a bizarre crime gets wide publicity, sick minds try the same thing, whether it be kidnapping or giving children apples with razor blades in them for Halloween."[8]

When a criminal commits a shocking crime, as did Ralph and the Tylenol killer, a gut reaction on the part of the average citizen is to conclude that he must be crazy. But this reveals only the public's perceptions, and nothing about the workings of the criminal's mind.

If a criminal commits a serious crime and believes that the evidence is strong enough to convict him, he may resort to the insanity defense to beat the rap, as Ralph did. In the streets, local jails, and other detention facilities, he has heard that if a person can convince the authorities that he is crazy, he will be sent to a hospital for treatment, not to a prison to serve a long sentence. In some jurisdictions, if a defendant is declared "not guilty by reason of insanity," he is free to walk the streets. In many instances a hospital is far more comfortable and has a freer environment than a prison. More important, the local lore is that if the criminal plays the psychiatric game, he will be considered improved and will be released far sooner than he ever would from prison. (This applies only in cases where a long sentence is imminent.)

To convince the examining psychiatrists and the court that he is insane, a criminal must satisfy one of several legal definitions of insanity, depending on the legal test used in a particular jurisdiction. Does he know right from wrong (1843 McNaughton rule)? Is the crime a product of a mental disease or defect (1954 Durham rule)? Does the defendant lack substantial capacity to appreciate the criminality of his conduct or to conform his conduct to the requirements of the law (1972 American Law Institute Model Penal Code)?

In some instances a determination of guilt or innocence is separate from a determination of the individual's mental condition. Arizona enacted a "guilty but insane" law in 1995, in which the defendant is tried on the merits of the evidence. If found guilty but then determined to be insane, he can spend time in the Arizona State Hospital instead of in jail. He is to serve the equivalent there of whatever prison sentence he would have received. However, if the hospital staff determines that treatment has rendered him sane and no longer dangerous before the sentence ends, the offender can be released, then monitored by a mental health agency.

Just as his crimes have been rational and deliberate acts, so is the criminal's scheming of his insanity defense. In the jails or wherever else criminals are sent for observation, one learns from another, the psychologically sophisticated tutoring the unsophisticated. Some also get tips from their lawyers. Attempts to fake mental illness range from the subtle to the bizarre, depending on what the criminal surmises will be convincing. He may claim that he hears the voice of the devil commanding him to do evil. He may proclaim that he acted as a messenger of God. He may feign delusions of persecution, asserting that people are plotting to do him in, or that poison is being added to his food. He may pretend to be confused and disoriented. All this malingering is designed to demonstrate that he is irrational and out of contact with reality and thus not responsible for his crime.

A suicidal gesture may accomplish what the criminal wants. He informs his cellmate that he will hang himself at 7:00 P.M. and asks that a guard be summoned at that time to cut him down. He figures that if he is considered a suicide risk, he will be shipped immediately to a hospital.[9]

Seventeen-year-old Tracey landed in the juvenile detention center after repeated truancy, stealing, and destruction of property. Needless to say, this teenager did not enjoy her living quarters. Peering into the window of the door to her room, a staff member was alarmed to see that Tracey had tossed a bedsheet over a rafter and was fashioning a noose. Immediately the staff member burst into the room and reasonably concluded the girl was suicidal. Tracey was stripped of most personal belongings and placed on a special suicide watch. (It is standard practice for staff to remove all items, including many articles of clothing, that a suicidal individual could use to inflict self-harm.)

When I interviewed Tracey shortly thereafter, she was indignant and irate. She declared that she was not in the least depressed, much less suicidal. When I inquired about the purpose of the sheet and noose, she muttered that all she'd tried to do was convince the staff she was depressed so they'd transfer her to the community hospital's psychiatric unit. There, in an unlocked facility, her boyfriend could visit, and they could plan her escape. I told Tracey that the detention center staff had no way to divine her motives. Correctly, they had taken steps to prevent Tracey's harming herself. This delinquent girl was too clever for her own good. She ended up with more rather than fewer restrictions.

There are many other ways to convince others of the presence of a mental illness to mount a legal defense of insanity, including feigning epileptic seizures, mumbling incoherently, staring into space, pretending to hallucinate, and mutilating oneself. A case for amnesia may be concocted even before the defendant's first interrogation by police.

One man acknowledged to me that he took precautions to lay the groundwork for a psychiatric finding of amnesia. Upon learning that the police were closing in on him for a crime, he abandoned his car, tossed the keys into the river, buried all identification, and wandered into a clinic looking dazed. He was hospitalized for three months and then released on convalescent status. There was no attempt to prosecute him.

The display of symptoms of mental illness may be dramatic in jail, during courtroom proceedings, or at a hospital where the criminal is sent for observation. For example, when a defendant behaves erratically and inappropriately in a courtroom, he is likely to know that his behavior will raise doubts about his sanity or at least his competency to stand trial. One defendant was derisive of the flamboyance with which another was faking. He thought the man was overdoing it and told him, "You try to save your ass your way, and I will save mine my way." He had made a study of psychological tests. In a quiet manner, he let signs of psychopathology seep out during the testing. Appearing withdrawn and anxious, he showed difficulty with memory and concentration, often losing his train of thought. He gave responses that were mutually contradictory. On the ink-blot tests, his reticence vanished, and he said he saw breasts, vaginas, and lots of blood spilling over the cards. Later he told a buddy, "What you have to do is see pussy in every picture." He was declared not guilty by reason of insanity, and was sent to a hospital. By a successful insanity defense, he beat a potential sentence of twenty years for his crime of armed robbery and another five years for possession of the illegal weapon used in the crime, a sawed-off shotgun.

Elizabeth murdered two human beings, the homicides occurring many years apart and in two different states. One was a man at whom she became enraged. The other was an elderly landlady. She was declared insane for the first, sane for the second. In the latter case, Elizabeth's attorney attempted to convince the jury that his client was seriously mentally ill by capitalizing upon her lifelong history of irresponsible and erratic behavior.

As a teenager, Elizabeth shoplifted, constantly defied her parents, and used drugs. She successfully concealed a great deal of her antisocial conduct by presenting the façade of an all-American girl who was a cheerleader and student council president. Although highly intelligent, Elizabeth detested schoolwork and did just enough to graduate from high school. Sick of being told what to do by others, she had no more interest in formal education. She never developed a work ethic and failed to acquire marketable job skills. Searching for excitement, she quit job after job and drifted from place to place. Once in a while, Elizabeth grew despondent and ended up as a patient in regional hospitals by ingesting a combination of alcohol and pills. There were times when she sought hospitalization or help from outpatient mental health facilities because she was homeless and knew she could enlist others who knew the ropes and could help her obtain free services, including food stamps and assistance in locating an inexpensive place to live. By persuading a counselor that she was chronically and severely mentally ill, Elizabeth qualified for social security disability status. Then she could receive a regular check and not have to worry about employment. During a ten-year period, this woman received numerous diagnoses, including "schizoaffective disorder," "bipolar disorder," "acute paranoid psychosis," "possible personality disorder," and "unspecified neurotic disorder." One hospital chart noted, "During the course of her various hospitalizations, she had received practically every type of medication." By the time she committed the first homicide, Elizabeth's psychiatric history had grown so extensive that she was readily acquitted by reason of insanity.

Years later, Elizabeth killed again. The crime occurred in a different state, and the real Elizabeth was finally unmasked. When she came to trial, Elizabeth's attorneys relied heavily on a stack of psychiatric records to fortify their claim that she was mentally ill and legally insane when she committed the crime. Her volatile, explosive conduct in jail added to this documentation. But after many hours spent combing through her voluminous records and interviewing Elizabeth at the jail, I concluded that she had known exactly what she was doing. A jury agreed and found her guilty of first-degree murder.

Elizabeth had been renting a room from an elderly woman whom she came to despise. When I interviewed her, Elizabeth explained, "She wanted to regulate my activities with men. She was going to say how I lived in her home." Elizabeth also resented the landlady's criticizing her for idly sitting around the house and not working. The landlady urged her to become more sociable and offered many suggestions as to how to improve her situation. Ever since she was a child, Elizabeth had not taken kindly to others telling her what to do, and she regarded all this well-intended advice as meddling. She complained to an acquaintance that she was fed up with her landlady and remarked that she "would probably kill her if I got into a fight." Elizabeth confessed that on many occasions she became so enraged that she contemplated killing the woman. Eventually she shoplifted a knife, stabbed the landlady to death, then rinsed the blood off her hands and the knife, and left the house.

How is it that highly trained professional psychiatrists and psychologists are sometimes fooled? Never for a minute does the criminal really believe that he is mentally ill. In fact, he is offended if anyone calls him crazy. However, he is willing to be called just about anything if he can beat a charge. He is a pro at examining people, having an uncanny knack for finding out what they want to hear and then feeding it to them. The strange behavior of the criminal at the time of the examination and/or the sordid nature of the offense may be sufficient to convince the examiner that he is dealing with a sick person. Thus the fact that the defendant has murdered his victim, hacked up the body, and then buried the pieces may by itself convince the examiner that he is dealing with an insane killer. A routine case of armed robbery is unlikely to be viewed the same way. But what may be extraordinary is not the crime but the defendant's apparent incoherence, mumbling, confusion, and general disorientation. If both the crime and the behavior during examination seem bizarre, the defendant has it made. He will be whisked from jail to hospital.

The experts may be misled in yet another way. If the defendant has a history of brain injury or disease, he may make the most of that condition by claiming that it caused him to act without awareness or intent. Accurate or not, it makes for a tidy explanation. The examiner may conclude that the crime was a product of the disease and come up with a finding of diminished responsibility.

The criminal's behavior can be so extreme and variable that even well-trained professionals have difficulty assessing him. They are confronted by the oscillating peaks and swamps of his moods, the contrast between his savage brutality and maudlin sentimentality, his apparent conformity and brazen defiance of authority. I have interviewed youngsters and adults who committed numerous crimes, some extremely serious, but managed to avoid detection by law enforcement authorities and instead were referred by their distraught and baffled families, schools, or community agencies to mental health professionals.

The antisocial person shifts from unbridled optimism and a sense of invulnerability to unmitigated pessimism and despair. His changes in outlook and demeanor may be visible to others. The oscillation does not signify the presence of a mental illness, such as "bipolar disorder" (known formerly as manic-depressive illness)! The highs and lows stem from the criminal's reactions to living in a world that neither corroborates his inflated sense of his own importance nor fulfills his unrealistic expectations.

No sooner has the criminal been declared "not guilty by reason of insanity" and been admitted to the hospital than he starts working his way out. He participates in programs striving to convince the staff that he is earnest about change and is improving. In the hospital, the staff regards each activity as therapy. If the patient plays basketball, it is recreational therapy. If he makes a leather wallet, it is occupational therapy. If he has ground privileges and rakes leaves, it is industrial therapy. But the place to make a major impression is in therapy with the doctor, who will make the most influential recommendation about his release. In group psychotherapy, individual psychotherapy, and the therapeutic community, he feeds the doctor and the rest of the staff what he thinks they want to hear. He ventilates his feelings, delves into his past, and demonstrates insight into his mental condition. He also abides by hospital rules—at least to all appearances. The hospital's evaluation of him is based primarily on his cooperation and insight. Said one hospitalized patient, "They don't care what you did on the outside as much as how you are doing inside."

No matter how he got there, both the adult criminal and the juvenile offender have contempt for the hospital staff and programs. Seventeen-year-old Edward told me, "Most kids don't realize their rights." He said that he refused "to bow down and kiss the butts" of the doctors and nurses, who he proclaimed could easily be outsmarted. His goal while in the hospital was to "educate the kids in how to beat the system."

Playing the psychiatric game is exciting. Just like a crime, it offers a criminal opportunity to outwit the system and make fools of everyone. About the only time that he is certain to fail is when the hospital staff is fearful of releasing him because he has committed a highly publicized atrocity. Then a decision is made to bury him in confinement. But he may have yet another alternative open to him. By becoming a troublemaker and an administrative headache, he may succeed in pushing the staff to discharge him. One man kept filing grievances and writs against the hospital where he was confined. The administration became so weary of responding to his charges that it accelerated granting him privileges and eventually placed him on outpatient status. But if a patient is considered a truly dangerous case or has attracted publicity in the past, he may instead spend considerable time locked in seclusion.

To the criminal, the hospital is a permissive prison. Because he is considered sick, his crimes of the past and violations of the present are treated therapeutically, not punitively. This means to him that he will be able to get away with a lot more than he ever could in prison. He figures, often correctly, that he can do as he pleases as long as he shows remorse and psychological insight later. If he assaults another patient, he can talk about his pent-up hostility. If he uses illicit drugs, he can rationalize it as seeking relief from overwhelming anxiety. If he tries to escape, he can relate it to intense depression. Sometimes he gets away with such psychological rationalizations and may even be praised for them. Though he is ostensibly sick, at times the hospital will treat him as totally rational and responsible. Under the banner of the therapeutic use of authority, it may seclude or restrict him, or deny him privileges. The criminal is never sure how the staff will react at any given time, but he worries about that *after* an infraction. He commits crime on the hospital wards and on hospital grounds as he preys on vulnerable noncriminal patients, many of whom are genuinely mentally ill. Robberies are frequent, drug rings flourish, sex with patients becomes a way of life, assaults and occasionally homicides occur. Criminals misuse privileges and leave the grounds without authorization, wreaking havoc in the community and on their return importing contraband into the hospital.

There are some criminals, although relatively few, whose psychological defenses crumble after arrest and in confinement. Observers erroneously conclude that such a mental state must have prevailed at the time of the crime. Criminals showing signs of psychosis are often far too confused and disoriented to scheme and execute crimes that require an alert and precise mind.

Carla had been hospitalized on an inpatient psychiatric unit after threatening a teenager with a knife. Twenty-four-hour-a-day observation of her behavior convinced the staff that she was truly psychotic, not malingering. She shuffled through the ward with her head bowed and hands in a prayerful pose. She told me that her hands were contaminated by semen and she was praying to be cleansed of sin. With medication, Carla's condition improved gradually. Her delusional thinking vanished, and she seemed ready for discharge to what was called a family care home. Less than a month later, I received reports that Carla was violating the rules of the halfway facility. She stayed out past curfew and became sexually involved with different men. The psychosis had lifted only to reveal a criminal personality. The delusion she suffered in the hospital seemed to result from a backlash of conscience. Formerly promiscuous and violent, in her psychosis Carla sought absolution and purity. With the psychosis in remission, she was far more dangerous to herself and others.

Some criminals like Carla cycle through alternating periods of crime and psychosis, the psychosis lasting as long as several months. But when the psychosis lifts, often with the help of medication, the patient who was irrational becomes totally lucid and in control of his behavior. There is no evidence to indicate that the transient psychotic phases *cause* the criminality.

The above suggests that all criminals are rational and that crime is never caused by a mental illness. I can speak only from my own clinical experience during the past thirty-four years. Clearly the issue is open to debate and needs further study. There are several caveats for those who undertake these evaluations. One is that it takes many hours of probing to penetrate the defendant's self-serving statements and to understand his thinking processes. Second, it should not be assumed that because a person is psychotic at the time of the evaluation, he was psychotic at the time of the crime. Finally, even if it can be ascertained that the person was mentally ill when he committed the crime, it does not necessarily follow that he was powerless to act other than he did.

With respect to this last point, I am familiar with a case in which a young man murdered a former girlfriend. Sufficient evidence was collected by psychiatrists over many years to indicate that the defendant was in fact a "paranoid schizophrenic." Despite his delusions of persecution, however, he schemed and carried out the homicide with deliberation and an awareness of consequences. He not only purchased a gun and stored it while thinking about the crime, but he also took steps to locate the girl and cased out the place where she worked. Beforehand, he had a discussion, ostensibly hypothetical, with a psychiatrist as to what would happen were a person diagnosed with his condition to commit a serious crime. He concluded that he would be found mentally ill, remanded to the hospital, and thereby avoid prison. This is precisely what happened.

Psychiatric hospitalization gives the criminal an excuse for more crime. Each time he is treated at a psychiatric facility, there is additional documentation of mental instability. Whenever he is arrested, he will be regarded as an offender with a psychiatric condition. Consequently, for a new offense he may wind up again in a hospital rather than a prison. There he will continue his efforts to outfox the shrinks.

MENTAL RETARDATION

A controversy has been simmering over whether people who are mentally retarded can distinguish right from wrong and thereby be held responsible for their crimes. IQ scores have been offered as the key criterion for establishing mental retardation. Decades ago, David Wechsler, originator of the still widely used Wechsler Adult Intelligence Scale (WAIS) and the Wechsler Intelligence Scale for Children (WISC) defined intelligence as "the aggregate or global capacity of the individual to act purposefully, to think rationally and to deal effectively with his environment."[10]

A case that I was involved in as the prosecution's psychological expert reached the United States Supreme Court.[11] A man with an IQ of 59 had been sentenced to death by a jury in Virginia. He had committed a brutal homicide requiring deliberation and planning, then faked an injury and obtained treatment at a hospital in order to establish an alibi as to his whereabouts. The defendant's conversations with me covered many subjects, including rap lyrics he had composed, his recipe for cooking chicken, and his references to biblical parables (he correctly used the word "parable"). He was able to name the current president of the United States, recalled who was president before him, and identified the governor of the state. Among the words that he used correctly were *déjà vu, psychic, theory,* and *forensics.* He boasted about figuring out solutions before the contestants during a television game show. The defendant's school records did not contain one mention of his being unable to do school work. Frequent observations were made that he refused to work and was uncooperative and disruptive.

An IQ score depends to a considerable extent upon acquiring information during one's schooling (e.g., as on vocabulary and arithmetic subtests), and it also relies on a person's willingness to stay focused when a task on the test becomes difficult. There is no way that a person who held the conversations I did with this man could reasonably conclude that he was mentally retarded, despite his low IQ score. This individual was able, in Wechsler's words, to "act purposefully" and "think rationally." Hearing the appeal of this man's capital murder sentence, the U.S. Supreme Court ruled that imposing a death sentence on a person who was mentally retarded constituted cruel and unusual punishment prohibited by the Eighth Amendment. However, the Court left it to each state to establish criteria for defining mental retardation.[12]

MENTAL DETERIORATION AND CRIMES COMMITTED BY PEOPLE SUFFERING FROM "DEMENTIA"

As people live longer, the population of the elderly suffering from some type of dementia (a medical condition), such as Alzheimer's disease, is increasing. These individuals show changes in mood, behavior, and personality as well as loss of memory and difficulty completing tasks that were familiar. Important legal and social policy questions arise as to how society should respond to men and women suffering from dementia who commit prosecutable acts of property damage or attack and seriously injure others. Do such individuals, if criminally charged, belong in correctional facilities, psychiatric institutions, or some other type of specialized facility?

Sentencing a disoriented, terrified person suffering from a form of dementia such as Alzheimer's disease to jail or prison seems inhumane. With the dismantling of the state hospital system throughout America, few facilities exist for long-term care of the mentally ill. Assisted living and nursing facilities may be ill-equipped to manage these fractious and unpredictable individuals.

Given my findings that the "out of character" crime does not exist, I wonder about people with dementia who commit crimes. (This is not a population I have studied.) Millions of men and women who are afflicted with conditions such as Alzheimer's disease become confused, disoriented, and withdrawn, eventually becoming totally dysfunctional. Although difficult to care for, they do not pose a physical danger to others. Does this disease bring out and magnify tendencies that already, at some level, have resided within the personality of the individual? Or are the differences between those who are dangerous and those who are not explainable solely in terms of organic pathology? I do not have the answer. Perhaps it does not matter in terms of developing a policy to deal with the problem.

When a mental health professional evaluates a criminal, there are actually two evaluations occurring simultaneously. The criminal is doing what he has done throughout his life—casing out the other person so he can figure out the best way to achieve his objective. He has spent most of his life sharpening this skill as he has been confronted by parents, neighbors, teachers, counselors, law enforcement officers, and others who have attempted to hold him accountable for misconduct and breaking the law.

By evaluating the evaluator, the criminal seeks to discover a way to sidetrack him from focusing on the gravity of the particular offense and to convince him there are mitigating factors for what he did. By claiming mental instability of one sort or another, he'll deny or minimize his culpability and hope to get off lightly. If he has a genuine but temporary mental disorder, this may become the focus of treatment, and he may improve. But the criminal personality remains untouched, and more injury to others is a certain result.

10

LOCKED UP

IN MID-1982, WHEN THE FIRST edition of this book was being written, there were 394,380 inmates in prison in the United States.[1] As of June 30, 2002, the total number of inmates in state or federal prisons or in local jails was a record 2,015,475.[2] In addition, toward the end of 1997, there were 125,805 juveniles in public or private residential placements charged with or convicted of an offense.[3]

With this upward trend in incarceration, the prison reform movement has continued to gather strength, especially with the advent of so-called "supermax" institutions, which I shall describe later in the chapter. Much of the criticism leveled at correctional facilities has been constructive. However, one major criticism that is inaccurate and misleading is that correctional institutions are schools for crime, which implies that those incarcerated in them are turned into something that they weren't before.

Prison is a breeding ground for crime only insofar as a criminal expands his associations and finds support for antisocial patterns of thought and behavior. He hears new ideas for crime in prison, but *he* is the one who accepts or rejects those ideas. No one forces him to continue a life of crime either within the institution or when he returns to society. He is not a hapless victim who is corrupted by fellow inmates. He has made choices in the past and continues to make choices.

Criminals exhibit the same behavioral patterns inside prison as on the streets. Being locked up does not alter a criminal's perception that he is top dog. Once he adjusts to his surroundings, he becomes determined to establish himself, his stance being "If you serve time, let time serve you." And so he continues his manipulations and power plays. Some inmates abide by the rules, but not because of any inner personality transformation. Rather, they are building themselves up as model inmates in order to gain special status or privileges. There are inmates who find incarceration to be truly a low point in their lives. They make genuine efforts to change, even seeking the help of institutional counselors, but the counseling that they receive usually turns out to be inadequate.

Wherever he is sent, the criminal believes that confinement is the final injustice in a string of injustices that began with his arrest. In the past, laws and others' rights meant little to him, but now that he is confined, he becomes highly legalistic about asserting his own rights. One inmate who was serving a sentence for a string of burglaries acknowledged, "You break a law to get what you want and treasure the law when it gets you what you want." The criminal looks for a way to beat a charge, and even long after he has begun serving time, he seeks a means to overturn a verdict or reduce his sentence. Some spend hours poring over law books in the prison library and weeks laboring over writs. Among them are men who make a career in prison as jailhouse lawyers, conducting legal research and preparing documents for themselves and other inmates, collecting as a fee, in the latter instance, money, property, and personal favors.

The assertion of rights continues throughout confinement and extends far beyond a preoccupation with legal statutes and procedures. As the criminal demands protection of his rights, he tries to intimidate members of the staff, who fear both lawsuits and violence. He insists on his right to join an activity if it appeals to him, or asserts the right not to participate if he finds it distasteful. At different times he may assume opposite stands on the very same issue. He may demand treatment and threaten to sue to get it. Just as readily, he may invoke his right to refuse treatment.

When the doors of prison first lock behind them, some criminals are temporarily frightened, remorseful, and depressed. These emotions are not alien, because criminals experience them occasionally on the street when they tire of the daily grind and of looking over their shoulders, and regret disappointing people who care about them. Even on the outside, there were moments when life seemed no longer worth living. Behind bars, they have plenty of time to think. Old fears loom larger than ever and are more difficult to dispel. The present is grim, and the future seems bleak. Early in their confinement, some immerse themselves in prayer and Bible reading. Others ponder how to end it all. "I was just getting tired," said a twenty-eight-year-old armed robber, "getting to the point where I wasn't getting anywhere. I didn't see anything tangible I could call success. When my kids grew up, what kind of guy were they going to see? You never see anything accomplished. You're a nothing. You're scared." The turmoil and fear experienced by these criminals does not last. The man who trembles upon his entry to prison may, in time, turn as tough as nails.

Although even some of the most seasoned criminals begin their sentences in despair, others enter prison hardboiled. If a man has committed crimes but never before served time, going to prison gives him status. Now that he has made the "pen," he is in the big leagues. A distraught mother wrote to a judge begging for information about her eighteen-year-old son's adjustment to his first incarceration. He had been sentenced to two years for arson. In reply, the judge wrote, "He does not assume personal responsibility for his behavior and tends to negate it. So far, he does not even appear to be uncomfortable in prison. Rather, it appears that he is getting some status from it."

The behavior of an inmate may be geared initially to what he has heard about an institution before he enters it. Prisons gain reputations among their alumni and among other criminals who hear about them through the grapevine but have never been inside them. Some are maximum-security institutions, notorious for being the end of the road for convicts who are unmanageable elsewhere.[4] These are often formidable fortresses with high barbed-wire fences, tall watchtowers monitored by armed guards, electronically controlled gates, and interior surveillance by correctional officers and closed-circuit television. Elaborate and costly security measures do not prevent highly volatile inmates from stabbing, raping, engaging in gang warfare, and rioting. The highest priority of an inmate is to survive. A new inmate knows that he will have to demonstrate from the beginning that he is as tough as the next guy. In institutions like this, the staff struggles to prevent inmates from taking over. Inmates occasionally win out and have the staff so intimidated that it depends on the prisoners to keep order.

At the opposite extreme are minimum-security facilities, which resemble college campuses. Inmates wearing their own clothing rather than regulation uniforms stroll to and from classes in education, art, music, and vocational training. They play tennis, engage in community-sponsored social activities, participate in work-release programs, and go on home visits. The atmosphere is casual, regimentation minimal. Such an environment is possible as the institution houses offenders considered less dangerous because they have not been convicted of violent crimes.

"Supermax" prisons have been constructed throughout the United States. These institutions are intended for inmates that have proven to be so dangerous they cannot be safely contained in the general population of even maximum-security penitentiaries. The supermax facilities have been controversial because they are so restrictive. These prisons have become the targets of lawsuits by plaintiffs who contend that inmates suffer unduly from prolonged isolation in a harsh, psychologically traumatizing environment.[5]

To better understand who gets housed in a supermax facility, consider Gordon—incarcerated for murder and other violent crimes. The leader of a prison gang, Gordon's institutional record showed dozens of write-ups for disobeying orders, disruptive conduct, theft, possession of contraband, and use of mind-altering substances. On two occasions he incited riots, one of which resulted in the serious injury of a correctional officer and in the staff having difficulty securing the unit.

Most supermax inmates have been violent in the free world. They also have demonstrated an unwillingness to abide by institutional regulations, and continue to be a danger to others. Like Gordon, they must "earn" their way into a supermax facility by posing threats to safety, establishing themselves as escape risks, instigating disturbances, or engaging in violent behavior toward staff or other inmates. Once housed in supermax, a system is laid out so that they can earn greater freedom and eventually work their way into a less restrictive prison. Some cooperate while others balk. It is the inmate's choice.

The toughness of the inmates and the tightness of the security are not the only factors determining an institution's reputation. Prisons are also known for their physical conditions. Some are antiquated buildings that are crowded, dingy, ovenlike in summer, and freezing in winter. Others are modern but still stark with their gleaming metal and tiny windows. What also matters to inmates is whether it's a "joint" with a lot of programs expounding rehabilitative goals or a no-nonsense lockup where the staff goes strictly by the book. Given humane conditions, many prefer the latter because all they have to do is follow institutional rules and serve their time, without playing what they call the "head games" of rehabilitation.

Despite being behind bars, the criminal still expects to do as he pleases. This is not surprising, because it is a lifelong attitude. However, inmates have different methods of getting what they want in prison just as they did outside. Some wage open warfare individually or in gangs with staff members, flouting authority and brazenly defying regulations. One teenager bragged about his defiance in a state institution: "I tore up my room. I loved hearing glass break." At another juvenile facility, several ringleaders assembled all the kids of one unit, barricaded the staff out of the lounge, and demolished the place. Some prisoners prefer to be locked in their cells or banished to "the hole" rather than capitulate to anyone. Even in their cells they can create a commotion by setting bedding afire, or cause floods by stuffing up toilets. Said one inmate, "I am going to play my cards the way I want to and when I want to. Go straight—hell! I would rather remain a hoodlum than let anyone walk over me. No one is going to stop me unless they kill me."

In a struggle for status among fellow cons, the physically aggressive inmate is quick to lash out with a stream of profanity or throw a punch whenever he feels infringed upon. A prisoner who calls him a string of names may wind up with a fork jammed in his gut. A melee may erupt when someone switches the channel on the television. An unaware staff member may suffer a fractured skull from a flying chair after denying an inmate's request. One irascible inmate, displeased with the vegetable soup served at lunch, stared into his bowl, glowered at the man serving him, and complained that he had received the "dregs of the pot." He declared the "slop" unfit to eat and demanded another portion. When the worker ignored him, he threw the soup in his face.

An inmate may conclude that direct confrontations with staff or fellow prisoners are futile, that there is wisdom in restraint. The model inmate is the consummate actor. Contemptuous of everyone from the warden to the guards, he still plays up to them. By lining up allies, he expects to make life easier. Even the toughest con may decide that to score brownie points it is worthwhile to scrub his cell, buff the floors each morning until they gleam, and work diligently at his institutional job. Good behavior has its rewards, including the possibility of early parole. (Some states have eliminated parole entirely. The full sentence must be served.) In some systems, an inmate can earn "good time" credits. Whenever a specified number of days passes without an infraction, one day is lopped off his sentence.

Gerald was given a lengthy prison sentence for severely beating a woman who refused to have sex. Once incarcerated, he obeyed all prison regulations. Gerald joined a music appreciation group, participated in athletic programs, took college courses in finance and philosophy, and excelled in an interpersonal skills program. Staff regarded him as a model and an inspiration to other inmates. Finding him to be an insightful participant in individual and group therapy, the psychologist invited him to be a co-leader of a therapy group. Gerald was evaluated as having progressed so that his attitude, previously aggressive, was now normal toward women. The staff decided that Gerald had been sufficiently punished. With his psychologist predicting he would maintain his gains and make further progress, Gerald was paroled to a halfway house. There the counselor was so impressed that he concluded that Gerald's days of criminality were over. No one could fathom that the worst was yet to come. To this date, no one knows how many innocent young women this "model inmate" slaughtered in the years after his release. When he was finally caught again and put on trial, he received the death penalty in two different jurisdictions based on evidence of his atrocities that persuaded both juries to convict him.

Whether he locks horns with the staff or cons his way into their good graces, the criminal wages psychological warfare. With his customary finesse, he preys upon human insecurity, weakness, greed, and prejudice. Knowing how staff members feel about him and other inmates may be of considerable advantage. If he can touch a sensitive nerve, he may provoke a staff member into losing control. It is a triumph to divert attention from himself and put the other person, or even the whole institution, on the defensive.

Serving time for forgery, Gary, a tall, wiry man of thirty, stayed to himself, determined to avoid a fight at all costs. However, he had his own way of causing trouble. Without a trace of anger, Gary one day informed the social worker on the psychiatric unit where he was housed that he planned to file no fewer than ten lawsuits, each alleging a specific form of malpractice as well as denial of psychiatric treatment. He declared, "I'll keep records on everything. I'll write down every irregularity. If the food isn't hot, I'll write it down." One of Gary's ploys had been to fake agonizing pain stemming from earlier surgery. His purpose was to persuade the physician to prescribe a narcotic drug. Denied the medication, Gary used the threat of a lawsuit to pressure doctors to transfer him to a different facility. He knew that all his legal maneuvering might amount to nothing, but he boasted to his friends that he would be long remembered for exposing staff incompetence and forcing the administration to defend itself.

The criminal is quick to detect dissension among staff members and exploit it. In many institutions, racial tensions run high. Fully aware of this, the inmate will invoke race where it is completely irrelevant to the issue but expedient for him. He cries discrimination to shift attention from what he has done wrong to a consideration of whether the staff is prejudiced. He injects race if he loses a privilege, if he is spoken to harshly, if he is ordered to do something he finds disagreeable, or if he has been caught for an infraction and is about to be punished.

In prison, just as on the street, the dilemma of whom to trust hangs heavily in the air. Criminals don't know what trust is. If they use the word, it usually means that a person won't betray them. "Don't snitch" is a code among inmates. The price of squealing on another con may be a beating or even death. Even so, the inmate realizes that every man is out for himself and that even his best buddy may turn informant to save his own skin or to acquire privileges. Although convicts share an understanding of "no snitching," the dominant ethos in prison is, as it was outside, "fuck everybody else but me." Writing decades ago in *Corrections Magazine,* Stephen Gettinger made an observation that still holds. He reported, "Some prison observers say that the inmate code's prohibitions against informing are more honored in the breach than in the observance. The trading of information is as common, and as necessary, to the daily life of any prison as taking the count."[6]

As he serves time, the criminal experiences psychological changes. There are periods of profound depression, similar to that which overwhelmed some upon arrival. As the days, weeks, and months drag by, prison life grates upon the inmate. The criminal never tolerated much in the way of a routine in the free world, but the regimen in prison is incomparably duller and more oppressive than anything he ever knew. Other people control his schedule, and there is little variation in what he will be doing each day during the months or years of his sentence. Outside, the criminal expected the world to suit him, and in prison he's no different. He seems to expect the institution to accommodate him as though he were a guest paying for a deluxe hotel room. His complaints resound with righteous indignation, as he ignores the fact that he is where he is as a consequence of the choices he has made.

Besides complaints there are genuine regrets. In contrast to the bleakness of prison existence, inmates glimpse life outside through radio, television, letters, periodicals, and occasional visitors. They are aging, and life is passing them by. Their children are growing up, and their wives are finding new interests, sometimes other men. They have much to regret—not just their present incarceration but their previous indifference or opposition to the many opportunities to live a different kind of life. There is plenty of time to look in the mirror and reflect upon a life in the gutter, an immersion in what one man called "a life of filth and slime."

Martin, an alumnus of jails, prisons, and residential drug treatment, spoke candidly about his many regrets. His self-loathing was obvious as he condemned himself for selling his children's new Easter shoes to raise drug money. Martin stole far more than shoes. His children were robbed of a father. "When they were really young, and like really, really needed me, I wasn't there," he said somberly. He neglected not just his family but himself. He was so occupied prowling the streets in search of drugs and committing crimes that for months he didn't even take a shower. Remarked Martin, "I was just existing. I wasn't really living. I was already dead."[7]

A twenty-five-year-old vicious felon named Ryan was serving a long sentence for a bank holdup, but had never been caught for a string of armed robberies in which he had assaulted and maimed innocent people. In prison he was doing a lot of thinking about his life and commented wryly, "I feel like a guy who was viewing the Virgin Mother and her child but who was so totally rotten that all he could think of was raping Mary and having sex with the child."

One outcome of such revulsion toward the self is to resolve to go straight. The inmate decides to avoid the incessant feuding and intrigues of the prison community and stays to himself. He cooperates with the staff, but this time he's not conning. Other inmates are highly suspicious of him, certain that he is putting on an act. If not that, they mark him as trouble because they think that he has sold out to the staff and become an informant. When their hunches turn out to be wrong, they may become convinced that he is sincere and really does want to change. But they remain skeptical because they know from their own experience that such determination never lasts. The basis for their skepticism is usually borne out. The man who aspires to straighten out finds that life without criminal excitement is intolerable. Gradually his commitment to change erodes, usually in prison, but certainly after he gets out.

An alternative to change is suicide. Some criminals had suicidal thoughts on the streets when things weren't working out. In confinement, an inmate's state of mind is such that he becomes despondent over the meaninglessness of his life, yet is also raging at a world that he thinks never gave him a fair shake. Sighed one inmate who was considering suicide, "I wouldn't have to put up with shit anymore." There are no readily available statistics about the number of suicides in prison. Certainly, suicidal gestures dramatizing the inmate's plight are more common. A heavy but not lethal dose of drugs, a wrist-slashing with a crude, handmade knife, or an inept job of hanging himself compels others to take notice and do something to help the inmate. He may wind up in a less harsh environment, such as a prison hospital or psychiatric unit.

The despondent inmate may seek salvation in religion. Some criminals study the Bible, applying its passages to their own lives. They send for religious materials and ask their families or prison personnel to provide them with still more. They flock to the prison chaplain's discussion groups, sing in choir, share in readings of the liturgy in chapel services, and participate in other religious programs. Some experience a sudden flood of religious inspiration and overnight become converts to a particular faith. The "Biblebacks," as other inmates call them, quote scripture, zealously imparting their insights to others. These are not conversions of convenience calculated to impress the authorities. The institutional life of these inmates becomes pervaded by religion. They tune their radios to church services and to gospel singing. They infuse their artwork with religious motifs. Their poetry, letters, and other writings resound with religious themes. Some inmates, less public about their absorption in religion, withdraw and quietly devote hours to reading and prayer.

Institutional staff members have no way of knowing whether the depression, spirituality, or attempts at reformation are genuine or whether the criminal is up to his old tricks. When genuine, these phases may last for months at a time. But phases they are. When they end, the criminal emerges with his basic outlook intact.

No criminal wants to return to prison, and no criminal expects to do so. For offenders who serve time, the thought of being confined again may in itself be a powerful deterrent to further criminal activity. Some do not repeat. By some process, known only to themselves, they change the way they think and their behavior. I am not talking about the ones who become slicker at what they do so they don't get caught, but about individuals who make far-reaching, lasting changes. These obviously are not the people who are referred to me or to other change agents. There are no studies of these people and no statistics as to how numerous they are.

A criminal's absorption with crime does not necessarily diminish just because he is locked up. Despite the restrictive environment, he schemes, talks about, and continues to engage in illicit activities. Any external stimulus, such as a television crime show, a detective movie, or a lurid crime story in the paper feeds an already busy mind, as do his daily conversations with other inmates about crime. Through letters and visitors, the criminal hangs on to old ties in addition to establishing new ones in prison. To some, confinement poses a greater challenge than ever to get away with illicit activities. Theft is rampant in prisons. Anything that a man wants to hold on to must be kept on his person or surrendered to a trustworthy staff member. An inmate may be robbed when he sleeps (if he shares a cell or dormitory), while he takes a shower, or at any other moment when he relaxes his guard. Inmates not only steal from one another, but also pilfer personal belongings from the staff and food and other supplies from the institution.

Just as the criminal made sexual conquests outside confinement, he may attempt to do the same within. Homosexuality occurs not simply because the criminal is without a woman. Sex in prison is a powerful weapon to obligate and control others. A consenting sexual act may occur between two inmates in which sex is bartered for cigarettes, food, personal possessions, or money. Each criminal gets what he wants from the other and gives up little of importance. But sex in prison is often far less civilized. The threat of rape can command respect and breed fear among other inmates. Many pairs of eyes rove up and down the body of each new young man who enters the institution, especially if he is of slight build and physically attractive. In his bed at night, a new inmate may be beset by a gang of inmates who threaten him with far worse than rape or sodomy if he resists or informs. It is a jungle in which the strong subjugate the weak. To obtain protection, an inmate may submit to becoming the lackey and sexual slave of one of the most feared inmates.

Rape in prison often goes unnoticed or ignored by staff. It has largely been regarded as a hazard of life in prison, almost a routine occurrence in some institutions. A movement to protect inmates from sexual assault has gathered backing from reformers and publicity in the media. This is part of a more general raising of consciousness with respect to fostering humane treatment of men, women, and children behind bars.

Criminals attempt to solicit sex from staff members whom they think they can compromise. They test out personnel by telling dirty jokes and making suggestive remarks. Sexual rendezvous are most easily held in settings where criminals have their own quarters or have earned the privilege of leaving the unit accompanied by staff. If an inmate succeeds in having sex with a staff member, he owns him and can extract special favors in the future. For example, one inmate threatened to report a female attendant with whom he had a sexual liaison unless she testified favorably in his behalf. At a hearing, she did as instructed.

Staff members must be trained so that they are alert to the wiles of the criminal and are not compromised on the job. The product catalog of the American Correctional Association lists numerous publications that instruct correctional employees how to protect themselves psychologically as well as physically.[8] Titles of publications include "Games Criminals Play: How You Can Profit by Knowing Them," "The Art of the Con: Avoiding Offender Manipulation," and "Game Over! Strategies for Redirecting Inmate Deception."

Gambling is also a way of life in the institution. Like sex, it is a means by which criminals obligate others and build themselves up. Bets are placed on card games, pool, chess, outside sports events, and virtually every other activity in which the outcome is unknown. The gambling may be organized, as in daily numbers games linked to a downtown connection by a staff member. In most facilities, regulations prohibit criminals from having money on their person. Yet there are inmates who are flush with cash they have acquired by gambling, from visitors, or by doing favors for staff. In some gambling operations, inmates net more than a staff member earns in weeks. If cash is not available, anything that is valued can be currency in a wager: cigarettes (where allowed), items from the canteen, personal possessions. Some staff members are regulars in the gambling. When the inmate wins, he may acquire more than the sum bet. In lieu of demanding immediate total payment or charging losers usurious interest rates, he may cancel debts if the indebted staff member closes his eyes to particular violations and helps the inmate gain privileges.

Many a fight in prison has begun over an unpaid debt. One inmate was heard screaming at another man who owed him a pack of cigarettes, "You pay up, or I'll go through you like a hurricane."

Correctional facilities take precautions to prevent contraband from being brought in, but criminals are ingenious. A shakedown of virtually any correctional facility will yield a variety of contraband items, especially handmade weapons. Silverware may be smuggled from the dining rooms, although many institutions are meticulous in trying to account for every piece after each meal. In prison industries, metal or woodworking shops, and during other activities, inmates are in regular contact with sharp, heavy, and breakable objects that they can turn into weapons. Even a mop handle makes a good club. Inmates of one penitentiary collected all the glass containers left from Christmas gifts given to them by family and friends. One night, angry at the early shutoff of the television, they urinated into the jars. The correctional officers were startled when they were barraged with glass and showered with urine as jars without tops were hurled down from the upper tiers of a cell block. From then on, glass jars were designated contraband.

Illicit drugs are nearly always floating around prisons and psychiatric hospitals housing criminal offenders. Friends ingeniously conceal drugs in packages that they send by mail. An innocent-looking apple may have a drug injected into its core. A tempting chocolate cake may have drugs baked between layers. A sugary powder surrounding hard candy may really be heroin. Visiting at many institutions occurs without personal contact, inmate and visitor looking at each other through a pane of glass and talking through a telephone receiver. But institutions that allow contact visits experience an influx of drugs. A long kiss may not be an expression of love, but a means of transmitting capsules. Staff may bring in contraband from the outside or, knowing the sources for drugs inside the prison, may rifle the stock of unit medical supplies, the warehouse, or the pharmacy. The staff member knows that he has a permanent market and an easy way to make money. Instead of selling directly to inmates, the staff dealer finds one inmate whom he can trust to serve as distributor and conceal the source of the supply. For a job reliably done, the distributor is well compensated. He, too, stays behind the scenes, lining up other prisoners who will actually make the sales. Everyone gets a piece of the action, and the staff member remains insulated by others fronting for him. The total take from a prison drug ring may run into hundreds of dollars a week. Some criminals who leave on pass for home visits or work release engage in drug-related activities as well. The first stop en route home may be at a phone to arrange to meet his connection and stock up. If the risks are not too great, he conveys the drugs to the institution himself. However, if he is stripped and searched each time he returns, he buys the drugs but arranges with a visitor or staff member to bring them to the prison.

How widespread staff collusion with inmates and direct staff participation in illegal activities is in America's correctional institutions is impossible to say. Only rarely does a scandal hit the papers, since such matters are usually handled internally. Whereas most employees in corrections are conscientious and responsible, some desire to work with or near criminals because they identify with them and find them exciting. Such individuals relish listening to inmates' accounts of their exploits, and they sometimes join in the endless bantering about crime, drugs, and sex. Such staff members would abhor working with the retarded, the physically handicapped, or the elderly; it would be far too tedious. Criminals intuitively sense which employees are very much like themselves, and carefully test the waters to see who can be compromised. Some staff members will not risk their positions by direct involvement in criminal activity, but they get their kicks vicariously. Others are ready for action, and collaborate with inmates in gambling, drug trafficking, theft, sex, and whatever else opportunity presents. The relationships are mutually exploitative. The staffer has his excitement, and his job becomes more than just work. The criminal expects to gain a potential ally who will not turn him in for infractions and who will help bail him out of trouble. If such expectations are not met, the inmate has the weapons for blackmail. The staff member, in turn, can threaten to report the criminal for any of a number of real or made-up offenses and thereby imperil his eligibility for privileges or release. If enough employees of criminal character work in any one part of an institution, their actions inevitably sabotage their conscientious colleagues, who then become disillusioned and demoralized.

All of the above is intended to underscore the point that criminals are criminals, no matter where they are. In prison, their personality remains as it was. What may vary is the degree of risk they will take and the method by which they operate. Those abstaining from crime still miss it, but they content themselves with fantasy and conversation about crime. One offender commented matter-of-factly that were he released, he'd steal my money. He quickly cautioned me not to take this personally, but he just knew he'd steal whenever he had the opportunity. Even after years of incarceration, his desire to steal was as strong as ever.

Contrary to what many people believe, most criminals can and do learn from experience, but it is not what society wants to teach them. In prison, criminals have ample time and opportunity to sharpen their skills for future crimes. Some resolve that upon release they will lie low, limit themselves to smaller crimes, and forgo the big-time ventures. Or perhaps they will mastermind a crime but stay behind the scenes rather than participate directly. Such intentions are short-lived. Once they step outside the prison doors, their appetites become voracious for the excitement of the old life. Some do in fact become more successful criminals, immersing themselves in crime but being slick enough to avoid apprehension. Others avoid arrest for a long time but eventually land back in the slammer. Then there are the big losers. Hardly has the prison disgorged them into society than they slip up, get caught, and are charged with a new offense.

It is widely believed that criminals outgrow crime or "burn out." The burnout theory may be based on the fact that some older criminals cease to get arrested for street crimes, and so they don't return to prison. It is true that as the street criminal ages, he is not as agile and literally cannot run as fast as he used to. He has mellowed only in that he takes fewer big risks and his offenses may be less serious. But his criminal personality remains unchanged, and people still suffer at his hands.

James grew up in the slums of a large eastern seaboard city. He recalls his parents struggling to provide for him on what little his father earned working long hours for a moving company. Both parents were intent on his having advantages in life that they lacked. Though neither had more than a grade-school education, they emphasized the value of learning and bought James books. His mother took him to the zoo, on picnics, and to parades. But none of this really interested James, who at eight years of age found hanging around street corners far more to his liking. As a teenager he practically lived on the streets and in the alleys, committing crimes daily. After serving prison sentences for violent crimes and after treatment in a mental hospital, at fifty James was a free man. People who were acquainted with him thought that he was burnt out, mostly because he seemed less combative and had sworn off hard drugs.

A handsome African-American man with a neatly trimmed, graying beard, James wore suits wherever he went. He instantly appealed to many people because he had charm and charisma. He cornered people and spoke with great fervor as he interpreted social issues in terms of the Scriptures. (He was a self-educated man, having dropped out of school in the eighth grade.) Although some people regarded him as a religious fanatic, others admired him for his sincerity. Because he was required by the court to show evidence of employment, James waited on tables at a restaurant. Although he annoyed some customers by his inclination to preach, he kept his job. Management indulged his foibles because James seemed trustworthy and loyal.

James indeed appeared to be a changed man, but he had a lot of people fooled. Never did anyone at his job suspect that he was stealing from tips that belonged to busboys as well as pilfering food and utensils from the pantry. As soon as he was no longer under court supervision, James quit his job and launched a criminal operation. He began working ten hours a week as a phone solicitor for a company that sold household products such as lightbulbs and brooms. Using his employer's phone list, he told potential customers that he was a minister raising funds for his church. This was the beginning of an enterprise in which James defrauded the public for years. All the while, he was collecting welfare and social security benefits, which began when he was declared mentally disabled in the hospital. Appealing especially to the African-American community, James posted signs on soft-drink machines advertising counseling and pastoral services. Each week he rode a bus across town to upper-income white neighborhoods, where he hung around libraries and community centers, strumming his guitar and soliciting passersby for contributions to his church. He ingratiated himself with children, singing their favorite songs and offering free instruction on how to play the guitar. He'd find out where the youngsters lived and stop by their homes to ask their mothers and fathers for donations. It was awkward for parents to refuse this "reverend" who had been so kind to their children.

James had a talent for convincing people that he was personally interested in them, concerned about their welfare. If he heard that someone was sick, he promised to pray for that person and sent a card. His expressions of sympathy helped wring money out of ill patients and their families. James's enterprise flourished as he announced to potential donors that he was opening a small store. They would donate not only money but also furniture, clothing, and other belongings, thus helping the poor to purchase at cut-rate prices what they could never otherwise afford while at the same time supporting the church.

The business never opened, but James did manage to add to his wardrobe and apartment furnishings. From donations, social security, and welfare, James lived comfortably. He kept no accounting of his receipts and never filed an income tax return. By his own estimate, he had compiled a list of more than 400 names, whom he sporadically contacted by phone or letter. The most gratifying aspect of his activities was that James induced people to trust him with their hearts and respond generously with their pocketbooks. This was a triumph. It supported his belief that he could accomplish anything that he set his mind to.

James never severed his ties with other criminals. He once told a psychologist, "Some of my best friends are hardened criminals. What I admire is that they can make positive decisions. They are closer to being human than people who represent good, moral behavior." One day he was robbed of cash and some personal possessions. He turned this event to his advantage by proclaiming to potential donors that his ministry had been victimized and that it was imperative that the work of the Lord continue. Although he was not the lady's man that he had been in his youth, James still consorted with a twenty-seven-year-old prostitute and other irresponsible young women. He was off hard drugs, but smoked marijuana and occasionally drank heavily.

This fifty-year-old man was regarded as innocuous by those who had known him as a tough young street dude. Although no longer violent, James continued to live a criminal existence and in doing so inflicted more widespread, although not physical, injury than ever before. Neither years of confinement nor the process of aging had significantly altered his personality.

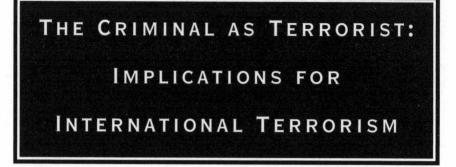

11

THE CRIMINAL AS TERRORIST: IMPLICATIONS FOR INTERNATIONAL TERRORISM

DURING YEARS OF INTERVIEWING and counseling criminals, I have encountered individuals who have spent major parts of their lives spreading terror in countless ways. No one knows when, where, or how these people will strike.

Having interviewed men and women who have committed almost any crime imaginable, my mind naturally has turned to thinking about the applicability to public figures of what I have observed, including heads of state who have committed atrocities against their own citizens, genocide included, and to the mentality of those who commit acts of international terrorism. Although I have had no direct contact with these people, I have good reason to surmise that the elements of the criminal personality that I have described in this book apply to them. Before turning to this topic, let's explore the broader concept of the career criminal as a terrorist.

Consider what the following men share in common: a rapist, a perpetrator of domestic violence, an arsonist, and a pair of snipers.

Jay began spying on young women who were alone in ground-floor offices after their co-workers had left for the day. He described his mounting excitement as he "prowled around fantasizing about the women I saw, using what I saw as material to masturbate." By casing out interiors of office buildings, Jay located secluded areas and spotted exits. He noted the parking spaces most conducive to making a rapid getaway. Having methodically done his homework and identified his prey, Jay was always prepared. He waited until the targeted employee was gathering her belongings and about to leave. He recalled, "There was a quick rush of excitement at the beginning of an attack due to not knowing what was going to happen." Barging into the office, Jay grabbed his victim, dragged her into a bathroom or other closed area, raped her, then made a quick escape. These rapes became the subject of feature news stories on television and in the press. Fearing that they might be next, thousands of women took extraordinary precautions and altered their routines. No longer could they take for granted the sense of safety that they had at work. Jay's reign of terror went on for more than a year, finally ending when he attacked the wrong person. Acting as a decoy, a female police officer attracted Jay's attention. She was prepared when he struck.

Marie never knew when her husband Max would erupt. She and her two children lived in fear of his fierce temper, which could ignite at something as minor as not being able to find the television remote control. Marie reported, "He'd slap the kids in the face. When I was pregnant, he beat me. I had bruises on my arms and chest." Max once punched her so hard that she went flying against a wall and perforated an eardrum. Marie claimed that her husband had amassed a huge collection of guns and repeatedly threatened to kill her, especially when he was inebriated.

When I checked out Marie's accounts, they stood up. A co-worker had seen the dark bruises. A son told me that his dad had hurled a chair at his mother and had given his sister a black eye. Both children knew about the guns, and one reported having watched his father point a pistol at their mom and threaten her. Marie never notified the police or social services, because she was terrified that Max would retaliate. She told me of having reached a point where "I felt I'd rather be shot than stay in the house." Still she was afraid to leave because Max had warned her that if she tried, he would shoot her or abduct the children. After yet another beating, Marie finally summoned the courage to take the children and flee.

★　　★　　★

A university community was plagued by a series of dormitory fires set by an arsonist who struck late at night. When the alarm sounded, students would be awakened and hurry from their residence halls while fire and rescue equipment screamed to the scene. Students, college staff, administrators, and families were terrified, never knowing when or where the campus arsonist would strike next. Anxious students kept clothes by their bedside in case they had to dress at a moment's notice and exit the building.

During three weeks of 2002, two snipers in the Washington, D.C., area killed ten people and critically wounded three others, ranging from thirteen to seventy-two years of age. The victims were gunned down in the pursuit of daily tasks—filling gas tanks, shopping, going to work, standing on a curb, waiting to enter a school building. As a result, the residents of the entire metropolitan area drastically altered aspects of their daily lives. People who don't scare easily were looking over their shoulders, quickening their pace while doing errands, and curtailing nonessential activities. Schools canceled outdoor events, including weekend and evening athletic competitions, field trips, even daily outdoor recess. Many parents accompanied their offspring to the school entrance rather than allow them to walk alone. An entire school system south of Washington shut down for a day. Large and small businesses suffered as customer traffic was much lighter than usual. As the shootings continued into mid-October, Halloween parties and parades were canceled. The siege of the Washington area ended on October 24, 2002, with the arrest of two men, and life returned to normal for those not directly affected by the shootings.

The rapist, the perpetrator of domestic violence, the arsonist, and the snipers all were terrorists. Jay terrorized a workforce of women throughout an entire county. Max was a controller whose family lived in perpetual terror of his explosive temper. The arsonist terrorized hundreds on a college campus. And the snipers terrorized millions of Washington, D.C., area residents.

My use of the term "terrorist" expands upon the dictionary definition: "the use of violence and threats to intimidate or coerce, esp. for political purposes."[1] Individual criminals operate as terrorists whether they victimize one person, a family, a community, or a whole society. This is as true of the white-collar criminal as of the serial killer. They just operate in different ways.

Dr. Carl Edwards, a psychologist and attorney, observed, "Terrorists fall into a particular class of murderers who operate on a larger scale."[2] The white-collar criminal may not terminate a life, but his acts can generate widespread apprehension, and he can ruin lives.[3] In the aftermath of the disclosures of corporate crime, millions of investors, whether or not they lost significant amounts of money, grew fearful about ever trusting financial advisers again or risking money in the stock market.

It is not a huge leap for one who understands the mental makeup of criminals and realizes that criminals operate in all strata of society to extrapolate to the personalities of despots and tyrants. Acting in the name of a cause, these ruthless individuals have terrorized and slaughtered their opponents, including family members and citizens of their own countries. Incidents in the Middle East and in the Russian region of Chechnya have demonstrated that women, too, can be effective terrorists, creating carnage by their suicide attacks.[4]

Like the true criminals they are, fallen tyrants tracked down by Italian journalist Riccardo Orizio protested their innocence and glorified themselves and their objectives. But they gave no thought to the ruthlessness of the means they employed, nor did they concern themselves with anyone's point of view but their own. In the aftermath of torture and bloodshed, these dictators lamented only the frustrating of their ambitions and blamed others as betrayers. Confronted with the devastation they inflicted upon their countrymen, they managed only a terse acknowledgment that "excesses" were necessary, given the circumstances.[5]

Whether they used primitive weapons centuries ago or employ modern, sophisticated technology today, criminals in positions of supreme power have tortured and killed millions, carrying out their barbaric acts as zealots for a purportedly noble purpose. Saddam Hussein of Iraq is but one malevolent dictator in a seemingly unending list throughout history. He stifled free speech not only by maintaining an iron grip on the government and media, but also by literally cutting out the tongues of dissidents and forcing physicians to hack off the ears of deserters from his army.[6] He, his sons, and his loyalists subjected men, women, and even children to gruesome tortures and executions. He used chemical weapons against citizens of his own nation. He is no different from other infamous despots who controlled their citizenry through terror. Investigation into his background revealed that his criminality went back at least to his teen years, when he bullied and physically attacked others. He attached himself to political causes that called for violence and assassinations. Ostensibly anticommunist, he found a hero after whom to model himself in Joseph Stalin, dictator of the former Soviet Union.

In the aftermath of the attacks of September 11, 2001, much has been written about the personalities of terrorists and those who lead terrorist organizations. Numerous articles from a variety of sources have characterized Osama bin Laden and his followers as criminals. Writing in the *Washington Post*, James Reston stated, "Everywhere I traveled—in Saudi Arabia, the United Arab Emirates, Lebanon and Egypt—bin Laden and his group were freely and frequently labeled as criminals. The al Qaeda leader . . . cares nothing for the Palestinian cause, but only about himself and his place in history—he's a classic megalomaniac."[7]

The criminal can make anything wrong right and anything right wrong. Right is what he wants to do at the time. Many observers commented that the perpetrators of terror, acting in the name of a holy war sanctioned by their religion, were perverting the teachings of that religion. Stanley Bedlington, also of the *Washington Post,* wrote that Bin Laden "defiled his own religion" and willingly transgressed "strict Koranic injunctions."[8] An article in *Time* pointed out, "The jihad [bin Laden] declared against the United States, in the eyes of most religious scholars, was never a holy war, it was a blatant fraud."[9]

Tashbih Sayyed, editor of *Pakistan Today,* suggested that extremists seeking to establish Islamic states gain "vitality, energy, and power" by inciting, then exploiting, resentment against the West to further their own political aims. Mr. Sayyed observed that the "authority of the pulpit" is then used to "distort and manipulate both Islamic history and theology."[10]

In an article in *USA Today*, Dinesh D'Souza noted that the September 11 hijackers, who were ostensibly deeply religious, "spent their last days in bars and strip joints sampling the licentious lifestyle they were about to strike out against."[11] In an unequivocal statement, King Abdullah II of Jordan wrote in the *Washington Post* about Islamic fundamentalists, "In fact, there is nothing fundamentally Islamic about these extremists. They are religious totalitarians, in a long line of extremists of various faiths who seek power by intimidation, violence, and thuggery."[12]

An article in the news.telegraph.co.uk pointed out that bin Laden distinguished between good and bad terror and asserted that what he and his followers practice is "good terror."[13]

A *Washington Post* article described thirty-seven-year-old Abdullah Shah as having "conducted a personal reign of terror in several provinces."[14] While claiming to be engaged in combating the Soviet presence in Afghanistan, Shah murdered neighbors, tortured his wives, extorted money from travelers, and even bit them. He also kidnapped villagers, holding them for ransom, dumped corpses in wells, and set a busload of refugee families on fire. According to reports, Shah and his followers "had weapons in the name of holy war [against the Soviet army], but they used them to kill poor people." It took many years for him to be tried and sentenced to death under the justice system newly established in Afghanistan during 2001 and 2002.

Reports have appeared of American criminals involving themselves in international terrorist groups. Doing so can be just one more expression of the person's criminality. A news item titled "U.S.-Born Latin Turns Islamic Terror Suspect" described a young killer who belonged to a teenage gang in Chicago.[15] He had served time in prison for a road-rage shooting incident. The *Washington Post* reported, "And now the menacing 31-year-old man who calls himself Abdullah al Muhair is the first accused al Qaeda operative with 'Jose' tattooed on his right arm." He converted to Islam and learned how to wire explosives in Afghanistan and Pakistan.

Under the cover of advancing his cause, a criminal can conceal his underlying motives, which have more to do with affirming his importance, consolidating his authority, and tightening his control than with bringing any genuine, heartfelt political or social agenda to fruition. Perhaps some terrorists are pure and believe they are just in their motivations. But many certainly appear to share characteristics of the criminal.

12

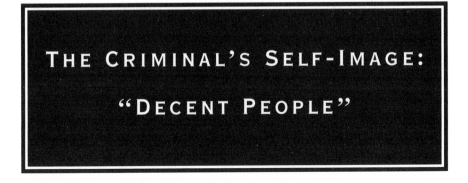

THE CRIMINAL'S SELF-IMAGE:
"DECENT PEOPLE"

THE PLACE IS THE OREGON STATE HOSPITAL, at a meeting of a therapy group where dangerous sex offenders are receiving psychiatric treatment. Among them is a man who raped babies, a fellow who sodomized a six-year-old boy, another who raped a fourteen-year-old girl at gunpoint, and ten others who have committed almost every other imaginable sexual offense as well as other types of crimes. The therapist has just asked the men why society has rules. One man replies, "We have rules to protect society and so people won't hurt others." Another speaks up, "Society would fall apart without rules. There'd be mass confusion." A third says, "Rules are designed to teach people their responsibilities."

All these responses are rational and to the point. They come from the lips of men who, without question, know that rape, kidnapping, child molestation, and other forms of sexual abuse are wrong and why they are wrong. These men will acknowledge that, from society's point of view, they are criminals. But not one really regards *himself* that way. Every member of that group believes that he is basically a decent human being. How is it possible for a criminal to believe that he is a good guy when he has left behind him a trail of destruction?

The criminal knows right from wrong. He may be more knowledgeable about the laws than many responsible citizens. When it suits him, he is law-abiding and even takes pride in being meticulous about it. One ruthless teenage gang member, for example, would never spit on a sidewalk or break the speed limit when he motorcycled through a school zone. Despite his knowledge of what is legal and illegal, the criminal decides that he can make exceptions for himself just because it suits him at a particular time. The fact that *he* wants to do it makes it right.

If a criminal regards something as wrong for him personally, he will not do it. An act is wrong if it is too risky. An act is also considered wrong by a criminal if he thinks it is too petty. A big-time operator may consider shoplifting wrong only because it is not worth bothering with. If a criminal makes an error in judgment and is caught, he will say that what he did was wrong, but only because he was caught.

The semantics of this last point are interesting. One teenager said that lately he had been "messing up" and he needed to stop doing that. To the untrained ear, it might have sounded as if this youth wanted to reform, but that was not so. If he hadn't been caught for a crime, he would not have called it "messing up." What was wrong was getting caught, not his commission of the offense.

The criminal not only knows right from wrong, but also believes that wrongdoers must be apprehended. Criminals are portrayed as hating the cops, but this is not so. As children, they admire policemen and imagine themselves in badge and uniform, brandishing a nightstick and revolver and driving a speeding cruiser. Fascination with the police continues into the criminal's adult years, and he is an avid viewer of police shows and detective thrillers. He regards police as absolutely necessary to lock up lawbreakers, and on occasion he may help them out. After assisting officers in the arrest of a burglar, one criminal wrote to a law enforcement agent, "You have impressed me as a very efficient, no-nonsense guy who won't tolerate inefficient police work, and I really hope that you will match any criminal power thrust with an overwhelming display of power on the side of law and order." The criminal has contempt for law enforcement officials mainly when they pose an immediate threat to him.

Although the criminal may not accept what others consider moral standards, he claims to have his own set of morals. Other people are liars, perverts, scoundrels, and criminals, not he. He looks down on them as depraved because they do things that he would not. Specific crimes are wrong and thus off-limits for him simply because he personally finds them offensive. Criminals differ as to what they find most revolting. One says that a child molester should be killed, while another advocates that a rapist be castrated. But each considers whatever he does as beyond reproach. One tough guy said that sneaking up on an adult male and mugging him is all in a day's work, but if he were to see anyone do the same to a child or elderly lady, he would rip the attacker to shreds. To his way of thinking, the two situations are completely different.

If there is something that the criminal wants, he knocks down every barrier until he gets it. If this requires maiming or killing, so be it. There is no need to justify a crime to himself either before or at the time he commits it. In cold-blooded fashion, he does whatever suits him; he is the only one who matters. A twenty-five-year-old man who served a sentence for two counts of assault and battery commented, "A realistic person will have to admit that this is a dog-eat-dog world and basically every man is for himself first, others second. Only the fit will survive. Take what you want out of life, without any qualms or doubts, ruthlessly if necessary. But above all be true to yourself." He went on to say, "The question of being right or wrong is not a major one, for when you are dead and gone some will say, 'He was a good son of a bitch' and some will say, 'He was a dirty son of a bitch.' Either way, you're a dead son of a bitch, and there won't be any dispute over that!"

The criminal does not think he has hurt anyone unless he draws blood. Even then, he has little concern for the victim. A seventeen-year-old boy fired a gun at a youth "who started beating on my car." Asked about the impact on the victim, the teenager replied, "I guess he was treated in the hospital. I don't think it harmed him in any way. It hurt him at that time. I can't think of any aftereffects." The offender does not see himself as harming his victims when he vandalizes their property, forges their checks, cons them out of savings, or breaks into their homes. Yet, if someone did any of these things to him or to his family, he would assist the police or personally seek revenge. One fifteen-year-old had recurrent thoughts of sneaking up on old people and robbing them, but when asked how he would respond if someone did this to his grandmother, he said, "If I found the person, I'd kill him."

When a criminal is confronted with tangible evidence that he has harmed someone, he blames the victim or minimizes the damage. At most, he passes it off as perhaps poor judgment on his part, but certainly not as reflecting anything negative about his character. One individual commented, "Just because I shot a couple of state troopers doesn't mean I'm a bad guy." Very rarely does the criminal feel any remorse or empathy for his victim. An exchange that I had with sixteen-year-old David reveals a characteristic attitude on the part of the offender.

David was very familiar with the operations of a restaurant where he had worked. As the place was closing and two employees were tallying receipts, preparing to make the night bank deposit, he and his buddy, wearing ski masks, burst in. While David pointed a gun, the other boy tied up the employees. The teenagers grabbed the money, jumped into a car, and fled. When I interviewed David at the detention center, I asked him about the impact of what he had done. He stared at me blankly and replied, "No one got hurt." No blood was shed, no bones broken. I pointed out that the employees might have suffered flashbacks, become terrified to return to work or to venture out at night. There likely was a severe impact on the victims' families and friends, and on employees of other businesses in the area. David shrugged and remarked, "I never thought of all that." Even though he knew full well he had done something very wrong, serious enough to land him in detention and perhaps to be tried as an adult, he did not think of himself as having inflicted any real harm. From his perspective, he was the only true victim because he was incarcerated. He regretted being caught, but had no remorse about having committed the crime.

Psychiatrist Willard Gaylin called guilt "the guardian of our goodness." He said that feeling guilt is so painful because "it is like tearing apart our inner structure."[1] The criminal agrees that feeling guilty is painful. One offender commented, "If I thought of myself as evil, I couldn't live." The point is that criminals experience guilt, but only in the most shallow sense. It is fleeting, and they can shut it off long enough to do whatever they please. When they commit a crime, they can shut off considerations of conscience as quickly and totally as they can switch off an electric light. Just the fact that the criminal can *feel* guilt, no matter how ineffective it is as a deterrent, helps him maintain the belief that he is decent.

What I'm saying is that the criminal is not totally without conscience. Whatever fragments of conscience he has occasionally do deter him. An embezzler described metaphorically how his conscience operated. "I was able to block it off. I could open a little door, and out would come the wrongness. I'd shut it back in a soundproof room and no one would hear the screaming. On the whole, it worked. At times, it didn't work, and I'd wake up in the middle of the night and worry." But he didn't worry enough to stop committing future crimes.

A man broke into an elderly person's home and stole her cherished heirlooms. When he learned that she was suffering from cancer, he was conscience-stricken enough to make sure that all her possessions were returned. Remorse in this situation did not deter him from committing additional break-ins. Experiencing remorse and making restitution for this one crime only bolstered his view of how compassionate a person he was.

The criminal thinks highly of himself because he has within him a deep reservoir of genuine sentiment. Amazingly, a murderer became impassioned about sparing the life of a bug, screaming at his wife not to squash it. A criminal who indulged in fantasies of knifepoint rape and homicide replied to his wife when she proposed that they go to a tree farm where they'd be allowed to chop down their own Christmas tree, "No, I will not destroy living matter." Even while en route to a crime, a criminal may perform a good deed. One man dropped by a bar, treated a homeless man to a meal, and, feeling pretty good about himself, robbed a bank. Then there is the multiple murderer who wrote poetry about self-control:

So keep your mental balance
When confronted by a foe

Be it enemy in ambush
Or some danger that you know.
Be self-controlled and responsible
When all around is strife
And know, my friend, you've mastered

The most vital thing in life.

Idealism is obviously not unique to the criminal. Perhaps all of us sustain a belief in our own goodness because of our ideals. We may stray from those ideals, but we do not compartmentalize them from daily living. It takes a particular kind of mentality to break into an apartment, terrorize and rape a woman, and then remain for forty-five minutes to talk to her about religion. The criminal's idealism and altruism are genuine and are integral parts of his good opinion of himself. Still, he continues to commit crimes. Asked about her faults, a female offender replied, "I have a big heart. My definition of a flaw is being an evil person." Evidence of her "big heart" included using credit cards without authorization to charge lavish gifts to bestow upon friends.

Sometimes the criminal persuades himself that a different environment will allow his goodness to prevail. He dreams of getting away from it all, retreating from the world and living a simple life in the country or mountains. Said one man incarcerated three years for felonious assault, "Damn, I don't ever want to own a bicycle or a car or any kind of transportation. I'd love to be on a farm or a ranch someplace alone for about five years and just sit there. No risks, no pressures, no nothing."

Many criminals are remarkably talented. Prison art shows display the work of gifted painters who have had little formal training. Some criminals are musically gifted, performing their own compositions on instruments that they learned to play totally by ear. Many who don't play an instrument may be music aficionados. An alumnus of a federal penitentiary with a passion for Bach declared, "To me, music is everything." Some criminals are excellent craftsmen, fashioning stylish leather goods and constructing handsome, sturdy furniture. Others have a knack for repairing just about anything.

If the criminal receives accolades from others for these accomplishments, his sense of his own worth is further enhanced. Frequently, others judge him solely on his artistry and envision great accomplishments in the future. Those familiar with his criminal record turn optimistic about his becoming a constructive citizen. But because he lacks self-discipline, the criminal is unlikely to develop his talents. He has little interest in training or apprenticeship programs, which entail drudgery and perseverance. Instead he expects to turn out a polished product or masterpiece overnight. Since that is seldom possible, he loses interest.

People who are not criminals also fail to make use of natural aptitudes or to cultivate their talents. They may set such unrealistically high standards for themselves that they quickly become discouraged and quit shortly after embarking on a new undertaking. Some talented individuals have such a neurotic fear of failing that they give up before facing evaluation by others.

The chief impediment to the criminal's actualizing his talents is that the *process* of doing so is devoid of meaning to him. The responsible person finds meaning in the process of achievement. He may be prouder of his determination in surmounting obstacles and sticking with an undertaking than of the final product. Not so with the criminal. When he is not an immediate success, he asserts himself in criminal enterprises, which are far more satisfying. Still, the criminal's view of himself as a good person is elevated merely because he possesses particular talents or skills, whether or not he ever develops them or anyone benefits.

The capacity to experience and express sentiment is another component in the criminal's maintaining an opinion of himself as a good human being. Many criminals feel their deepest sentimentality toward their mothers. (Some wear tattoos saying "Mom.") In most cases, the criminal's mother has believed in him, bailed him out of trouble, and never abandoned hope. On the one hand he adores her, but on the other he makes her life hell, cursing her when she opposes something he wants to do, stealing from her, threatening her, and causing her sleepless nights. Yet his mother remains forgiving, always willing to help him pick up the pieces of his life and help him start anew. When the criminal is despondent, she is one person to whom he can turn. His awareness of what he has done to her is likely to be most intense when he is in prison. One inmate wrote his mother: "To my beautiful Mom! I can't believe I chose this life for myself and my family. I know you say you forgive me, but do you really? I mean do you still love me the same after all this shit I've put you through? I sure hope so. I carry a picture of you on my I.D. I am so proud of my pretty Mom. You did everything right for me but for some reason I chose the wrong path. Honestly what do you think my future looks like? You always know all. Do you think I am gonna change? I've been doing wrong for so long."

Although the criminal violates everything for which his mother stands, he worries about her, especially about something horrible and unforeseen happening. One young man feared that, because his mom lived alone, she might become a victim of a criminal. He counseled her in a letter from prison, "You should devote several hours to a pure exercise in survival by just moving from one position in your room to another, imagining exactly what you would say and do if confronted by a robbery or assault." He went on to instruct his mother, "Who's gonna train you? That's right! *You are*. What can you say that will calm an attacker? 'I won't hurt you' is the best opener. If he's worried about being hurt, he'll calm down. You can't reason with whoever it is while he's scared. I'm gonna change subjects because it depresses the hell out of me to keep thinking about you being in the position we're talking about, but please prepare yourself for the possibility by doing the things I have told you. You'll feel foolish standing in the living room yelling at yourself, but so what? If you can handle the playacting right, you may just spontaneously do the right thing someday and not get shot." Then he posed the question "Do you know why most people who get killed in robberies get killed?" He rejoined, "They do not know how to be robbed. That sounds absurd to you, I'm sure, and it is sickening that we live in a world where a person should be trained as a victim." The fellow who wrote this letter was an authority on the subject, for he had committed numerous robberies.

The criminal's sentimentality about his mother has become so widely recognized that an advertising campaign to reduce crime was launched by appealing to its possible deterrent effect.[2] The ad urges young people to think about the impact on their mothers were they to commit a crime and get injured, killed, or sent to prison. In other words, the message is before you act, think of Mom.

Although sentimentality about their mothers may be deeply felt by most criminals, they differ greatly as to where their other sentiments lie. Some are so fond of animals that they will bring home an abandoned, injured animal and treat it more tenderly than their own children. These animal lovers will chew out and even assault anyone whom they find mistreating an animal. Other criminals abuse animals or are completely indifferent to them. Similarly, some love babies, anybody's baby. It tears them up to hear an infant cry, and they rush to pick up and soothe a baby. But there is also the criminal who doesn't care for babies at all, not even his own. A wailing infant may evoke murderous thoughts or a brutal physical response.

Usually the criminal conceals the soft side of his personality for fear that others will see him as a sissy. He is embarrassed if a buddy finds out that he went to an art gallery or that he listens to "longhair" music. To openly express affection is to be weak. The very qualities that the criminal hides from his buddies are pluses in the eyes of the responsible world. To others the bad doesn't seem so bad when socially redeeming features are also evident. The "good points" work to the criminal's advantage especially in confinement, because the staff thinks that there is hope for him when he returns to the outside world.

Responsible people frequently mistake fragments of sincerity and goodness for basic character. They are especially inclined to think this way if they observe the criminal during a period when he is temporarily abstaining from crime and behaving responsibly. They conclude that, at heart, the criminal really is a pretty decent fellow whom they can help change by drawing upon his good qualities and reinforcing them. The sad truth is that what appear to be socially redeeming features serve only to further the individual's criminality. The sentimentality, art, and music, the isolated acts of kindness all support the criminal's inherent view that he is a good person. He sincerely believes that any sin he might have committed is more than compensated for by the good that he has done. When others praise him for a good deed or for a talent or skill, he assumes that they are voicing their unqualified approval of him as a human being.

Some criminals are religious, and this figures prominently in their good opinion of themselves. Schooled in religion as youngsters, they took what they learned to heart. In the primary grades, they were not defiant or hell-raisers. Rather, they were super-good, regularly attending church and Sunday school, helping in the home, and looking out for kids who were the underdogs. Believing that a supreme divine being was watching them all the time, they tried to merit God's approval. One criminal reported that as an eight-year-old he pictured God dwelling in a tower like a church steeple, looking down upon him, and judging everything he did to determine whether he'd rest in heaven or burn in hell. Another, at eight, was convinced that if he was bad the devil would snatch him and he'd die before his ninth birthday. One boy crossed himself each time the word "damn" slipped out of his mouth. As children, these criminals were ready to condemn adults and other children for the slightest impropriety. As for themselves, they believed that to remain in God's good graces, they had to be better than good, purer than pure. Their determination, though sincere, did not last. In a manner typical of criminals, they shifted from one extreme to another.

As the youngster's world expanded beyond his family circle, there was both greater temptation and an ever more active mind that dwelled increasingly on the forbidden. The slow but steady erosion of his purity was almost impossible to observe. Those who thought they knew him were astounded when this model child suddenly exploded into antisocial activity. Yet religion was not abandoned forever. Criminals keep returning to it, some out of nostalgia for their childhood, others in a personal crisis when they long for the serenity of a church with its soothing music and familiar ritual. As with everything else, the criminal exploits religion to serve his own purposes. He not only presents God with his list of wants, but also asks God to be an accessory to his crimes. He prays for success in his ventures and later, when he gets himself into a jam, implores God to bail him out. After the police apprehended one man for an assault with a deadly weapon, he silently prayed from the patrol car, "God, if you'd only help me now, I won't do any more things." The criminal bargains with God for salvation after he is confined and resolves to mend his ways.

Fifteen-year-old Vic was shocked when a judge finally ordered him locked up after he had repeatedly violated probation. His first stint in confinement was sobering. There he began reading the Bible and a small book written by a minister. He devoted considerable thought to the nature of sin and resolved to sin no more. Vic found the smaller volume so absorbing that he considered swiping it to take it home. Then he was jolted by his parents' reminder that it was a sin to steal a book that he thought might keep him from sinning. Leaving the book where it belonged, he reflected more on the nature of sin and told his parents with tears in his eyes that he wanted them to help him reform. Vic's sincerity was temporary. Shortly after he was released from detention, he returned to crime.

Religion has little to do with how the criminal lives. As a child he may serve as an altar boy at a ten-o'clock service and two hours later go on a shoplifting spree. As an adult he may pray in church in the morning and that very evening put a gun to someone's head. Many members of organized crime profess to be religious. They have shrines in their homes, attend church, and give money to charity. But these acts do not stop them from executing their adversaries. For criminals, religion and evil exist side by side, one compartmentalized from the other. A striking example of this is a thirty-year-old who had murdered his girlfriend.

Sam had always considered himself a religious man. In his adult years, he still went to church, although not regularly. At the conclusion of one service, he went to the pulpit to talk with the minister and showed him a book on Christian ethics. Ethics book in hand, he lied to the minister by telling him that he had been released from confinement and was starting a new life. Actually, Sam was a fugitive from a federal institution, sought by the authorities.

The lament of most clergymen is that their regular congregants fail to live by the teachings of their religious faith. They emerge from church brimming with righteousness and feeling virtuous just because they managed to get out of bed and sit through a service. Then they curse their fellow congregants as they scramble to get out of the parking lot. But the fact remains that, despite their human frailties, unlike the criminal, they retain a sense of social boundaries, obey laws, and fulfill obligations. The criminal, on the other hand, has a remarkable capacity to shut off considerations of responsibility or morality from his thinking so totally that he can freely commit murder, rape, arson, extortion, and myriad other crimes. He perceives no contradiction between prayer and crime. Both are right for him, depending on what he wants at a particular time.

Ironically, the criminal's religiosity fosters crime for, when it is genuine, it bolsters his opinion of himself as an upstanding citizen. It is as though by having felt remorse, prayed, and confessed his sins to God, the criminal empties his cup of whatever evil it might have contained so that he has even more latitude to do as he pleases. Writing about Robert Hanssen, the FBI agent who sold top-secret information to the Soviets, biographer David Vise noted, "Hanssen reasoned that as long as he regularly confessed his sins to various priests and sought forgiveness, he would remain in a state of grace."[3]

Regarding himself as decent, the criminal approaches the responsible world with scorn. An ordinary life is a living death, clearly not for him. Said one youthful housebreaker and lockpicking expert, "I'd rather be dead than be a clerk." Yet the criminal occasionally envies the responsible person. He eyes the results of hard work and responsible living—a comfortable home, a car, a family, a high-paying job—and believes that the holder of these is on easy street. A seventeen-year-old delinquent said, "Sometimes I wish I was like regular kids." He saw his friends ready to graduate and driving cars that they bought with job earnings. He mused, "I could have had all that. Sometimes I feel like a fool." But this youth quit school, would have no part of working, and turned his back on a devoted family. The problem is that the criminal covets the trappings of living responsibly, but does not actually want to be responsible to obtain them.

There is a tendency on the part of others to resist seeing the criminal as he is. Many people have difficulty thinking of another human being as willingly and deliberately injuring others. They cling to the view that everyone is good at heart, that there are extenuating circumstances for even the most vicious crimes. Throughout his life, the criminal exploits this tendency of others to see him as basically good.

Fifteen-year-old Al, who had been roaming the streets, stealing, drinking, using drugs, disrupting classes, and assaulting students, was evaluated by a school social worker and a school psychologist. The social worker regarded Al as suffering from "undue environmental stress" and "inappropriate role expectations." The psychologist said that his behavior was "most probably the result of a relatively impoverished home life and some learning difficulties." During my evaluation, Al displayed blatantly antisocial attitudes, which had been long-standing. He asserted, "If people mess with me too much, I'll hit 'em." He guessed that if he had been arrested for all his crimes, he'd be locked up a long time. It is significant to note that in the same "impoverished home" lived two sisters and one brother, none of whom had been in trouble.

Because he is a minor and the full extent of his criminality is not known, people are inclined to want to help rather than punish kids like

Al. Unless he has been charged with a major crime and is considered dangerous, the delinquent may be let off with a warning or placed on probation. If he consents to receive psychological treatment, the charge may be dropped.

The adult criminal also is given breaks unless he has committed a violent crime or has a long police record. Those who deal with him, whether family, friends, or strangers, frequently fail to penetrate his thicket of lies, vagueness, and self-serving statements.

It sometimes happens that people lose sight of the criminal's basic character because they see him doing good deeds, and they want to believe in him. For raping and strangling a young woman to death, Harold was serving time in a hospital after being declared not guilty by reason of insanity. Hospital records documented that, over the years, Harold held elected offices on his ward, received high ratings at his job on the grounds, sang in the hospital choir, and assisted in activity programs for geriatric patients. Although he continued to live at the hospital, as a volunteer at a community agency he provided counseling and supportive services to indigent clients. He concealed from the organization that he was a patient in the forensic psychiatric ward at the hospital. Because he was involved in these worthwhile endeavors, Harold regarded himself as the model of a reformed man. However, hospital records over the years noted that he had violated numerous regulations, remained fascinated by and fantasized about sexually sadistic activities, manipulated other patients and staff, recently had purchased a beeper, which was against hospital policy, and continued having sex on the grounds with females. Harold declared, "I know right from wrong." He then commented that he needed more confidence—this from a man who had continually found ways to outwit staff members for years. Asked about his long-standing pattern of manipulating people for his own means, Harold retorted, "Everyone manipulates." He stated that he had become "a completely different person" from the man who had committed the brutal crime years ago. A well-meaning doctor, who knew the history of this man, set aside any doubts and believed Harold. The psychiatrist concluded that, through therapy, Harold had developed "a base of self-esteem from justifiably good deeds." The doctor asserted that no longer did he regard Harold as dangerous.

Thus criminals like Harold persist in regarding themselves as decent human beings. And others overlook telltale signs signifying a lack of change. Retaining a sense of his own goodness is not incompatible with the attitude displayed by an offender who, in all seriousness, inquired of his probation officer, "This empathy thing, what's in it for me?"

13

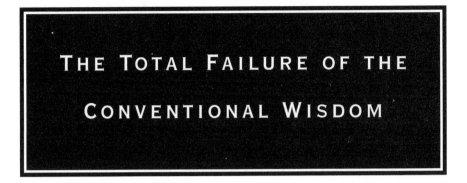

THE TOTAL FAILURE OF THE CONVENTIONAL WISDOM

SPECULATION ABOUT THE CAUSES of crime is as old as speculation about the nature of man. Human nature does not change, but theories and public opinion do, and it is these that guide a society in dealing with its criminals. The European "classical school" of criminology in the eighteenth and early nineteenth centuries saw man as responsible for his acts. It was thought that breaking the law was a willful act and that an offender should therefore pay the price by being punished. This applied not only to the adult criminal but also to the juvenile offender, for children were essentially regarded as miniature adults.

During the late nineteenth and early twentieth centuries, the "positivists" in Europe began to broaden the scope of investigations into criminal behavior. They began considering the role of forces both external to the individual and within his psyche. The impact of the positivist movement was that social responsibility for crime was emphasized and free will negated, for the positivists contended that it was up to society to make man responsible. If a man committed a crime, it was largely owing to a failure of society.

Sociological explanations of crime have long been dominant in the United States and in many other countries as well. Practically nothing is exempt from the sociologist's claim that the environment causes crime: urban poverty, suburban materialism, divorce, unemployment, racism, peer pressure, schools, television, violent video games, pornography, advertising, moral bankruptcy in society at large, alienation produced by technology, even global warming. The following headlines, culled from the press during the past quarter-century, are illustrative of the direct cause-and-effect relationship that is alleged to exist between social conditions and crime.

"Can What a Man Eats Turn Him into a Rapist?"[1]
"TV Blamed for Attack on Jogger"[2]
"Violent Song Lyrics May Lead to Violent Behavior"[3]
"Will Global Warming Inflame Our Tempers?"[4]
"Studies Suggest Link Between Lead, Violence"[5]
"Study Links Violence Rate to Cohesion in Community"[6]
"Day Care, Aggression Link Is Reinforced"[7]

In their environmental explanations of criminal behavior, sociologists have all but omitted consideration of the individual himself and the free choices he makes.

For example, it has been observed that a disproportionate number of inmates in correctional facilities are poor and from minority groups.[8] What does this reveal about the causes of crime? Certainly nothing about the characteristics of the poor or of minorities either as groups or as individuals. Most poor people are not criminals, and many well-off people are. And the overwhelming number of members of any minority group are law-abiding.

Sociologists can help in analyzing the operations of the criminal justice system and trends in the occurrence of different types of crimes, but their formulations about the causes of crime continue to be flawed and often misleading.

Sociologists have argued that it is the laws themselves that make a person a criminal. Dismissing the idea that there is a "criminal mind," they point out that a person may engage in an act that is legal in one state but be hauled off to jail in another for engaging in the same act. Some assert there would be fewer criminals if laws were changed and certain offenses decriminalized. The problem with this approach is that there are people who will break laws, whatever they are. One criminal said that if rape were legalized, he would not rape, but "I'd do something else." What he meant was that it was the kick of breaking the law that mattered, whatever the particular law happened to be. To understand crime, one must focus on the personality of the criminal, not on laws and social mores. Crime resides within the person, not the environment. There are people who will be exploitative, larcenous, and violent no matter what the laws are.

People persist in believing that improving social conditions will result in less crime. The 1960s witnessed a host of programs enacted to remedy social ills. A 1967 presidential commission prepared a report that is quoted even today. The commission declared, "Warring on poverty, inadequate housing, and unemployment is warring on crime. A civil rights law is a law against crime. Money for schools is money against crime."[9] Partly due to movements for social change originating in the 1960s, money has been poured into creating better housing and more opportunities for jobs and education.

The preceding chapters have shown that criminals have a similar manner of viewing themselves, regardless of racial, ethnic, economic, religious, or educational background. Their minds work the same way, regardless of their social environment. When policy makers and those making decisions about individual criminals regard them as victims of forces outside themselves, they only provide criminals with excuses for crime and grant them license to commit more crimes.

While changes in the environment have improved the quality of life for millions of citizens, the criminal remains a criminal. Offering a delinquent youngster or adult criminal a more desirable place to live does not change how he thinks! The fact that crime has not been significantly reduced by social programs does not invalidate those programs. Nor does it absolve policy makers of responsibility for improving living standards for people who need help to better themselves.

Psychiatrists and psychologists have approached criminality differently from sociologists in that they are interested more in a person's mind than in his environment. But they too stress the effect of environmental factors impinging on the individual, especially during his formative years. Even during generations before psychology gained a foothold, people believed that if a youngster was bad, his parents must have done something wrong. Psychological research seemed to support such thinking. In their 1936 book, *New Light on Delinquency and Its Treatment,* William Healy and Augusta Bronner reported that youngsters turned to crime largely because of "deeply emotionally felt discomfort" stemming from a lack of "satisfying emotional relationships in [the] family circle."[10] The "new light" was the focus on the family's role in crime causation. Their findings led them to assert that "reconstruction of the parental attitude" is mandatory "for the solution of the delinquent's problems."

The belief persists today that youngsters turn to crime because of their parents' dysfunctional behavior. This view, like that of the sociologists, is deterministic. It is essentially the position that the child enters the world like a formless lump of clay to be molded by parents and later by society. This perspective is not only clinically unsound but has proved damaging, especially to parents who have been unfairly blamed for things going wrong, even to the point of having state authorities prosecute them and take their kids away.

Reviewing a large body of research, psychologist David Cohen has concluded, "The influence of rearing and family life (nurture) is surprisingly weak."[11] He is critical of the "parent-blaming tradition" that has led to parents feeling far more guilty than the facts warrant. Research has documented what every parent of more than one child senses: children are born with different temperaments. Pediatrician William Carey defines temperament as "the stylistic part of personality; it is the distinguishing flavor, style, or characteristic that makes one's personality unique." He points out that temperament is "largely inborn."[12]

From the cradle, the infant's temperament has a considerable impact on how his parents treat him. A mother or father responds differently to a cooing, contented baby than to an infant who is colicky and cranky. In other words, the child raises the parents as well as vice versa. No one knows why the criminal opposes the social order from an early age. No one has yet been successful in identifying the critical factors that cause criminality. Efforts to help criminals change have met with even less success.

To understand antisocial conduct, professionals in the mental health field frequently are guided by the extensive literature on the psychopath (also termed the sociopath or antisocial personality). This has been misleading because the description of the psychopath reveals mainly the effect he has on others and very little accurate information about how his mind works. The psychopath is characterized as lacking a sense of responsibility, the capacity to profit from experience, and a conscience. He is described as impulsive, emotionally immature, grandiose and self-centered, and unable to experience guilt or form meaningful human relationships. Although diagnosticians may make distinctions between the psychopath and the criminal, for all ostensible purposes, one differs hardly at all from the other. Clinical descriptions of the psychopath are incomplete and in some important ways erroneous.[13] For example, to call him impulsive is to assert that he lacks self-control, whereas he actually has a rational, calculating mind that enables him to delay gratification if he deems it in his best interest. The criminal has moral values, but he shuts off considerations of conscience long enough to do what he wants.

The question of whether there is a "bad seed" or born criminal remains unanswered. Numerous studies have suggested that there may be a genetic predisposition or organic factors that play a role in criminality. Research findings increasingly suggest the contribution of genetic components to antisocial behavior. The *Harvard Mental Health Letter* indicates that some individuals "may be genetically vulnerable to psychopathy," and cites studies supportive of that possibility.[14] A study of twins conducted in Sweden and England pointed to a genetic role in "bullying behavior."[15]

Brain dysfunction, low levels of particular hormones, malfunctioning of neurotransmitter systems, and enzyme deficiency have been mentioned in the research literature. Although no one has suggested that one specific gene or biochemical deficiency will eventually be identified as causal, the possibility of a genetic predisposition toward criminality raises troubling questions.[16] In a book titled *Genetics and Criminality,* authors Dan W. Brock and Allen E. Buchanan ask, "Is it fair to hold people responsible and to blame and punish them for their behavior once we understand that behavior as having a substantial genetic basis?"[17] Writing in that same work, Rebecca Dresser surmises that if a genetic predisposition is found to be causal, once offenders "are on notice of their dangerous condition, they will be held responsible for adopting a lifestyle that prevents them from endangering others."[18]

Discovery of a genetic predisposition to criminality thus would not mean that some human beings are preordained to spend life in the penitentiary. It would not mean that we need lock up a predisposed child for life. Awareness of a genetic predisposition can induce a person to take preventive measures and receive help to combat it. Such preventive measures are often taken by children of alcoholics in light of the discovery of evidence of a hereditary predisposition to alcoholism. A person aware of such a familial tendency can choose whether to drink. A woman with a family history of breast cancer can take steps to prevent the disease, be watchful for early signs of it, then obtain treatment if necessary.

We are a long way from solving the puzzle of what causes criminality. Certainly, research into a possible genetic contribution should be continued while we remain sensitive to the possible misuse of findings.[19]

Professionals may offer a multitude of theories and explanations about *why* a criminal is the way he is, but these do not lead to effective solutions, and many turn out to be misleading. So consumed are those trying to *explain* an offender's behavior that they do not develop an understanding of how he actually views the world. Some fail to conceive of him as a human being who makes choices. Instead, they regard him as a victim of the environment, of a mental illness, or of an organic abnormality.

Sometimes it seems that, finally, a repudiation of the conventional wisdom regarding causes of crime is taking hold. Despite the steps forward, however, the psychological determinists are still very much alive. In a magazine for mental health professionals, Mary Sykes Wylie referred to a public "profoundly weary of a psychologizing 'abuse excuse' for any and every kind of bad behavior," and that favors instead "an increasingly Old Testament vision of justice."[20] She concluded her piece lamenting this trend and asked how children who kill can "be anything else," given that they "have rarely had anything like adequate emotional shelter from the rages and fears of ordinary, fantasy-soaked childhood." Wylie asserted that society is punishing children "for our failure to raise them in the first place."

In contrast to this point of view, there appears in some quarters a clear recognition of the role of choice. Appearing in the *Monitor* of the American Psychological Association is a discussion of a doctoral student in clinical psychology who grew up in a crime- and drug-infested neighborhood.[21] Mention is made of his having "chosen" to study—"a different path from many of his peers." The question is, had this young man landed in jail, would his plight be attributed to a choice he made to become a criminal, or merely to an inevitable consequence of growing up under undesirable circumstances? Having made a "good choice" is praise often given to someone who made an effort to improve himself and overcome adversity to become a worthwhile citizen. But society has difficulty conceiving that a person might make a "bad choice" purposefully and choose criminal behavior over responsible behavior.

Depth psychology may pay lip service to the possibility of a person's making choices, but in fact it remains highly deterministic. It posits that an individual acts in a certain manner "because." The "because" can include a slew of ostensible reasons, including some of which the individual allegedly lacks conscious awareness.

Effective in its analysis of many troubled individuals, depth psychology is not as successful in unraveling the complex personalities of criminals. A major reason for this was discussed earlier (chapter 9), namely, that psychiatrists and psychologists derive their clinical data from a highly unreliable source—the criminal. He simply is not an honest reporter of his own history. Another problem is that any knowledge the criminal gleans from depth psychology he converts into excuses. The result is more "incite" than insight. He becomes incited to blame even more people or circumstances than he did previously.

Another barrier to understanding the criminal mind is that those who evaluate offenders use interviewing techniques that are appropriate for many types of clients or patients, but are counterproductive when utilized with a criminal population. While providing some information, conventional mental status examinations and psychological tests reveal little that is truly helpful in illuminating the criminal's view of himself and the world. Questions designed to gain a psychodynamic explanation of underlying motives afford the criminal opportunity to deceive the interviewer and offer any justification. Said one offender about his psychiatrist, "She had her theory. I fed her what she wanted to hear until she thought I was cured."

Perhaps the most formidable obstacle in trying to understand a criminal is that people approach the task with theories and concepts that simply do not apply to criminals, although they may apply to other individuals. In fact, in my days as a psychodynamically oriented psychologist, I totally missed the boat in evaluating delinquent kids. In one instance I wrote an article that was published in a professional journal about Paul, a fifteen-year-old adolescent patient whom I treated on a university hospital psychiatric unit.[22] That case shows how easy it is to develop a misconception about a person even when one conscientiously applies the diagnostic tools he has been trained to use.

I assumed that Paul's truancy, shoplifting, drug abuse, and car theft were symptoms of a deep underlying personality conflict. I thought that a major source of anxiety and trauma had been that Paul's parents had defaulted on a promise years earlier to arrange for him to have an operation to bring down an undescended left testicle. I wrote in my case summary that Paul had been unsuccessful in getting the help he wanted with his undescended testicle. Over time, he felt betrayed and lost faith in adults' ability to be gratifying or stand for anything. His attitude became one of defiance, to get away with things until he was forced to quit, then to turn to something different. I regarded Paul's delinquent acts as symptomatic of his frustration and anger about the undescended testicle. During Paul's psychiatric hospitalization, he requested and had an operation in which the undescended testicle, which had atrophied, was removed and a prosthesis was inserted into the scrotum. I wrote: "The 'ultimate deception' was no more. The operation had been promised to Paul by his therapist, and it had occurred." Thus the expectation that he would no longer act out his frustration and anger about this matter. For a while, Paul's behavior on the unit did improve, but this was only temporary. The last I heard was that after Paul had been discharged from the hospital, he became involved in more serious crimes, including possession and use of a firearm.

As I look back, I recognize that there was nothing in my entire report that shed light on the boy's antisocial behavior, nothing about his delight in deception, his search for kicks, his belief that the world was his chessboard. In fact, this evaluation could as well have described a neurotic adolescent with little inclination to commit crimes.

The appeal of psychodynamic psychology is that it seems to offer answers. After the fact, it can explain anything. The human mind desires closure and especially to make sense out of what appears senseless. Unfortunately, it is not so simple. As it has turned out, conventional theories from modern depth psychology are largely irrelevant or misleading in understanding the criminal. Ultimately, it is more important and beneficial to piece together the structure of his thinking, to understand his world, to grasp what makes life meaningful for him. Probing and then reporting on an offender's *thinking* about himself and the world can be of inestimable value to a judge, a probation officer, or anyone else who will make decisions about him. Such an approach is of far greater value than an expedition into the criminal's past to dredge up what can only lead to conjecture as to what might have caused him to do what he did.

During most of the twentieth century and at the dawn of the twenty-first century, theories about crime and solutions for crime reduction have been deeply rooted in beliefs about causality. Those who have thought that the environment causes crime have recommended changes in the environment as remedial and preventive. Some have searched for answers in psychology, believing that the individual rather than the environment must be the focus. Their thinking, however, was that criminality was a *symptom* of a deeper maladjustment and that it could be treated like other emotional disorders and problems of living. Psychological concepts and techniques that were effective in treating disturbed but responsible patients were utilized in clinical work with criminals. Hanging on to beliefs about root causes as an approach to reducing crime continues to result in an enormous waste of resources. The conventional wisdom remains alive and well. Based on concepts of causality, it remains a barrier to altering a situation in which the nation's prisons bulge and citizens are prisoners in their own homes.

14

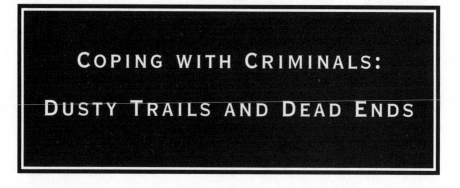

COPING WITH CRIMINALS:
DUSTY TRAILS AND DEAD ENDS

EFFORTS TO HELP CRIMINALS become responsible usually fail because they are based on shopworn and inapplicable theories, ingrained preconceptions, myths, fads, and emotion. Because so many people in the criminal justice system and in the community at large do not understand how criminals think, they have slavishly followed dusty old trails or else all too rapidly dashed down unexplored paths that resulted in a dead end. Punishment and rehabilitation both have failed to reform criminals. Rehabilitative programs have been rooted in theories about crime causation instead of in an understanding of how criminals think. Based on erroneous premises and misconceptions, rehabilitation's failure was inevitable. This does not mean, however, that criminals cannot change. There are times when they are open to making far-reaching changes. What has been missing is an accurate conception of the scope of the task of change and the tools to effect it.

In the wake of the failure to rehabilitate or successfully deter criminals through punishment, society remains polarized between the so-called bleeding hearts who want to help the criminal and the so-called law-and-order forces who want to lock him up for long periods and forget him.

What does the criminal think about this? He regards punishment as unjust because it interferes with the life he wants to lead. He is restricted, although not totally stopped, from pursuing the triumphs and conquests that fortify his self-image. While he is behind bars, society is protected. But some argue that he becomes hardened and more of a public enemy in the long run. As I pointed out in chapter 10, imprisonment does not alter a criminal's basic personality. Whether he is on the streets or in prison, he develops contacts, learns new tricks of the trade, and passes on a few tips of his own to others. Both the streets and correctional facilities can serve as schools for crime. Although one thirty-year-old said to me, "Incarceration has given me the credits to become a teacher of crime," he was already quite knowledgeable in that area before he was ever behind bars.

For some offenders who have not made crime a way of life, prison has a deterrent effect in that once they are released from custody they refrain from committing new crimes. But for the chronic offender, confinement is simply a time-out from his customary activities.

The terms "corrections" and "reformatory" suggest that the criminal justice system intends to correct and reform, yet deep pessimism prevails with respect to the feasibility of rehabilitating criminals. Nonetheless, attempts to discredit rehabilitation have not totally succeeded. Never has there been complete abandonment of the rehabilitative ideal, even under presidential administrations known for conservatism on social issues. During the Reagan administration, a conference convened by the White House recommended in its 1988 report, "All jails and prisons should establish drug-treatment programs."[1]

America is especially reluctant to give up on its youth, to write off any youngster as a hopeless delinquent or criminal. With the new millennium approaching, the U.S. Department of Justice affirmed that rehabilitation remains a "viable goal" of juvenile justice.[2] In 1996 the U.S. Office of Justice Programs called for juvenile correctional facilities to offer "comprehensive treatment programs that focus on reversing criminal behavior patterns."[3] And an article appearing in the *Washington Post* on July 26, 2003, made reference to "the rehabilitative emphasis that is a cornerstone of the juvenile justice system."[4]

Belief in the viability of rehabilitating adult offenders has not vanished even during times of diminishing financial resources and public skepticism. An editorial in a 1995 publication of the American Probation and Parole Association proclaimed, "We possess the capability to intervene and influence change in antisocial activities among offenders on a daily basis."[5]

Clearly indicative that the rehabilitative mission is very much alive is an announcement that the Maryland prison system will be hiring 210 additional teachers and drug counselors—"the first step in a plan to reduce crime by emphasizing rehabilitation."[6] This is being done by a state that had been allocating very little to that endeavor. During 2004, the Illinois Department of Corrections planned to open a $78 million dollar women's prison offering "a wide range of therapeutic programs" in a "holistic approach" to rehabilitation of substance abusers.[7]

The thousands of correctional counselors, case workers, educators, vocational teachers, and mental health professionals employed by juvenile and adult institutions consider themselves to be more than custodians of a warehouse. Most prisons and psychiatric facilities for criminals offer inmates a variety of programs. Some are mere timefillers, but most claim to prepare the criminal to reenter society. What is being done today in the name of "rehabilitation"?

Vocational training still is given top priority by many in corrections, their rationale being that a person without job skills will continue to prey upon society because he has no legitimate way to earn a living. Prison industries provide inmates an opportunity to learn a trade and earn small sums of money. For example, Pennsylvania Correctional Industries (PCI) advertises to the public its line of "Big House Products." These include the manufacturing of storage bags, construction of "heirloom quality wood furniture," production of institutional uniforms, and preparation of a line of canned foods.[8] Some institutions hire special teachers and purchase elaborate equipment so that inmates can learn a trade, such as carpentry or auto mechanics, or a skill, such as computer keyboard mastery. Local correctional facilities, such as jails, permit some inmates to hold jobs outside the institution on workrelease programs. But these programs often come under fire when inmates take liberties with the lack of supervision and are caught committing crimes while they are supposed to be on the job.

Cynics may contend that the criminal exploits vocational training by trying to impress others and earn his way out of confinement. Even though this sometimes happens, it is no indictment of job training. If a criminal lacks job skills, there is every reason to help him acquire them.

But the result of doing *only* that is a criminal with job skills rather than a criminal without them. He remains a criminal, with the same patterns of thinking and behavior that he had before.

That one can engage in "career planning" with an unchanged criminal is a misconception and results in an enormous waste of time and resources. A counselor may discuss career alternatives in terms of skills, aptitudes, and interests that develop over a lifetime, but the criminal is thinking quite differently. Behind a criminal's seemingly sensible discussion of his career plans lie unrealistic expectations and colossal pretensions. Before he attends his first vocational training class, he considers himself the top man in the program and later the best at the job. He envisions spending his earnings before he acquires any proficiency. Career planning is futile until the criminal sees himself more realistically and develops a set of attitudes basic to getting along with people in any kind of work. Of what use to an employer is a skilled employee who flares up at the slightest criticism, refuses to follow directions, and is erratic in attendance? (I wish I could say one can identify that rare prisoner who can go "legitimate" with only proper career training, but I can't—because I haven't met one yet.)

There is a strikingly high incidence of illiteracy in America's juvenile and adult correctional institutions. According to one prison study in Virginia, 75 percent of the inmates had reading levels of fourth grade or lower.[9] Proponents of prison education assert that without remedial instruction, inmates who can't read and write will remain barred from opportunities and, consequently, out of frustration, will continue their criminal careers. The high rate of illiteracy does not indicate that illiterate people are more likely to commit crimes. Rather, it suggests that many criminals are likely to refuse to make the effort to acquire reading skills.

When they were in school, some criminals defiantly rejected the most dedicated efforts of those who endeavored to teach them to read. Recalling the sheer drudgery in learning to read, one youth in a correctional facility commented, "I can't stand reading a book. I have to really concentrate. It's like working. I'd rather see the movie. The last book I read was *Curious George* [a book for preschoolers]." That such individuals are quite capable of learning to read is often borne out while they are confined in an institution. With time on their hands and little to do, they amaze teachers by how rapidly they catch on and begin to read. A report from an Oklahoma correctional facility attested to the fact that, in a year or less, young men between the ages of sixteen and twenty-five were able to progress from below a sixth-grade educational level to mastering the equivalent of high school subject matter.[10]

Institutions offer a range of services, from individual tutoring in basic reading skills to permitting inmates to attend college classes on a nearby campus. Some inmates find the educational program inherently worthwhile, whereas others are interested mainly in impressing the staff or avoiding more disagreeable tasks. Those who attend classes outside the institution may exploit the opportunity in the same manner that fellow inmates misuse work-release—committing crimes outside prison walls and importing contraband upon their return. A high school diploma or other educational achievement does not alter a person's criminal lifestyle. He simply becomes a more educated criminal who later may utilize his newly acquired knowledge to gain entrée into new arenas for committing crimes.

Courses in practical matters such as nutrition and money management are designed primarily to prepare the criminal to reenter the community. One class of youngsters in a correctional facility selected a hypothetical stock portfolio that appreciated more than those of all other contestants, including teams from prestigious schools.[11] The jury is out as to whether these delinquent youths—champion stock pickers—will work hard and one day invest their own earnings successfully or will turn out to be the corporate crooks of the future.

Because inmates are isolated from the community, the community comes to the inmates. More than a quarter million volunteers throughout the nation are demonstrating that they care about prisoners. They establish relationships through tutoring, counseling, coaching sports, coordinating social events, and providing cultural enrichment. To inspire civil concern and leadership, community organizations invite inmates to become members of prison chapters.

Those who would help the criminal become a social being assume that although his needs are the same as those of most people, he does not know how to fulfill them in an acceptable manner. Programs are designed to teach offenders "the importance of interpersonal relationships as a source of happiness, enrichment, and satisfaction."[12] Although this is a worthy objective, it is totally misdirected when geared to the criminal, who has a very different set of needs. "Happiness" is the charge he gets from knocking off a bank, the kick out of cracking a safe, the thrill of incinerating a building. The "enrichment" he seeks from relationships is profit through a con game. "Satisfaction," if it is ever experienced, is the short-lived flush of triumph experienced after a "big score." Criminals may find human relations classes an agreeable way to pass the time, but to teach a criminal social skills without addressing lifelong thinking patterns is as useless as pouring a delectable sauce over a slice of burnt, rancid meat.

The prisons are bulging with talent. Millions of dollars are spent on programs designed to discover and nurture the inmate's creative potential. It is reasoned that he will think more highly of himself and, in the process, discover a constructive and rewarding hobby, perhaps even a full-time occupation.

The short-term outcome of such endeavors may be positive. Programs that occupy inmates constructively reduce tension and contribute to a better institutional climate. But they fail to alter significantly a criminal's outlook on life. In the unlikely event that he channels his talents into a full-time occupation, he remains without integrity and thus becomes a crooked artist or craftsman.

Because criminality has been seen as symptomatic of an underlying psychological disturbance, psychotherapy has been utilized as another rehabilitative tool in institutions. (The underlying principles are often identical to those utilized in treating responsible people who have a wide range of emotional disorders.) Treatment is expensive, and there appears to be greater reliance on it with juveniles than with adults. Because intensive individual psychological treatment is time-consuming and very costly, it has never been widely available to offenders, even to those who have been patients in psychiatric facilities. Group therapy is regarded as having a greater impact than individual therapy because of the prospect of harnessing peer pressure as a positive force for change. Also, presumably it is harder to deceive a group than to fool one individual.

In all correctional facilities, the staff rewards desirable behavior and ignores or punishes that which is undesirable. When the approach is couched in the psychological language of "behavior modification," it is still centuries-old reward and punishment, but with an attempt to be consistent. The inmate earns points for cleaning his living area, completing other chores, working diligently at his job or schooling, and participating in activities. Points are converted into privileges, which permit the inmate increasing amounts of freedom. The criminal finds this one of the easiest systems to exploit, because he does not have to guess what the staff or therapist wants. With behavior modification programs spelling out expectations, the inmate finds compliance easy unless he considers it selling out even to go through the motion of doing things on others' terms. At best, behavior modification results in token temporary changes by the criminal. The staff has less trouble with him, and he earns his privileges. Still, he remains a criminal.

Monitoring and counseling offenders in the community (referred to as "community corrections") is regarded as not only less expensive but more humane than confinement because, instead of being caged with others like himself, the criminal can be "reintegrated" into the mainstream of society.

The desire to find alternatives to full-time incarceration has given rise to a proliferation of community programs. Halfway houses have been established for offenders as a transition between prison and freedom. Community facilities offer offenders education, vocational training, and counseling.

Since the late nineteenth century, offenders have been placed on probation and allowed to live in society provided that they report at regular intervals to a probation officer.[13] In 2002, there were nearly 4 million offenders on probation in the United States.[14] Community correctional programs are available to some offenders after they serve a portion of their sentence and are released from prison on parole. Probation and parole are designed to keep track of offenders and in some cases to counsel them. But in many communities, probation and parole have no teeth; they are hardly an inconvenience to the offender, much less a sanction. A half-hour appointment every other week (or even less often) hardly provides enough time for an overburdened probation or parole officer to complete paperwork, much less hold a meaningful discussion. Some probation officers have such heavy caseloads that they would not recognize many of their clients if they saw them on the street.

Repaying the victim or public-service work, commonly referred to as "restorative justice," may be court-ordered as a condition of probation and an alternative to serving a sentence. Restitution programs may have deterrent value for some offenders who have to labor many weeks to compensate their victims. But how does a rapist, or an arsonist who sets a multimillion-dollar fire, make restitution? For the repeat offender, it is possible that making restitution will have an effect opposite to what is intended. The criminal does not regard the victim as a victim at all. *He* is the victim for having been caught. Compensating a person who society claims is a victim may bolster a criminal's already elevated view of himself as a decent person and thereby give him even greater license for crime.

Restitution may leave the victim better off, and that is a huge plus. The fact that the chronic offender is unlikely to be deterred or rehabilitated is by no means reason to discard restitution altogether. However, it argues for selectivity in its application. The shortcomings lie not with restitution or, for that matter, with any other program, but rather with its sponsors' unrealistic expectations of its power to change criminals. Like the institutional programs described above, many community correctional programs help criminals acquire skills or pay a debt to society, but they have very little effect on how they live their lives.

Eighteen-year-old Frank was on probation for unauthorized use of a motor vehicle. He had not been caught for a string of other car thefts, shoplifting, and drug use. Even he admitted that he had a "rotten temper" that had resulted in vicious assaults, especially when he was drinking. Having just graduated from high school, Frank wanted his own apartment because he was fed up with his parents telling him what to do. He was eager to work because "I like to spend money." After being fired from three jobs, he was unemployed for several weeks, maintaining that he could not find a job "where I'd feel right." Frank had turned down positions as a waiter, fast-food cook, and others that didn't "feel right" because he considered them beneath him.

Frank decided that a job-training program was the path to high earnings, and persuaded a high school counselor to refer him to the

Department of Vocational Rehabilitation. The state was willing to foot the bill for the training if a case could be made that Frank had a "diagnosable emotional disability." Frank was referred to me for an assessment. In my report, I concluded, "The Division of Vocational Rehabilitation would be wasting its time and resources by offering Frank opportunities that others would better utilize." I then predicted, "Frank might begin job training with enthusiasm, but become bored and disenchanted. Competing desires for excitement might result in his quitting. This is not a young man with serious ambitions to launch a career and lead a responsible life. There is no diagnosable emotional disturbance." Because one of the people at DVR who knew Frank insisted that he deserved a chance, he was accepted.

Sure enough, after initial enthusiasm, Frank lost interest, became irregular in his attendance, and finally dropped out. Meanwhile, he was continuing to use drugs and was arrested for possession of a substantial quantity of marijuana. His probation period was extended for that offense. He knew he had to work, and couldn't afford to be too choosy as to where. Immediately he got a job at a restaurant, where things went well until he was accused of stealing from the cash register and was fired. Frank's probation officer never knew of this because management did not press charges. Not wanting to endanger his probation, Frank quickly landed a job as a stock boy in a supermarket. As soon as he set aside several hundred dollars, Frank purchased a car, but eventually defaulted on the payments. As long as he was working and avoided arrest, he remained in good standing with the probation officer, whom he saw once a month for thirty minutes. However, his drug use and drinking continued, and he was still stealing.

Because Frank hadn't raped or murdered anyone, he appeared to be a suitable candidate for community corrections. However, community programs do not help offenders like Frank make fundamental and lasting changes. But neither does prison.

Community corrections has a major challenge. Rather than continue to offer palliative and superficial measures, community corrections must offer well-thought-out, intensive programs that will equip criminals with a new set of concepts that correct lifelong patterns of thought and action. In the long run, this will be less costly than building more prisons.

Unless criminals are serving terms of life without parole, which very few do, they will be free eventually to prey upon us all. There is still a job for corrections to do in the institution and the community—that is, to *correct*. But rehabilitation as it has been practiced cannot possibly be effective, because it is based on a total misconception. To rehabilitate is to restore to a former constructive capacity or condition. *There is nothing to which to rehabilitate a criminal.* There is no earlier condition of being responsible to which to restore him. He never learned the ways of getting along in this world that most of us learned as children. Just as rehabilitation is a misconception, so too is the notion of "reintegrating the criminal into the community." It is absurd to speak of reintegrating him when he was never integrated in the first place. The criminal has long stood apart from the community, contemptuous of people who lived responsibly.

Some people in the criminal justice system and in the community at large equate helping a criminal change with inducing him to give up crime. But to conceive of the task in this limited way is like calling a patient healthy when two cancerous kidneys are removed and he is offered no transplant. If a criminal gives up crime, what will replace it? Change demands more than keeping his hands off others' property or his fly zipped. It requires giving up a whole way of life. Rehabilitation specialists recognize that the criminal must be offered an alternative. They endeavor to provide him with opportunities for "success experiences," which they think he has been denied in the past. This too is a misconception. The criminal doesn't think he's a failure except when he gets caught for a crime. If he failed at school, work, and elsewhere, it is because of choices that he made. It is not his self-esteem that needs building. He is not a shy, neurotic individual who feels he can't do anything right. Rather, he thinks of himself as an exceptional person who is superior to others. If people want to pat him on the back as he learns new skills and does what he is supposed to, that is fine with him. While receiving praise for success in their programs, he is scheming his next holdup or thinking about where to find the most potent heroin.

Sometimes a criminal convinces himself that he'd straighten out if he could resolve just one problem that he thinks is the key to all others. He may genuinely desire to cut back on his drinking, stop using hard drugs, or control his temper better. "My drinking governs my whole attitude toward life, myself, and the world," declared one gunman. If a counselor concentrates on a single problem such as alcohol consumption, he is only beginning to deal with a criminal's irresponsibility. In fact, if a counselor can get the criminal to stay off the bottle, he may inadvertently help him become more adept in crime, for if the criminal stops drinking, his thinking becomes clearer and his coordination improves. Similarly, if a criminal is detoxified and stays off narcotics, he doesn't run the risks in the drug world of dealing with shady characters, buying contaminated drugs, or worrying about dosage and undesirable side effects.

Many states make special provision for psychological treatment of sex offenders. Sex offender treatment programs proliferated in the late 1990s, particularly after some states enacted statutes requiring offenders still considered dangerous to remain confined even after they completed serving their prison sentence. Psychologists have developed methods of conditioning sexual responses of offenders. While the offender views slides of different types of sexual behavior, his arousal is registered by a gauge attached to his penis. As he reacts to the slides, an aversive stimulus is introduced, such as a shock, loud noise, or foul odor. Consequently, just the thought of the deviant act becomes an adverse stimulus. Counseling or therapy frequently focuses on sex-related problems, a practice comparable to spraying one leaf of a philodendron to cure a totally bug-infested plant. A rape or child molestation is a dot on the landscape of the criminal's irresponsibility. Even if one conditioned a criminal so that deviant sexual behavior no longer appealed to him, that would not stop him from injuring people in other ways. Sex is only one outlet for the excitement that he seeks at the expense of other people. Issues more basic than specific sexual practices must be addressed.[15]

Not only is there a conventional wisdom about causation of crime and treatment of criminals, but there is also a conventional wisdom about how to tell whether a program is successful. Assessment of change is sometimes based on observations of the criminal's adjustment to institutional life. An environment may be offered in which criminals find it worthwhile to abide by the rules and participate cooperatively, even enthusiastically, in programs and activities. If you were an observer in such a situation, you might be so impressed by the normalcy of the residents' behavior that you would wonder why they were confined at all.

On one offender treatment unit, I saw residents who were well-groomed, neatly dressed, polite, highly involved in treatment, and productively occupied throughout the entire day. They also seemed to discuss problems with considerable frankness during their therapy groups. In reality, the residents had adapted to their environment, but their outlook on life was little different from what it had been on the street. In fact, I heard one patient proclaim that his life prior to confinement was "exciting and exhilarating." He said that in this program he would "take my classes, become more sociable, and increase my awareness in some areas." Finally, he confessed, "My intention is to be a higher-plane criminal, more of a white-collar type." Upon hearing this, another fellow acknowledged, "There isn't a day that goes by that I don't think to myself, 'I'm here picking up things to tighten my game up.'" By this he meant he was learning to be more cautious so he could avoid getting caught in the future. These revelations, unusual only because they were so explicit, underscore the peril of equating compliance with inner change. When a criminal voices intentions to change, but simply adapts to confinement, a corrosion in his attitude and behavior will occur once he is released, if not before. Furthermore, successful adaptation to a highly regimented environment by no means ensures that a person will cope responsibly with the pressures and temptations of the real world.

"Boot camps" have been utilized in recent years as a cost-saving alternative to confining lawbreakers in correctional facilities. With a military-like regimen and emphasis on discipline, many of these camps also contain rehabilitative components such as literacy programs and counseling. A Department of Justice study of three demonstration boot camps for juveniles concluded that "short-term success was possible in the (90 day) residential treatment programs."[16] Analysis of the after-care phase showed the success to be short-lived: "Without the 24-hour surveillance and regimentation of boot camp, youths soon reverted to old patterns of behavior."

With the aim of doing something quickly and inexpensively, programs have been developed to scare youthful offenders into living responsibly. "Scared Straight," a New Jersey program, was the pioneer and the best known of such efforts. The idea was to bring youthful offenders face-to-face with adult inmates who would tell them in graphic terms what doing hard time was like. A report published in the *Harvard Mental Health Letter* indicates that these programs not only fail but actually "increase the rate of offenses by 60–70%." In some instances the offenders serve as "models rather than bad examples."[17]

Recidivism is the major measure of change. Although the term generally refers to the repetition of criminal behavior, it most frequently refers to rearrest. Reliance on arrest statistics is heavy because these are not subjective assessments and can be readily obtained from official sources. Recidivism statistics are not encouraging. Of 300,000 prisoners released during 1994 in fifteen states, 67.5 percent were rearrested within three years.[18] Statistics tell only part of the story because they do not reflect how the criminal is living his life day by day. They reveal nothing of his honesty, his dependability, his decision making, or his concern for other people. Throughout his life the criminal has always gotten away with far more than has been discovered. After a taste of prison, he may become shrewder and more cautious, but he continues his exploitative way of life and commits crimes. Recidivism statistics indicate only whether he has been careless enough to be caught.

The total expenditure for the entire criminal justice system—federal, state, and local—in fiscal 1997 was close to $129 billion.[19] Yet, despite this massive outlay of funds, precious little has been effective in helping criminals change.

The dismal failure of one program after another has turned the public cynical about whether it is even feasible for criminals to change. Is it reasonable to conclude that criminals, by nature, are unchangeable just because so far efforts to help them reform have been unsuccessful? This, too, would be a misconception.

A criminal is most likely to have doubts about his way of life after he has been apprehended for a crime and is facing unknown consequences. The door of a detention center locking behind him may render an adult or juvenile especially vulnerable to thinking about change, especially if it is his first incarceration.

I interviewed Dick, age twenty-one, shortly after he was locked up and experiencing his first taste of confinement. He said that he started "going wild" at fifteen, when he hung out with the wrong crowd, became a tough guy, and was "screwing around with dope." Since then he had used practically every kind of drug floating around the streets, indulging in long binges of amphetamine and barbiturate use. Finally he was arrested and charged with two counts of armed robbery, two counts of larceny, and carrying a pistol without a license. He told me that the first five days in jail he was so scared that he vomited every time he ate solid food. So terrified was he that he hardly slept a night during the first two weeks. He was not so much afraid of other inmates as he was about his future. Night after night he lay awake thinking and reading. He called himself a "social retard" and cried because his way of life was emotionally "killing" his father. He was also depressed because his girlfriend had written him a "Dear John" letter. "I want to change," Dick said with considerable fervor. "I just can't do it myself, and I have nobody to help me. But my desperate desire to change is what I feel is most important."

Does a criminal like Dick say he wants to change just as one more con? Does he say it because he is momentarily afraid and seeks reassurance about his future? At any particular time, it is impossible to be certain how genuine such a state of mind is. The important point is that there are times when a criminal is vulnerable, when his life is not working out as he hopes, and he casts about for an alternative. Vulnerability is highest when the criminal is faced with losing something he values, usually his freedom, possibly also a girlfriend or his family. He may also be vulnerable after he has lost his freedom and he has had time to think and become despondent about the course of his life. At such times, straightening out has its strongest appeal. Even when not incarcerated, the criminal has periods when he becomes fed up with himself and wants to straighten out and start a new life. He is sick of running, looking over his shoulder, and disappointing and injuring those who care for him. He has neglected and exploited his family as well as many others.

Lloyd, twenty-two, had committed many crimes but never served a day in jail. Still, as he perceived his life going to pieces, he was becoming increasingly apprehensive. He had lost job after job, his girlfriend was on the verge of leaving, friends had deserted him, and his family was ready to disown him. Lloyd wrote a letter to me in which he said,

"I am completely estranged from my family and girlfriend. I realize that I don't have friends because I treat them irresponsibly. I stopped collecting unemployment, determined to change, and am now nonarrestable. My working hours have increased, and I am a full-time student. But I cannot continue these activities knowing what I know about myself." Going on, he wrote somewhat despairingly, "I have no real conception of what is expected of me now, and I keep going back to my original tendencies to make myself feel better. I have been in many kinds of therapy. It didn't work—none of it. Internally I am frightened and I realize I am not functioning as a human being. Fortunately, I have never been caught for a serious crime, although I have committed them. If it weren't for various members of my family bailing me out, I would have been incarcerated by now." The best time to reach a criminal, then, is when he is vulnerable, like Lloyd when he wrote the letter, for otherwise his sincerity about change will slip away, and he will continue the only life he has ever known. The work of habilitation can begin in prison or in the community. The critical factor is not where it takes place, but the state of mind of the criminal.

Reflecting on his wasted life, a middle-aged inmate of a state penitentiary posed to me what really is a challenge to society. First, he said that people like himself were rarely reached by current methods. Then he despaired that it might not be possible to change at all. "In my opinion," he said, "the human mind is ever reduplicating itself, acquiring more finesse, sophistication, technique, subtlety, and science. I am sure that a controlled setting that is humane in its approach, that is moral, principled, and courageous, can inspire the most lowly to become a working and functional part of this country." Said another criminal, "I know it is not easy to change someone's whole concept and evil ways, but I am aware of this. For me to become a law-abiding citizen would be my greatest triumph."

Little has changed since I wrote in the 1984 edition of this book about what passes for rehabilitation. Token measures continue to be instituted in sometimes frantic, usually fruitless, attempts to do something rather than nothing, and do it as quickly and cheaply as possible. The words of the National Academy of Science, written more than a quarter of a century ago, still ring true: "The Panel believes that the magnitude of the task of reforming criminal offenders has been consistently underestimated. It is clear that far more intensive and extensive interventions will be required if rehabilitation is to be possible."[20]

I ask today the same question I did twenty years ago: Will society effectively utilize its resources to help criminals become responsible, or will it continue to throw billions of dollars into human warehouses or down the drain into well-intentioned, but misguided, partial solutions that turn out not to be solutions at all?

15

TO CHANGE A CRIMINAL

WITH THE EXCEPTION OF A FOLLOW-UP note at the end, this chapter appears exactly as it was written for the 1984 edition. The rationale for leaving the content unaltered is that it presents the essence of an effective approach to helping criminals change. Many readers of the earlier edition told me that they found the sojourn of Leroy both instructive and inspirational.

A tall, gaunt, white-haired, elderly psychiatrist was doing most of the talking as he leaned back in the chair across from Leroy, a bearded black housebreaker and armed robber, who appeared cowed into silence. In a direct yet polite manner, Dr. Samuel Yochelson was telling Leroy that he was a menace to society.

Yochelson had dealt with criminals this way many times before, but he was a different man in his approach to them than he had been ten years earlier in 1961, when he arrived at St. Elizabeths Hospital in Washington, D.C., to begin a second career. One of Buffalo's most eminent psychiatrists, he was known not only as a successful practitioner but also for his contribution to the public's knowledge of psychiatry through his regular appearances on a local television series. As he approached his mid-fifties, the time had come when he aspired to make a contribution to this field that would be both scholarly and practical. From being a public figure in Buffalo, he chose the obscurity of a new environment where he would not be heard from for fifteen years. Yochelson undertook the research-treatment program in criminal behavior at a hospital rather than a prison because he thought that a treatment environment would be more conducive to a clinical study, and in addition he could draw upon the expertise of the huge hospital's medical and social work departments.

When he began the research, Yochelson didn't consider his patients "criminals." Rather, he regarded them as disturbed people who were products of adverse family situations and oppressive social conditions. He spent hundreds of hours taking detailed histories and hundreds more treating them in individual and group psychotherapy using traditional techniques with which he had been successful in Buffalo. Yochelson believed that if he could help the St. Elizabeths patients gain insight into their past behavior, they could resolve their conflicts and would no longer commit crimes. After several years of probing into their early experiences and psychosocial development, he observed something quite sobering. Despite all their insight, these men still were committing crimes right on the hospital grounds and, when caught, used their newfound insight as justification.

Undaunted, Yochelson realized that he would have to take a new tack. Having discovered that the search for causes was futile and contributed only to rationalization, he stopped swallowing his patients' self-serving stories and concentrated on their current thinking. As he did this, he saw that they were rational, not crazy at all. He concluded that the insanity defense through which they had escaped imprisonment was a farce. In fact, they were no different from criminals whom he studied who never were hospitalized for a psychiatric condition.

Increasingly, Yochelson became a hard-liner, not in the sense of wanting to punish criminals but in insisting that they be treated as responsible for their behavior and held accountable. Only by seeing them as the victimizers they were, not as the victims they claimed to be, could he surmount the barriers that they set up to confuse and distract not only him but everyone else they encountered.

The work with these men whom he now called criminals was arduous and unrewarding for a long time. But Yochelson persisted, meticulously recording on thousands of pages all of his observations, even those he couldn't immediately make sense of. Eventually he realized that significant and lasting change in the behavior of criminals could occur only with a 180-degree alteration in their thinking. He developed a technique to teach criminals to report their thinking so that it could be monitored and errors pointed out and corrected.

In its format, Yochelson's new program resembled a classroom more than a therapy group. The procedures that he developed are time-consuming to apply, but they offer promise of revolutionizing practices in many parts of the criminal justice system and in the mental health field.

Leroy did not walk into the doctor's office from the streets begging for help. Yochelson had encountered a few criminals who did this. Some wanted to kick a drug habit or lay off booze. Others were momentarily depressed or anxious and wanted him to get a wife or parent off their backs. But they were not interested in making profound changes in themselves. Leroy declared that he had nothing to show for his thirty years. He had abandoned his wife and children for sex, heroin, alcohol, guns, and other excitement in the streets of Washington, D.C. After beating a charge for bank robbery by faking insanity, Leroy was committed to St. Elizabeths Hospital, where he met Yochelson. Now he wanted two things—to get out of the hospital and to make changes in his life. What changes he wasn't sure, but he was certain that he wanted things to be different.

Yochelson began by stating that he knew Leroy sized up everyone whom he met. Since the purpose of the first meeting was primarily to let Leroy know whom he was dealing with, the psychiatrist did not worry about establishing rapport. Instead he assumed control of the interview by presenting his own view of what Leroy was like. Yochelson was not searching for explanations, which Leroy would readily feed him in the form of self-serving stories and excuses. He declared that he would not fall prey to Leroy's diversions, excuses, and other attempts to mislead and confuse him. Leroy would be offered no chance to ramble on about his mother, his father, his "bad breaks" in life, or even his crimes. Yochelson knew practically nothing about Leroy's background, nor was he interested. He didn't even know the charge on which Leroy had been declared not guilty by reason of insanity. But having studied many criminals in depth and having found identical elements in many of their thought patterns, the doctor knew a great deal about the workings of Leroy's mind.

Yochelson asked Leroy to listen to his statements and then tell him whether he agreed. He asserted that very early in life Leroy had carved out a path different from most of those around him, that he had lived a secret life and gloried in being slick enough to fool others. Yochelson pointed out that Leroy's early and frequent violations grew out of a demand that the world suit Leroy rather than that Leroy suit the world. He cited Leroy's insistence that others respect him while he respected no one. Whereas Leroy paid lip service to responsibility, he actually had scorned all but extremely successful people, whom he thought he could surpass in brilliance and accomplishment. He stated that Leroy had a "glass jaw"; he could dish out abuse but couldn't take even the slightest criticism. He told Leroy that although he might brag about his friends, he didn't know what friendship was. He contended that by a twist of mind, Leroy considered himself decent despite having committed crime after crime and having neglected and then abandoned his wife and children, whom he still professed to love. After each statement, Yochelson would pause, gaze intently at Leroy, and ask him, "Am I right?" Sometimes Leroy nodded solemnly. At other times he would shrug his shoulders and remark, "You could say that." Yochelson would pounce on that statement and point out that it showed Leroy to be a coward who presented a tough exterior to the world, but who didn't have the guts to face up to who he is. When Leroy replied, "I don't know," Yochelson said that "I don't know" is typical of a criminal who fears tarnishing his image by being truthful. Yochelson demonstrated how everything that Leroy said was revealing of his personality.

Like a bloodhound, Yochelson pressed on for close to three hours, unmasking Leroy. Leroy didn't like what he was hearing, but he found it hard to deny. He quibbled with a word or phrase here or there, but found his resistance crumbling. Later Leroy admitted that early in the interview he had sensed that this wasn't another "shrink" whom he could lead by the nose, that it was going to be a lot tougher than he had expected to take on Yochelson. Leroy began to wonder if the doctor was reading his thoughts. Fleetingly he thought that because Yochelson knew so much about criminals, he might be one himself.

What amazed him most was that he was sitting there and taking it while this elderly man painted a dismal picture of him as a human being. Although he was being exposed, he did not feel attacked. Yochelson had remained calm and polite, even when he expressed his total opposition to Leroy's way of life. He did not ridicule Leroy, browbeat him, berate him, or treat him with anything less than respect. So Leroy continued to sit there and take it, almost mesmerized while Yochelson picked him apart and presented him with a mirror image of himself.

This was only the beginning. The doctor invited him to return for more of the same. Leroy had heard about Yochelson's program, but in the interview not a word about it had been mentioned. The doctor stated that until he completed laying out Leroy's personality, there would be no discussion of a program.

Leroy did return for further interviews. No aspect of his life was sacred, not even Leroy's new girlfriend, whom he regarded as responsible because she had gone to college. Yochelson's probing questions revealed that she was not the Madonna-like figure he portrayed. She smoked marijuana, was an "easy lay," and offered to be an accessory to his crimes by concealing his guns in her home. After several meetings it became apparent that Yochelson did not detect any redeeming feature in Leroy. Even his musical talents had been misused, as he played in dives where criminals hung out. Bluntly, Yochelson told him that he was a thoroughbred criminal and that three options were possible: Leroy could continue in crime and experience the consequences; he could commit suicide, in which case society would be better off; or he could learn to live like a civilized human being and become a responsible person. Leroy had ruled out the first two. That left only change, which he thought would be a snap.

Behavior follows in the wake of thought. To eliminate criminal behavior, it is essential first to change the way a man like Leroy thinks. This is by no means a fast or easy process. The task requires demolishing old thinking patterns, laying a new foundation by teaching new concepts, and building a new structure wherein the criminal puts into action what he is taught. All his life, Leroy had heard the word "responsibility" bandied about, a word used so promiscuously that it means everything and nothing. Leroy was used to parroting the word, even though he knew nothing about being responsible. To him, to be responsible meant to erect a façade and *appear* respectable. He commented, "Once a person is responsible, he can get away with a hell of a lot." Responsibility also meant to be a big wheel, to acquire fame and fortune overnight by any means that he could think of. But in the program that Leroy was about to enter, responsibility embraced all it takes to be an effective, constructive person with total integrity. It meant learning and putting into practice specific patterns of thinking that are second nature to most people but brand-new to the criminal.

Leroy was told that none of his hard-luck stories was relevant. The circumstances of his life were of no concern. He was not a victim. At the heart of this program is the premise that man can choose between good and evil. Rather than relieve Leroy's fears and guilt, Yochelson would try to intensify them. Having had some psychotherapy, Leroy was used to expressing feelings, ventilating anger. He was surprised that Yochelson, a psychiatrist, had no interest in his feelings. There would be nothing in this program to make Leroy "feel better" about himself or accept himself. Rather, in order to change he would have to grow intensely fed up with himself. Leroy was intrigued, but, more important, he saw no choice but to trust this man and see what the program was all about. He told Yochelson he would make an "honest effort." Refusing to let that phrase slip by, Yochelson pointed out that there could be no effort that wasn't honest. He asserted that Leroy seemed to be placing the program on trial. If things did not go the way he wanted, Leroy would then do what he pleased, secure in the belief that he had tried. Yochelson continued to unmask Leroy by dissecting his every statement or question.

Leroy was then permitted to join a group of five men who already were at different points in the change process. Groups were organized in this manner so that a new man could see how others were functioning and the current members could see themselves all over again as they heard the questions, arguments, and excuses of a totally unchanged criminal. Leroy had been accustomed to therapy groups where patients decided what to discuss and where the doctor said little. Yochelson's group did not begin to resemble those freewheeling discussions. In this situation the doctor, not the criminals, was running the meeting. From a sheaf of notes made during the past twenty-four hours, each criminal reported what he had been thinking—thoughts about other patients on the ward, thoughts about the nursing staff, thoughts about family, thoughts about a violent movie on television, thoughts about the group, thoughts about Yochelson, thoughts during masturbation. The others listened in silence until Yochelson broke in to comment on a particular thought or sequence of thoughts. That became the focus of discussion, with Yochelson applying corrective concepts to everyone in the group, not just to the man who was giving the report.

When Leroy entered the program, he had been given a preview of the life he would lead. Yochelson warned that it would seem like the cloistered existence of a monk. He would have to sever ties with other criminals. There would be no drugs, not even a beer; no sex until he learned how to have a responsible sexual relationship. Every day he would have to attend group meetings. Even after he left the hospital, participation would still be required. His existence would seem regimented and frustrating as Leroy encountered problems that he never knew existed. Leroy heard these words and pondered them. The program sounded extreme to him, but what other choice did he have? His disgust for the past and his fear about the future were strong enough for him to make a beginning.

Neither Leroy nor any other criminal can be passionately committed to change from the outset. It is impossible for a person to embrace immediately a way of life that he has previously scorned and about which he knows nothing. Commitment grows with experience. It's like learning to play tennis. This analogy made sense to Leroy, who had learned tennis while in the hospital. At first the sport seemed glamorous, and he was eager to try it. After chasing the ball around on one of Washington's miserably humid August days and fighting off the gnats, Leroy was anything but committed to tennis. However, with lessons and practice, he improved. The harder he tried, the more skillful he became and the greater his eagerness to play and improve. Unfortunately, he had not made the generalization from tennis to life. Yochelson did, however, and told Leroy that with more experience and knowledge, commitment to change would develop just as had commitment to tennis.

Yochelson had no way of knowing why Leroy had agreed to be in the program. Was it to impress the hospital authorities so they'd let him out earlier? In his years of experience with criminals, Yochelson had learned to be neither gullible nor cynical. He knew if he believed everything that Leroy said, Leroy would manipulate him and lose respect for him. But Yochelson also knew that if he constantly disbelieved Leroy, there could be no dialogue between them. He made no immediate judgments, preferring to take the position that "time will tell." As he saw it, Leroy's life was at stake. The burden was on him to be truthful and then to put what he was learning into practice. Otherwise the failure would be Leroy's, not Yochelson's.

Having heard that Yochelson's group met all morning every day, Leroy wondered what in the world consumed so much time. He quickly found out. Discussion was not limited to events or problems. Events may be few and unremarkable, especially during a routine prison or hospital day. A criminal considers himself having a "problem" only when he gets into a jam by doing what he isn't supposed to. So there was little point in limiting discussion to that. The heart of the meeting was the daily report of thinking. Then even the person who languished in bed all day with the flu would have plenty to report. First, Leroy had to be taught to stop and recollect what he had thought, then to make notes on paper. He was instructed to think of this exercise as though a tape recording of his thinking were being played back. The reason for the emphasis on thinking was that today's thoughts contain the seed of tomorrow's crime. Leroy began to understand this very quickly.

One morning he reported being furious when he was called into an office and accused by a nursing assistant of being high on marijuana. He was especially outraged because he had used no drugs for a week, now that he was in the program. The thought flashed through his mind, "I'll bust the SOB's head wide open." In the group meeting, Leroy's thought of assaulting the attendant was treated as seriously as if he had actually done it. Yochelson knew that unless such thinking was controlled, it would be only a matter of time before Leroy became violent. But it was not only thoughts about committing crimes that were considered important. No element of Leroy's thinking was to remain obscured. As an unchanged criminal, he was in no position to determine what was important. What seemed trivial to him could provide the substance for a morning-long discussion. As reports were made, Yochelson listened carefully and, from the hodgepodge of thoughts, selected a focus. One criminal living in the community happened to mention that en route to the meeting, he had thought of cutting off a driver who abruptly pulled out in front of him. This thinking flashed by, consuming seconds out of a twenty-four-hour day. Though most people would forget it instantly, this man had been trained to turn a magnifying glass on his thinking. Reporting this seemingly insignificant incident provided substance for a discussion that could have been approached on the basis of several themes—the criminal's expectation of other people, his attempt to control others, his fears, and his anger.

Leroy found that the morning meetings were like a classroom in that they were structured and orderly. But they were not in any sense dry or academic, because the teaching was directly related to group members' immediate experiences. Leroy initially wanted to impress others by showing how perceptive he was. During the first meeting, one criminal was arguing heatedly with Yochelson. In a self-righteous tone, Leroy lambasted the other man for arguing at the expense of learning something. He advised the criminal, "Doc knows what he's talking about. You better listen!" Leroy expected praise, but was taken aback by Yochelson's informing him that the purpose of the meeting was not to criticize one another but to *learn* from others' mistakes and experiences. Yochelson observed that all his life Leroy was quick to pick others apart, but rarely applied his criticisms to himself. The doctor's most frequent question to each criminal in the group was "What did you learn?" Early in the program, Leroy persisted in pointing out flaws in the group members or in Yochelson, but shrank from looking at himself. He had never believed that he was a criminal, and fought that notion with all his being.

One afternoon an attendant offered him a ride from the tennis court to his living quarters. Leroy accepted, only to find that the attendant went by way of the grocery store and purchased beer. Leroy took a few gulps and returned to the ward. No one had missed him, and no one knew about the beer except for the attendant, who wouldn't tell. When Leroy reported the incident to the group meeting, Yochelson reacted to it as though he had murdered someone. Leroy saw no big deal because "everyone" wandered off the grounds. For an experienced criminal, it was easy to get past the guards. Beer didn't hurt anyone. No one was the wiser. Wasn't he entitled to a slip? He wasn't perfect. In this single incident lay many errors in thinking. First, he had committed two violations of hospital regulations as well as a violation of the program by leaving the grounds without permission and drinking. Then there was Leroy's insistence that he could make exceptions for himself. It was the old story of making what was wrong right because he considered it right for him at the time. It wasn't the danger of a few gulps of beer that was at issue, but Leroy's lifelong practice of making exceptions, with one offense leading to another. Furthermore, Leroy rarely stopped at one beer. Rather, beer was the first link in a chain of Scotch, heroin, women, crime. His claim that he had slipped and wasn't perfect only meant that he had not exercised the necessary restraints to eliminate old patterns. Whether everyone went off the grounds and drank was irrelevant, a lame excuse. Everyone was not in the program. Leroy was. The main question was whether a beer was worth the sacrifice of his opportunity to become a responsible member of society.

One of the obstacles that criminals pose to nearly every interviewer or change agent is the argument that "everyone does it," or "people are like that." Criminals point an accusing finger at society for being corrupt, and claim that the only difference between them and others is that they have been caught. They'll point out how people in business and government get away with things, citing specific scandals. Leroy did his share of this. While acknowledging that many offenders avoid getting caught, or if caught don't get punished, Yochelson refused to be diverted from the task at hand—dealing with Leroy's irresponsibility.

The standards in Yochelson's program were stricter than almost any Leroy would find in the straight world itself. Leroy found it difficult to accept the fact that to change he had to go from one extreme to another. He didn't view himself as an evil person to begin with. Coming to terms with the truth about himself was excruciatingly painful, the most difficult undertaking he had ever experienced. The criminal's reluctance to face the truth was verbalized by one group member, who confessed, "The reason I don't examine this stuff is that when I really look at it, it's like touching a live wire." The most basic requirement of the program is that the criminal report his thinking without embellishing, editing, or omitting. Leroy deliberately concocted some lies because he didn't want to touch the "live wire." At other times, lies spilled out of his mouth automatically. He would deny something, admit to only a part of the truth, or shade his answer to make himself look good. As he pointed out, he had lied since he could talk, so lying was second nature to him.

Because of the criminal's habitual lying, it is important that in a program like this the agent of change maintain contact with a responsible person who knows the criminal well, such as a parent, wife, or employer. This must be done regularly with the criminal's knowledge and consent, especially once he is released. Yochelson was able to talk to the institutional staff who lived around the clock with Leroy and later to family members, once Leroy was in the community. Access to an outside source is essential to evaluate the criminal's progress and also because another person may see a problem brewing that the criminal fails to recognize because of a lack of experience in the responsible world.

Leroy found the first month of the program new and exciting. He was sure that he could change faster and more completely than anyone else. He got a high out of small accomplishments. On a pass, he went to the cleaner's and asked to purchase some storage bags. The owner graciously gave them to him. He stopped by the grocery store to ask for cartons, and was loaded up with more than he could carry. His asking was a real change. In the past, he'd just take whatever he wanted. Leroy proclaimed that he was getting high on responsibility. The trouble was that he still was in search of highs. It wasn't long before the novelty of the program wore off and Leroy grew bored. Whereas he had had tremendous stamina in his criminal life, he had little endurance for this. In the past, he always did things his way and found shortcuts, but in this program there were no shortcuts, only endless drudgery. Every time he opened his mouth, the doctor discovered something to criticize. There were no rewards for doing the expected. Yochelson would ask, "Do you want orchids for living like a civilized human being?" Observing that there seemed to be so much to learn at once, Leroy commented, "The more I do, the more there is to do." He found the whole program literally a pain in the neck and complained frequently of tension in his neck and a blistering headache. Although Leroy had been off drugs for months, he suffered other symptoms identical to those he had experienced during withdrawal from heroin. He knew that stomachaches, sweating, and other miseries would disappear if he cheated on the program. "Violation is the only comfort," he thought.

This man, who had always considered himself at the top of the heap, in control of all around him, suddenly seemed a helpless victim, if not of others, then of his own makeup. He acted as though his emotions arose from outside himself and he had nothing to do with them. Leroy claimed that because he couldn't control his anger, he slapped his girlfriend during an argument when she came to visit. He said he resorted to smoking reefer because he was so bored and depressed. He skipped a ward meeting because he was so anxious he couldn't sit still. It was up to Yochelson to alter his feelings and interest him in change.

Leroy's feelings had governed his interests, and so he'd repeatedly balk at others' requests, saying, "I don't feel like it," or "I'm not interested." In fact, Leroy thought it was the duty of others to give him reasons why he should fulfill an obligation that he didn't recognize as an obligation at all. The hospital eventually permitted Leroy to work in the community, returning to the institution just for sleeping. He was also allowed passes on weekends. Yochelson had stressed repeatedly the importance of programming time, especially on weekends. On one of his first Saturdays out, feelings prevailed. Leroy didn't feel like doing much at all and made no plans. After visiting his mother, he went to the heart of the drug and crime area at 14th and U Streets. Despite ideal spring weather, he didn't give tennis a thought. He had no interest in visiting friends of the family. He wandered by the bars and roamed through pool halls, feeling as if he wanted to get drunk more than anything else. He paused in front of one of his old haunts, told himself no, and returned to his mother's. On Sunday he had a couple of beers, returned to the hospital grounds, and began flirting with a female patient. As the sexual repartee grew increasingly animated, Leroy grinned and patted her buttocks. The woman was ready for anything, but Leroy stopped, asked himself what he was doing, and returned to his ward. Monday morning, he complained that he just couldn't get interested in the program. He was angry at Yochelson for trying to make him a lackey and rob him of his manhood. He exclaimed that he wasn't going to be like "no white man." Throughout the program, every time Leroy injected the racial issue he was angry and seeking an excuse for irresponsibility. Then Yochelson was a "no-good honky."

Leroy discovered that Yochelson was on a crusade against anger—quite the opposite of Leroy's earlier psychiatric treatment, in which doctors encouraged him to express his anger. Yochelson asserted that the angry criminal does far too much damage "ventilating" his fury. Whenever the world does not suit him, whenever he fails to control a situation, the criminal flies off the handle. Anger is his habitual response whenever he thinks he's being threatened, and this happens many times every day of his life. When a responsible person is angry, he may offend others, think less clearly, and be less efficient at whatever he is doing at the time. But the anger usually stops there. For the criminal, anger is a malignancy that must be removed before it spreads and results in a crime. Leroy was shocked when Yochelson told him to swallow his anger rather than unleash it. Yochelson advised Leroy that for the present it was better to risk an ulcer than for someone to suffer a cracked skull.

But neither ventilation nor suppression is an adequate solution. What must be done with a criminal like Leroy is to help him gain a realistic view of himself and of the world, so that fewer things bother him and so he reacts constructively when things go wrong. The thin-skinned criminal has to learn to benefit from criticism, cope with rejection, and roll with life's punches. Columnist Ben Stein put it succinctly when he wrote that life requires "taking the lumps and calling them sugar."[1]

But the criminal must do even more than that. He must learn to anticipate situations in which he might be angry, and think them through in advance. For example, if he leaves his car at a repair shop, he already knows from experience that mishaps are likely. The car won't be ready on time, the car will not be fixed, the bill will be higher than expected, the wrong thing will be fixed, or, worst of all, the service manager won't be able to find the car anywhere on the lot. A customer can be realistic in his expectations and thereby avoid anger. He can phone before leaving to check if the car is ready. He can request an estimate before a repair is made. He can instruct the shop to notify him before making any additional repairs. En route to pick up his car, he can remind himself that even though he has taken precautions, something still may go wrong. This does not mean that he will be a doormat for others to step on. But by anticipating problems, he can preempt anger. If the need arises, he can be firm without being angry. Psychologist Paul Hauck makes the point that it is possible to live without anger: "It is perfectly possible to raise children who will not get angry over most normally provoking situations." He asserts, "One can be as solid as the Rock of Gibraltar and as peaceful as a sunny day, both at the same time."[2]

The responsible person may not take such steps to avoid anger. But the consequences of his anger are usually far less devastating than what ensues when the criminal becomes enraged. Criminals like Leroy establish their place in the world through anger, often at enormous cost to others. Who is Leroy if he can't control people? What is life if others don't jump to his command and anticipate his every wish? From a report of a single episode of anger, the role of anger in his life is examined.

One Saturday, Leroy dropped by his girlfriend Jackie's apartment. When her phone rang, he grabbed it and heard a man ask to speak to Jackie. He handed the receiver to her and stood next to her, straining to hear both ends of the conversation. She tried to get rid of the caller by pretending that he had reached the wrong party. Leroy accused her of lying about not knowing the caller, since he had asked for her by name. Jackie denied it, and Leroy had sense enough to drop it. That evening they went to a nightclub. While Jackie was in the ladies' room, a buxom, stylishly dressed girl asked Leroy to dance. Jackie returned and, seeing the couple cheek to cheek on the dance floor, created a commotion that wound up with Leroy's proclaiming that no "bitch" was going to tell him what to do, particularly after being called by every guy in the city. As Jackie rose from her chair to leave, he wheeled around and slapped her across the face. This was how Leroy handled life.

Leroy had not yet relinquished his view of himself as divine monarch, nor was he putting himself in the place of other people. He expected to be Jackie's "man," her one and only, no matter how many women he had or how he mistreated her. When others did not fulfill

Leroy's expectations, he was outraged. And so he lived in a perpetual state of anger. To help him become more realistic, Yochelson introduced Leroy to "Murphy's Law," which says that if anything can go wrong, it will. Leroy heard a group member quip that he had discovered a corollary to Murphy's Law; things that he was absolutely positive couldn't go wrong also went wrong. For the rest of his life, Leroy could expect to be plagued by Murphy. Murphy's Law was only one tool. Basic questions to be addressed throughout the program were Who are you, Leroy? How do you affect people? What do you want to become? What do you expect of others?

Despite doubts about the program and whether the whole thing was worth it, Leroy saw little choice other than to stick with it. Leroy's state of mind was captured by thoughts he jotted down late one Friday afternoon.

"Near the first gate where I spend some afternoons, I saw a guy who I talk with often," Leroy reported. "I don't know his name and doubt seriously if he knows mine. We talked, and it was very obvious he had been drinking and was feeling no pain. I thought to myself that everybody I came in contact with was high on something and enjoying themselves. Then I wondered is the square life worth it, with all its loneliness and no fun. As the pretty cars left the grounds through the gates, I thought the cars were only just a small portion of what square people have along with homes, children, sweet, beautiful wives who love them, relatives and friends who respect them, and many other small but wonderful things. Then I felt my struggle and fight would bring to me those wonderful things, or I could get hip again and go no place, but the hell with it all, it's agony." His report ended with his writing, "I don't know why, but right now I feel like crying. So I'll stop and continue tomorrow. I hate this feeling, so help me God."

The worst problem Leroy faced in the early period was that as an unchanged criminal, criminal thoughts flooded his mind every day. The only barrier between himself and his life on the streets was a fear of getting caught and a threadbare conscience. These had not been very potent before, and he knew he could not rely on them in the future. Yochelson began to teach him ways to deter criminal thinking. The first method was to consider the many consequences of acting on a thought. At his job as a clerk, Leroy was positive that the boss was prejudiced against blacks and was afraid that he would be passed over for promotions. Each day he took a dimmer view of his boss, who appeared indifferent, if not antagonistic, to him while being cordial to the other personnel, all of whom were white. One day Leroy was reprimanded for coming in late. He had never seen anyone else spoken to so sharply. He held himself in check, but stalked into the group meeting vowing that he wasn't going to take "shit from that motherfucker" any longer. The next time he was going to let him have it. Patiently, Yochelson pointed out that this declaration told the story of Leroy's life. If something didn't go as he wanted, he'd teach the other person a lesson. If a situation was bad, he'd make it worse. He had always demanded fair play but had treated others shabbily.

Yochelson pointed out that, in typical fashion, Leroy was jumping to conclusions after only a few months on the job. He warned Leroy that he would encounter situations far more trying than this. In fact, Yochelson advised criminals to be grateful for things going wrong so that they could learn to cope with adversity and be better equipped for it in the future. If Leroy told off the boss, he'd not only enrage him, but if the boss was racially prejudiced, Leroy's behavior would reinforce that prejudice as well. Furthermore, Leroy would make other enemies in the office and find it more difficult to get work done. He might be fired and lose a job reference. Most important, his anger would unleash a chain of events that would be apt to culminate in his committing a crime, for this had been his pattern. Thinking of the consequences in advance was one form of deterrence. Later, Leroy would learn new concepts that would offer greater insurance against repeating old response patterns. He would understand the need for long-range thinking, the necessity of teamwork, and the importance of putting himself in the place of others. But until then, it was critical to equip him with deterrents for immediate use. Just as the criminal learns to abort anger, he also learns to nip criminal thinking in the bud before it flowers into criminal activity. He does this by preparing himself for any adversity.

Mark, one of the men most advanced in change in the group, reported that he and his wife, Liz, were driving to the mountains for a holiday weekend. In the past, the two of them had had arguments, long, cold silences, tears, and bitter recriminations whenever they were together, but especially on vacation. Weekends and trips had totally fallen apart over the most inconsequential incidents because Mark had always insisted on having his way. He tried to control Liz, even to the point of deciding what she should order from the menu for dinner. This time, Mark was trying to anticipate everything that could possibly go wrong—getting lost, car trouble, illness, dirty accommodations, cold weather, rain, weak coffee, inconsiderate people, crowds at recreational facilities, a wife wanting to do something he didn't have any interest in, her moving at a slower pace, her having her period and refusing sex.

This was all new to Leroy, who had planned little in his life other than a bank robbery. In this program he was taught to think not only about future *events*, but also about what his *thinking* might be. Yochelson stressed the importance of *thinking about thinking*.

Summer was approaching, and the days were hot and sultry. Pete, another member of the group, reported being "dizzy with desire" as he gazed at young women in shorts, halters, and bikinis. He contrasted the "lush female animal" on the third-floor balcony across the way with his "old hag" wife, who actually was neither old nor a hag. He caught himself thinking this way and reported to Yochelson that he had put a stop to it. If he had allowed it to proceed, he would have mentally stripped her nude and imagined "balling her like she had never been balled before." From past experience, he knew that then he would go beyond fantasy, prowling the corridor, seeking an opportunity to accost her and drag her into an area where he would tear her clothes off and gratify his desires.

Leroy was impressed with how quickly Pete had put the brakes on thinking. But Leroy pointed out that there were occasions when he didn't have time to ponder the consequences. Furthermore, he couldn't anticipate everything he'd think about, much less do. There had to be a more efficient way to deal with his immediate desires. How could he quickly squelch thinking about the pleasures of snorting coke when the thoughts seemed to hit him out of the blue? Yochelson suggested that perhaps the best way to deal with thoughts about drugs or other violations was simply to ask himself if they were worth throwing away his life and returning to the gutter. If Leroy answered no, he could direct his thinking elsewhere. This Leroy tried.

At the office, Leroy saw a young woman removing a splinter from her foot with a needle from a syringe. Immediately he thought about drugs. He dealt with this thinking by reminding himself that "drugs are death," then thinking about something else.

Pete reported spotting a pair of rubber gloves lying on a shelf in a physician's examining room. He thought about putting them on, grabbing the nurse, and raping her. Immediately, Pete stopped this stream of thought and began to think about problems at work. Another man reported going out to buy a quart of milk and passing a liquor store. He instructed himself, "Keep your mind on the milk." The thought that the responsible person can allow himself to think and perhaps savor is dynamite to the criminal, who will elaborate on it and translate it into action.

Finally, a deterrent process that Yochelson emphasized repeatedly was teaching each of the men to take stock of himself. Yochelson had been holding a mirror up to Leroy, rubbing his nose in the slime of the past. Now it was time that Leroy held it up to himself. Alcoholics Anonymous requires its members to conduct a "searching moral inventory." In the same way, if a criminal does not make a habit of reflecting on his life, he will not progress because there is little incentive to change.

Inculcating fear and guilt are essential to change inasmuch as they prompt consideration of other people and the making of responsible decisions. Leroy knew well the spine-tingling fear and knot in his stomach that came whenever he was approaching the scene of the crime and leaving it to make his getaway. The only conscience he knew was that of momentary remorse when he realized he had hurt or disappointed someone. Leroy could shut anything out of his mind long enough to do whatever he wanted. The criminal must learn that fear is built into life. Some people diet out of fear. They exercise because of fear, and drive safely because they are afraid. Fear is an incentive to do better. Out of fear of hurting others, people take precautions before they act. Fearing for the future, a person does what he must for his family and himself. He purchases life insurance, saves money, schedules health checkups, services the car. Leroy was told that if he hurt someone or acted thoughtlessly, he should experience pangs of guilt. Without fear and guilt, he could never live responsibly. Leroy's fear and guilt would grow only by subjecting his irresponsible thinking to scrutiny, then by struggling to grasp corrective concepts, and finally by putting them into practice.

Leroy believed that once he learned to be responsible, he would have no worries, but Yochelson warned him that he'd be tension-free only when he was dead. Through new experiences, Leroy was learning what the doctor meant. He began to worry about work because he had processed fewer requisitions in November than in October. It wasn't just that or the boss hassling him. There were constant interruptions, incompetent co-workers asking asinine questions, unreasonable deadlines, being placed interminably on hold while people in other agencies looked up information that turned out to be inaccurate so that eventually he had to redo work. Leroy complained that all this was meaningless. There'd be a ray of sunshine as one problem was solved, and then clouds seemed to descend—another day, another set of problems. Leroy wanted to say the hell with it. Why should *he* bother? Why should *he* worry? If this was life, it was not what he bargained for. Patiently, Yochelson did what he had done so many times before. He asked Leroy what alternative he had. Every job had its difficulties. Yochelson was having his own with St. Elizabeths. Life was full of problems. It was only reasonable to expect that before one was solved, another would crop up. Did Leroy want to return to hustling, holdups, and heroin? Did he want to kill himself? If not, the only other course was to press on and do what had to be done.

The program requires massive amounts of endurance, because life itself demands that. This is a quality that Leroy was short on. He was forever expecting to reach the summit of achievement without taking the beginning steps, and was angry when it didn't happen. His had been a life of emergencies, all of his own making. There were no goals, only an interminable series of conquests to shore up an inflated but precarious self-image. Leroy could not see any light at the end of the tunnel. He couldn't understand why anyone would work and work and work without a guarantee that it would all pay off. He demanded insurance against failure, and by failure he meant being anything less than tops at whatever he did. He said, "For some reason or other, I'm unable to go into a situation where there's a chance of failure." Since a guarantee of success was not forthcoming, Leroy began to doubt everything. "What's the purpose of it all?" he asked. "Every day is like you have to put on your armor to fight a battle. It's too much."

While Leroy was entertaining doubts, the hospital thought he was doing superbly and discharged him on a conditional release. By this time he was immersed enough in Yochelson's program to keep attending the group meetings each day. Although there was a momentary flurry of elation at being released, Leroy still found himself in a prison, the prison of a program that demanded making what he considered extreme sacrifices. All he could see was deprivation, not opportunity to start life anew. He had rejoined the wife and children whom he had abandoned years before. But still, what was life? Day after day, it was work, home, and the program.

Leroy lamented that all he had gotten out of the program was an aching head, upset stomach, and constant fatigue. He had reached the point of saying what he had said all his life when he tired of something: "Fuck it." At this point he had ruled out crime, but not other things. After working overtime one Saturday, Leroy came home late in the afternoon and found that his wife, Mary, was not yet back from shopping. He strolled down to the corner and started chatting with some of the winos hanging around. As he was talking, friends of Mary's called to him and offered him a ride home, chiding him about his poor choice of companions. Leroy replied that he was lonely. Seeing that Mary was still not home, he knocked on the landlady's door, and she invited him in to a party. Leroy had a drink or two and eyed a young lady who seemed to be about twenty. She was aware that he was watching her, and soon came over to him. They bantered flirtatiously. He nuzzled her cheek, then planted a kiss on her lips, and finally drew her into the bedroom, shutting the door behind them. After embracing and kissing, they undressed, and the girl began lionizing Leroy, telling him what a great build he had and admiring and fondling his penis. In a frenzied manner, they had intercourse and dressed. In the nick of time, Leroy returned to the party to find his wife just bursting in the door, looking for him. Mary accused him of nothing, but he was angry because "she shouldn't have been checking up on me." Leroy saw no harm whatsoever in this rendezvous. He claimed he was entitled to a "release." Yochelson viewed it differently, asking Leroy if a quick tumble with a tramp was worth risking the loss of his wife and children and the stability of the life that he was trying to build. He was not sexually deprived. He had sex with his wife almost every night. Finally, Yochelson reminded Leroy that once he made an exception for himself, it would be only the beginning. Whenever he said "fuck it" because of a momentary dissatisfaction, he came perilously close to abandoning the entire effort to become responsible. It was a question of his choice and will. Leroy became contrite, admitted he had erred, and moaned that he was a hopeless case. Yochelson was unrelenting. He reminded Leroy that he said "I can't" only when he didn't want to do something. "Are you a man or a mouse?" queried the doctor. Then he asked Leroy if he'd take criticism like a man and improve, or give up and blame others.

In Yochelson's program, the theme of the criminal's injury to others always hung heavily in the air. Leroy knew what injury was when his own home was burglarized. He knew what injury was when his son was threatened by a boy with a knife. But he never thought of himself as injuring others. He equated injury with drawing blood, something he rarely did. But he was completely oblivious to others' rights and feelings. A fellow in the group reflected, "I do have feelings for other people. If I saw people trapped in a burning house, I'd experience a certain horror." The man continued, "And yet I really don't have any feeling for those I hurt. Were I to rape a woman, I wouldn't feel one second of her pain or anguish. I can't explain the contradiction between my pain for those in the burning building and my complete lack of feelings for my victims. I think it's because, where my own interests and pleasures are concerned, my feelings for others are automatically so totally suppressed and discarded as to be totally absent. I don't know. I only know that if I could appreciate the sufferings of my victims, they wouldn't be my victims."

Learning what constitutes injury is critical to learning about oneself. Throughout the program, Leroy experienced new waves of awareness and then disgust as to the scope of the damage that he had inflicted in almost three decades as a criminal. Beyond physical suffering and financial loss, injury extends to the emotional damage, to the climate of fear engendered in the aftermath of a crime, and to the disruption of lives. A small violation has a far-reaching effect. If a man pays for a meal with a bad check, the business suffers a direct loss. But the customers are hurt, too, because if enough of these losses occur, management will refuse to take checks and customers will have to pay by cash or credit card. Furthermore, because the cost of losses is passed on to customers, the offender's own mother will have to pay more in that very restaurant. One of the men in Yochelson's group had committed burglaries and had been in a few fights. But he hadn't fought or broken into anyplace lately. He asserted that he wasn't much of a criminal because he "only dealt drugs." Yochelson pointed out that there was no telling how much injury this man contributed to through his drug sales. The criminal did remember that one of his buyers, after purchasing some heroin, had held up a store, terrorized the customers, and shot the lady behind the cash register. But never before had he thought about these or other injuries resulting from his drug trafficking.

The criminal's habit of blaming others is a persistent obstacle to the process of change. Yochelson told Leroy that what others did made no difference in this program. Only what he did mattered. Does he create a bad situation? Does he make an already bad situation worse by anger or poor judgment? He must evaluate himself before criticizing others. If his wife is unreasonable, the important issue is how *he* reacts. If he fails to meet a deadline at work because of someone else's incompetence, what matters is not the shortcomings of the other person, but how *he* deals with the situation. Even were he to be attacked totally without provocation, the focus in the group meeting would be his thinking about his assailant and what *he* actually did. Leroy and the others were totally accountable for changing their own lives. Blaming circumstances was futile and only gave vent to anger. One of the fellows reflected, "When you look over your whole life and you see the total harm, it is up to you to create a new life for yourself. Nobody else does it for you."

As Leroy learned new ways to think and behave, he gradually emerged from his own private universe into a world of sharing, teamwork, loyalty, and trust. His attitude shifted from "screw everybody else but me" to "I have to learn how to share. I don't even know what it means." He slowly relinquished his perch of solitary grandeur to discover the give-and-take of relationships. In the group meeting, he found out what a discussion is, witnessing that it is possible to disagree with a person without insulting him. He learned to listen. In the past, Leroy didn't think anyone could teach him anything because he knew it all to begin with. First in the group and then at work and with his family, he began to learn and practice the rudiments of civilized behavior. He became a team member instead of demanding to be the captain. As Leroy traveled along this new road in life, unremarkable everyday events called up memories of his sordid past.

Leroy and Mary were discussing their priorities in fixing up the apartment. Because both were working, they had been able to set aside more than $500 for the project. But they needed so many things, it was hard to decide whether to purchase a couch, chairs and a lamp, or some drapes and a coffee table. They listed each item they hoped to buy, and what it was likely to cost. The next morning, as he rode the bus to work, Leroy was absorbed in thinking about their discussion. He winced to himself as he thought about the way he used to "borrow" Mary's hard-earned wages on false pretenses and spend it on drugs and other women. He gasped as he realized what they could have owned by now had he been a responsible person.

Two other fellows who had been in the program longer reported sobering reflections arising from their current progress. Pete had done well in sales and had received a promotion. Now he was authorized by management to attend an out-of-town convention. Pete picked up the phone book to look up the airlines number to make reservations. As he ran his finger down the page, he thought of the obscene phone calls he had made to clerks at nearly all the airlines, as he tried to find a female agent who would engage in sexual repartee while he clung to the other end of the line, masturbating and fantasizing. As these recollections flashed through Pete's mind, he was revolted to the point of feeling physically nauseated.

Tony talked about his experience reading a psychology book in the library now that he was out of prison and in school part time. He reported with satisfaction that by concentrating for two full hours, he had absorbed a tremendous amount. His head was swimming with ideas, and he was bubbling over with enthusiasm. However, he remembered that before prison, his library habits were very different. He rarely could sit still for two hours, and when he did, only fifteen minutes were spent in study. The rest of the time his mind was in the streets or he was staring at girls' legs or breasts. He also reflected how during that period of his life he'd wasted thousands of the dollars that his parents had saved over the years for his college education.

Several years before meeting Yochelson, Leroy had been a patient in psychotherapy in which the therapist probed his unconscious mind and searched for hidden complexes. He also had participated in programs where he was rewarded or punished for his behavior. Yochelson's program was neither as complicated as the psychodynamic approach nor as simplistic as behavior modification. He found its concepts made sense, and he could glimpse progress when he allowed himself to be guided by them. The more he learned, the more starkly the present contrasted with the past, and the more he saw there was to learn. Leroy was surprised to learn that he knew virtually nothing about making decisions responsibly. He had been one of those people who didn't like to ask a question because to do so was a humiliating admission of ignorance. He had no need to plan ahead except in scheming a crime. He recalled, "I thought about tomorrow, tomorrow." Now he was beginning to realize that to admit ignorance was wiser than pretending to know it all. Leroy began to weigh alternative courses of action and consider both short- and long-range consequences.

There are other programs that teach criminals how to make decisions as well as acquire many other skills. However, they focus upon situational problem solving and feelings, not upon thinking patterns that are all-pervasive. Yochelson's program aimed to help a criminal change 180 degrees by learning an entirely new way of thinking and acting that would permeate his entire life. Leroy continued to be amazed at the tremendous attention to tiny details. For example, he reported that from time to time he put a quarter in a pay phone rather than twenty cents because he didn't want to take time to get the proper change. Yochelson developed this pattern into a major theme for discussion— the criminal's view of money. Leroy had never valued money. A nickel, a quarter, even a thousand dollars meant little. More money had passed through his hands in a few weeks than most people earn in years. To manage money, Leroy first would have to keep track of it. Again, it was the matter of going from one extreme to the other, from squandering thousands of dollars to counting every penny. Establishing the discipline of saving was what mattered, not whether the phone company gained five extra cents on the pay phone. In this program, the smallest breach of integrity became a major issue, even when no one was hurt by it. One of the men in the group ate ham at Thanksgiving rather than turkey. When asked by a friend whether he enjoyed his turkey, he responded that he had. This was a lie, a trivial one to be sure, but it was one that was not only unnecessary but that a criminal can ill afford. Leroy and the others in the group had lied all their lives, even when there seemed to be no advantage to it. One lie had led to another. To destroy this pattern, a criminal must maintain total integrity. Leroy's friend in the group could have replied, "This year it was ham." The discipline in being totally truthful is important in the same way as the discipline in accounting for every cent.

Leroy had ups and downs in change, as did all the men. As Leroy achieved more and more in the responsible world, it became increasingly hard to think of turning back. He viewed the old life as a living death. It was true that meeting deadlines at work, worrying about bills, balancing his checkbook, enduring the stresses of children, and working out differences with his wife were not the highs he was accustomed to. There were periods of self-pity and departures from the program— a nip of sherry, followed by a tumbler of Scotch, staying home from work on a day when he just didn't feel like going, slapping Mary in a fit of pique because now *she* was spending too much money. But from each such departure, Leroy learned. The most important reinforcer of change was that by adhering to the program, he was accomplishing new goals *he* had set. Leroy and Mary bought a small house in which Leroy took great pride. After coping with delays in securing financing and the drudgery of moving, he plunged into fixing up the place, spending practically every spare moment plastering, painting, cleaning, and working on the yard. Tending a vegetable garden became almost an obsession. After months of physical labor he was finally able to say, "As soon as you hit the corner, my house stands out." But many more projects remained—repairing the fence, enlarging the garden, sodding the front lawn, and painting the bedrooms.

Leroy's family life meant more and more. His boys, approaching adolescence, looked to him for approval and guidance. He fought back tears of joy as Tommy powered his school football team to victory with the encouraging cheers of the fans. Leroy had always believed he had to have more than one woman or else he was not a man. But he was starting to change his mind about this.

One day in the group, Leroy reported that a "sexy-looking thing" was waiting at the bus stop. Catching himself thinking, "She'd be a nice piece to have," he shifted his gaze, then boarded the bus and buried himself in the newspaper. She made her way down the aisle, plopped down beside him, and brushed her thigh against his. Leroy shifted his leg and responded politely to the conversation. Deciding to keep things light, he discussed the weather and bus breakdowns. When he got off, he thought he was a "damn idiot" for not taking her phone number. But as he walked to his office building, he had an image of Mary, who had suffered so much in the past because of him. Now she was beginning to trust him, to plan a life with him as her husband and the father of their two boys. He felt ashamed of his thoughts about the girl on the bus and dug into the work piled up on his desk.

As things continued to go relatively smoothly at home, Leroy found he was thinking less about other women and looking less, too. "I look once and don't allow myself to look again," he reported. "I am never going to let myself go. It makes me feel good to be in control of myself."

Leroy believed that he had gone through too much in the past and was working too hard now to soil a clean record. Hard work was yielding results—a promotion at work, an attractively decorated and immaculately clean home, two sons who loved him, a wife who depended on him, neighbors who respected him. Leroy had altered his spending habits. He and his wife had a savings certificate in a bank and had far fewer debts. Leroy said, "I value money. Excitement is when I have it stashed away." Leroy saw similar changes occurring in some of the other men in the group. One who had been insensitive and angry was referred to at his job as "the Easter bunny" because he was so affable. Another rose from busboy to manager of a large restaurant. Perhaps what Leroy and the others prized most was not so much the tangible accomplishments as the feeling of being clean. One man asserted, "I so prize the cleanliness that everything could go, including my health, but I'd still prize the cleanliness." What had been tempting was no longer tempting. Leroy severed his connections with other criminals, prostitutes, the drug world. No more looking over his shoulder for the police. He said with pride and some amazement, "That world is like a dream."

Leroy did not become complacent. The criminal life may have seemed like a dream, but Leroy knew it could quickly become real if he failed to be self-critical or ceased to struggle to improve himself. Although he was no longer legally accountable to the hospital, he put himself on parole, so to speak. Voluntarily, he continued to seek Yochelson's counsel long after the intensive phase of daily sessions was over. Meeting with Yochelson once a week, he spontaneously brought out his thinking. Rather than fearing the doctor's picking him apart as he used to, Leroy welcomed it. He was afraid of getting too cocky from compliments that were being showered upon him at work, at home, and by his friends. Leroy agreed with Pete, who drew an analogy between his current status and rowing a boat away from the brink of Niagara Falls. Pete contended that unless he kept straining at the oars, he'd drop over the edge of the falls. Another man put it this way: "My wife, our little apartment, the car, the stereo. It's like it's all sitting on sand that could be blown away with one little slip."

In November 1976, tragedy struck Leroy, something he'd never envisioned, although Yochelson had warned him it might occur. On Yochelson's first trip away from Washington to speak about his work, the seventy-year-old psychiatrist collapsed in the St. Louis airport and died a few days later. Leroy was stunned, but he knew what he had to do: "Damn what I feel, do I must. I have got to be stronger than ever." More than a year later, he was still watchful of his own thoughts, had received another promotion at work, and, above all, had continued to make the program his life.

As Yochelson had instructed him, Leroy continued engaging in a daily moral inventory. He knew that he would never reach a point at which he would "have it made." Rather, he was positive that the effort had to be constant and that he had to bear in mind what his life had been. This program seemed less and less burdensome because Leroy no longer harbored his former grandiose view of himself. The more he reaped the rewards of this new life, the more crime repulsed him. He lived a quiet life, one that he could never have imagined before, dividing his time among family, work, and a few friends. Leroy budgeted his money and his time, the latter being too short for all that he wanted to accomplish. He knew what had to be done to progress. He had the tools—the new patterns of thought that Yochelson had taught him. Leroy reflected, "It's easy to figure out things when my mind isn't bollixed up." Going back to crime was unthinkable. Declared Leroy, "There are too many things I want. I don't want anything interfering with my goals."

Twenty years since this was written, Leroy has maintained steady employment. He still lives with his wife, Mary. His children are grown. Leroy has a clean record—no arrests. He reports that he tries to take care of himself by exercising and remaining in good physical condition. He continues to abstain from the use of illegal drugs. The only major correction he reported making was voluntarily to attend meetings of Alcoholics Anonymous at a time when he realized his consumption of alcoholic beverages threatened to destabilize what had become a responsible and productive life.

16

"HABILITATION" OR

MORE CRIME?

FOR MORE THAN A QUARTER-CENTURY, I have presented and elaborated upon many of the ideas in this book at professional training seminars and workshops throughout the United States, Canada, and in England. Interest has grown among people who work day to day in the trenches with adult and juvenile offenders. I am referring here to professionals in the fields of corrections, mental health, education, law enforcement, social work, substance abuse, and the clergy. Dr. Yochelson's principles and approach to change ("habilitation") have been adapted and implemented in a variety of institutional and community programs. These efforts have demonstrated that a demanding program that corrects the thinking patterns of the criminal and holds him accountable for implementation of corrective patterns can be effective. In my outpatient clinical practice, I continue to find the approach powerful in helping criminals make far-reaching changes in their lives.

As he begins, no criminal can be aware of all that it will take to change. Some criminals will not be interested in finding out and, from the beginning, will reject any opportunity to reform. Some will make a stab at changing on their own, but in time abandon it. Criminals who refuse to change remain a danger, and society must be protected from them. In such cases, only two alternatives exist: lengthy confinement in humane institutions or release under a kind of close supervision that does not now exist. Supervision would require as a minimum that the offender meet weekly with an officer of the court, and that the officer make home visits and maintain regular contact with someone reliable who knows the offender well, such as a spouse, parent, or employer. Those criminals who are amenable should be offered the opportunity to participate in an intensive program designed to help them make fundamental changes in their thinking and behavior.

This is a tough approach to crime, because some criminals will have to be locked up for a long time, and because it stipulates that far more is necessary to effect *significant* and *lasting* change than current theories or practices suggest. Some criminals who want to change still must be confined in institutions for lengthy periods because no court will allow them to remain in the community after they've committed a heinous act. The institutional component must have trained staff who are in a position to evaluate criminals daily.

The most important part of the change process transpires in the community. It is a pipe dream to release a criminal from an institution and, without guidance, expect him to function responsibly in a world for which he is not equipped. It would be like insisting that a two-year-old construct an elaborate computer program. Once a criminal is released, the effort to help him change must continue in the community on an intensive basis. For those who are not confined at all, a period of "trial probation" is necessary. That is, the criminal could be placed on probation with the understanding that he participate in the intensive program for change. If he decided to leave the program, a court would determine whether probation should be continued under different conditions or revoked.

Because technology now exists to monitor offenders in the community more effectively than ever before, such a habilitative effort is somewhat less risky. Society need not rely on the criminal's good faith and the hit-or-miss efforts at supervision by overburdened overseers such as probation officers. Electronic surveillance can help in enforcing house arrest or in tracking the places an offender can go. It is possible to know where a criminal is at any given time through global positioning satellite technology.[1]

How long does the process of change take? Clearly, the task with the career criminal is the greatest. In a "habilitation" program, there is wide variation in the time required, depending upon how quickly a criminal gets down to business. If a criminal residing in the community on probation or parole seizes upon the opportunity to change as his "life line," he can complete the intensive phase of the program in one year of daily meetings, with regular follow-up meetings thereafter.

In describing the change process, I have referred to "the criminal" with few distinctions as to degree of severity. Obviously, not every person who commits a crime is a hard-core criminal. But still, crimes result from the way a person thinks. The program described in the previous chapter has been modified to help both youthful and adult offenders who are not career criminals become more responsible. However, the complete intensive process is mandatory for career criminals.

Change demands not only that an offender remain arrest-free, but that he also experience a diminution of his desire to commit crimes. Offenders must account for how they spend their money and time. Not only must they hold jobs, but they must establish stable work patterns. Those who have families must function in an accommodating and dependable manner. (This would be verified by interviews with family members.)

The program does not require new types of facilities or tremendous manpower. Personnel must be trained in order to become thoroughly familiar with the thinking and behavior patterns of criminals. When this book was first published in 1984, syndicated columnist William Raspberry stated: "I'm prepared to offer Samenow a deal: I'll give up the myth that criminals are caused by their environment if he'll give up the myth that they are cured by psychiatry."[2] Mr. Raspberry got the right idea about the "myth" of the environment as creating criminals. However, he got the wrong idea about the rest of it. Perhaps I failed to make it clear that a cadre of psychiatrists or psychologists is *not* required to help criminals change. (I have also never spoken in terms of "cure," which is best reserved when speaking of some physical illnesses.) Rather, the concepts and methods are straightforward and can be transmitted to people who do not hold advanced professional degrees, but who do have the dedication and stamina for this arduous work. It is essential that the men and women who operate such programs be responsible themselves, for there is little more futile than having one irresponsible person try to teach another irresponsible person how to become responsible. In other words, the personal qualities of those who are to help criminals change are important. To undertake this task, a person must have a blend of firmness, compassion, and a lot of patience, because quick results are unlikely.

Whether working in the institution or the community, the person guiding the criminal in this enterprise will show compassion not by shedding tears for him, but rather by devoting considerable time and effort to a monumental undertaking that has life-and-death importance to both society and the criminal.

The greatest obvious occupational hazard to people working with criminals may be the risk of physical assault. Also extremely inimical to a gratifying career is the prospect of a rapid burnout of enthusiasm, commitment, and interest. Mention the word "burnout" to seasoned people in corrections, and they know what you mean. Increasing numbers of idealistic, sincerely concerned young adults are entering corrections, eager to do a good job. Almost immediately they confront a formidable array of obstacles for which they are ill prepared. Despite the fact that their clients are among the most difficult anywhere, they think they are expected to accomplish what parents, teachers, employees, clergy, and others failed at for years. In addition, their caseloads are overwhelming. Time with clients is cut short by stacks of paperwork and lengthy meetings. The new employee encounters apathy, cynicism, and occasionally hostility from senior workers, who are battle-weary from struggles with criminals and the bureaucracy.

The new employee eagerly tries to establish a relationship with a criminal. Just as he thinks he is making headway, he discovers he's been "had." The criminal does what he's done time and again—providing one impression while concealing his true intentions and illicit activities. Just as the new worker starts to believe that his efforts are bearing fruit, he is jolted into a new awareness. For instance, he learns that during a shakedown of cells, the inmate whom he has been counseling has for weeks been stashing away contraband, including several homemade weapons. At first the new employee attributes his lack of success to inexperience. After repeated unwelcome surprises of this sort, his morale drops, and he wonders if he was really cut out for the job. Resentment mounts toward clients who defy his best efforts. Some workers start to believe that their clients are hopeless. Of course, some may be, but a prematurely defeatist attitude can turn into a self-fulfilling prophecy. One senior corrections official described the progression from enthusiasm to burnout. "The first year," he said, "the new guy can't do enough *for* the criminal. The second year, he can't do enough *to* the criminal. The third year, he doesn't give a damn." The human element vanishes when workers become cynical or indifferent. Some quit their jobs. Some persist and endure, grateful simply to survive each day and receive a paycheck. A minority plug along, still hoping to accomplish something worthwhile.

An effective program for change places total responsibility upon each criminal, who has the opportunity and capability of making new choices. The approach to the criminal involves focusing not on what happens to him, but on what he does to others. If his wife came at him with a frying pan, what had he done to provoke her? If truly nothing, then how did his response make the situation better or worse?

Criminals cannot be forced to change; they must reach a point in life when they are becoming fed up with themselves and, consequently, desire to change. There are just three paths—crime, change, or suicide. Many offenders have believed there is a fourth option—to *appear* responsible while engaging in violations on the side. Partial participation in this program is analogous to being a little bit pregnant. It is not a viable option. A person either shuts the door completely on crime or he does not. No middle ground exists. There is a parallel to Alcoholics Anonymous in that AA calls for total abstinence. A sip of alcohol becomes a glass, then a bottle, and in time the alcoholic reverts to where he was. So it is with the criminal. If he permits himself to lie, eventually lying becomes pervasive. If he takes home just a few inexpensive supplies from work, it is not long until he is cheating or stealing from his employer in other ways and then committing more serious offenses.

Prevention of criminal behavior is preferable to society's having to cope with an individual who becomes a one-man walking crime wave. People pay lip service to preventing criminal behavior in juveniles. However, there has been considerable foot-dragging in identifying at-risk children. Partly this paralysis arises out of a well-founded fear of mislabeling a child, prematurely tagging him as a future criminal. But surely we currently know enough to identify, without pejoratively labeling, youngsters who show expanding and intensifying *patterns* of destructive behavior.

Educators, mental health professionals, social workers, and counselors who have heard me speak have seen potential in the approach described above for intervening before youngsters are entrenched in a criminal lifestyle. They have regarded the concepts of responsibility as simple enough to transmit, in the proper format, to students in primary grades.

Questions about applying this work to prevention led me to write *Before It's Too Late: Why Some Kids Get into Trouble and What Parents Can Do About It.*[3] We try to identify children at risk for developing physical, emotional, and learning handicaps. Wouldn't it be more caring and a lot less expensive to use what we know and intervene early rather than to cage a child at an annual cost of between $35,000 and $64,000 as well as incur costs that cannot begin to be measured in dollars?[4] Conceivably, youngsters might be deterred by early systematic exposure to concepts that will help them think and behave responsibly.

Changing a person's thinking may suggest brainwashing or conjure up ominous images of prisoner-of-war indoctrination, treatment with mind-altering drugs, and other insidious or coercive measures. Procedures that I have described in this book do not remotely resemble any of these. Significant and enduring change is feasible only when a criminal is fed up with himself and consents to expose his thinking to criticism and correction. Decisions are not made for the criminal. The *process* of decision making is the focus, but the specific decision is made by the individual. Eventually he chooses his life's work and advances as far as his talents and effort allow. Within the limits of responsible functioning lie countless opportunities and many variations in lifestyle. The change process calls for criminals to acquire moral values that have enabled civilizations to survive. The objective is to teach them to live without injuring others.

The issues I've addressed here are as old as mankind: the power to choose, free will, good versus evil, response to temptation, courage or cowardice in the face of adversity. The Ten Commandments enjoin human beings from certain crimes, and the Golden Rule, "Love thy neighbor as thyself," offers a guide for living. The sacred books of most religions are filled with admonitions against deceit, anger, pride, and guilt. In addition, the Old Testament says, "As a man thinketh in his heart, so is he" (Proverbs 23:7).

We are as we think. It is impossible to help a person give up crime and live responsibly without helping him to change what is most basic—his thinking.

I have been criticized from both the left and right sides of the political spectrum. My work, spanning several decades, is based on research and clinical experience—thus it is apolitical. Nonetheless, I have been regarded as conservative because I maintain that crime resides within the individual, it is a matter of choice. But I also have been perceived as a dewy-eyed liberal because I am still here in the year 2004 asserting that as a society we must continue to seek more effective ways to help criminals change. The truth is that every man, woman, and child who is locked up will be released someday (except for the relative few sentenced to death or life without parole). When they are free in society, they most likely will have the same thought patterns that they had prior to their arrest. It is critically important that we help those offenders who are amenable so that they can habilitate themselves and become productive citizens. The savings to society will be incalculable if we are successful in that endeavor, even with only a minority of offenders.

NOTES

Preface to the New Edition
1. "Arrests of women for violent crimes increased 90% between 1985 and 1994 compared to 43% for men," reports Barry Yeoman in *Psychology Today*, November–December 1999, 57.

1. The Basic Myths About Criminals
1. U.S. Department of Justice, *Sourcebook of Criminal Justice Statistics*, 2000, 374.
2. Karnjariya Sukrung, "Tackling the Root of the Problem: Is Indulgent Child-rearing to Blame for the Recent Spate of Teenage Violence?" *Bangkok Post* (Outlook), June 21, 2003.
3. "Rampant Looting Across Iraq," *CNN.com./World*, April 17, 2003. "Czech Prostitution Is 'Price of Freedom'," *Chicago Tribune*, May 2, 1993. "Sex Toys, Stun Guns Are Poles' New Comrades," *Detroit News*, August 12, 1990. "Police Force 'Choking on a Flood of Crime' " (Moscow), *Washington Post*, November 7, 1993.
4. "Study Links TV Viewing, Aggression," *Washington Post*, March 19, 2002.
5. Ray Guarendi, *Back to the Family* (New York: Villard, 1990).
6. James Q. Wilson and Richard J. Hernstein, *Crime and Human Nature* (New York: Simon and Schuster, 1985), 148.
7. Dorothy Otnow Lewis, et al., "Neuropsychiatric Psychoeducational and Family Characteristics of 14 Juveniles Condemned to Death in the United States," *American Journal of Psychiatry* 145, no.5, May 1988, 585–89.
8. "Q&A with John Douglas, Ed.D.," *Forensic Examiner*, January / February 1966, 13.
9. Alfred Adler, "Individual Psychology and Crime," *Police Journal* 17, 1930, reprinted in *Quarterly Journal of Corrections*, 1977, 7–13.
10. Richard Conniff, "Rethinking Primate Aggression," *Smithsonian* 14, August 2003, 67.

2. Parents Don't Turn Children into Criminals
1. "Childhood Origins of Psychopathic Personality Trends," in S. A. Szurek and I. N. Berlin, *The Antisocial Child: His Family and His Community* (Palo Alto, Calif.: Science and Behavior Books, 1970), 2–12.

2. Robert Wallace, "Parents Smoke Pot; He Doesn't," *Telegram-Tribune* (San Luis Obispo, Calif.), November 8, 1979.
3. J. David Hawkins et al., "Predictors of Youth Violence," OJJDP *Juvenile Justice Bulletin*, April 2000, 6.
4. "Lasting Effects Found from Spanking Children," *Washington Post*, August 15, 1997.
5. "Society's Acceptance of Violence Backfires," *Monitor*, October 1994, 28.
6. "Yes, You Can Spank Responsibly," *USA Today*, November 14, 1999.
7. "Early in Life Learning How Not to Become a Bully," *Fairfax Journal*, February 25, 2003.
8. L. Joseph Stone and Joseph Church, *Childhood and Adolescence* (New York: Random House, 1968), 544.

3. Peer Pressure: No Excuse for Crime
1. E. H. Sutherland, *Principles of Criminology* (New York: Lippincott, 1939).
2. "The Columbine Tapes," *Time*, December 20, 1999, 40–41.
3. "'Columbine' Plot Failed, Police Say," *Washington Post*, July 8, 2003.
4. Nicholas Peleggi, *Wiseguy: Life in a Mafia Family* (New York: Simon & Schuster, 1985), 19.

4. "The Hell with School"
1. McGowan points out, "Children with risk-taking behaviors, such as those displayed in conduct disorder and oppositional defiant disorder, may exhibit symptoms that mimic ADHD/ADD, making accurate diagnosis difficult." Alicen J. McGowan, "ADHD: Attention Deficit Hyperactive Disorder and Its Relationship to Juvenile Delinquency and Criminal Behavior," *Forensic Examiner*, September–October 2000, 43.
2. "Feeling Safe in High School," *USA Today*, November 19, 1998.
3. "The Unteachables," *Daily Mail* (London), May 28, 2002.
4. From the Asklepieion Society Northwest, Minnesota Correctional Facility, Stillwater, Minnesota.
5. "Parent Handbook," Montgomery Blair High School, Montgomery County, Maryland, 2002–3, 14.

5. Work and the Criminal
1. Robert J. Samuelson, "A Weak Link Between Crime and Joblessness," *Washington Post*, May 10, 1983.
2. Exemplary in this respect is the array of services provided by the Alston Wilkes Society. Founded in 1962, this organization assists offenders in finding employment. "Alston Wilkes Society: Rebuilding Lives, Providing Second Chances," *Corrections Today*, August 2002, 14.
3. "Corporate Scandals Taking Toll on Markets," *Washington Post*, June 27, 2002.
4. "The Value of Trust," *The Economist*, June 8, 2002, 65.
5. Dale McGeehyon, "Greed Inc.," *University of Maryland Magazine*, Fall 2002, 31–35.

6. People as Pawns

1. Many years ago, the Rand Corporation found that thirty-four of forty-nine habitual felons had committed four or more types of offenses. Rand reported, "The picture is one of opportunism, and the offenders appear to have engaged in whatever types of crimes were available to them at the time and to have remained with them only as long as they were productive." Joan Petersilia, Peter W. Greenwood, and Marvin Lavin, *Criminal Careers of Habitual Felons* (Santa Monica, Calif.: Rand, 1977), 21.
2. U.S. Department of Justice, *Sourcebook of Criminal Justice Statistics*, 2000, 208.
3. "President's Task Force on Victims of Crime: Final Report" (Washington, D.C., U.S. Department of Justice), December 1982.
4. U.S. Department of Justice, *Sourcebook of Criminal Justice Statistics*, 2000, 385.

7. Ultimate Control: Crimes of Violence

1. Ann W. Burgess, Testimony Before the President's Task Force on Victims of Crime, Washington, D.C., September 15, 1982.
2. U.S. Department of Justice, "Strengthening Antistalking Statutes," January 2002, 1.
3. Ibid.
4. U.S. Department of Justice, "Intimate Partner Violence, 1993–2001," February 2003, 1.
5. Defense Task Force on Domestic Violence, *Initial Report* (Washington, D.C., U.S. Department of Defense, 2001), 72.
6. David Finkelhor and Richard Ormord, "Homicides of Children and Youth," *Juvenile Justice Bulletin*, October 2001, 6, 8.
7. U.S. Department of Justice, "Hate Crimes Reported in NIBRS, 1997–99," September 2001.
8. Edward Dunbar, "A Psychographic Analysis of Violent Hate Crime Perpetrators: Aggressive, Situational, and Ideological Characteristics of Bias Motivated Offenders," April 16, 1999 (unpublished).
9. "Gang Attacks Jews on Sports Field in France," *New York Times*, April 13, 2002.
10. American Psychological Association, "Hate Crimes Today: An Age-Old Foe in Modern Dress" (Washington, D.C.: American Psychological Association, 1998), 1.

8. "It's Thugs, Not Drugs; It's Thinking, Not Drinking"

1. "Opiate Abuse—Part I," *Harvard Medical School Mental Health Letter*, 3 January 1987, 4.
2. U.S. Department of Justice, *Sourcebook of Criminal Justice Statistics*, 2000, 252–53.
3. South Carolina Department of Alcohol and Other Drug Abuse Services, "Fact-Sheet: Marijuana" (Columbia, S.C.: 2001), 1.
4. The psychiatric literature acknowledges that having an "antisocial personality disorder" renders a person particularly susceptible to drug use. See "Drug abuse risk linked with antisocial disorder" *American Psychological Association Monitor*, February 1990, 12.
5. A Brown University publication noted, "Teens' use of condoms to prevent the

spread of AIDS or any sexually transmitted disease (STD) is deterred by their simultaneous use of drugs or alcohol, according to the Alcohol, Drug Abuse, and Mental Health Administration." "Effect of Alcohol, Drugs on Teen Use of Condoms," *Brown University Child Behavior and Development News Letter,* December 1990, 6.

6. K. S. Kendler, et al., "Illicit Psychoactive Substance Use, Heavy Use, and Dependence in a U.S. Population–Based Sample of Male Twins," *Archives of General Psychiatry* 57, March 2000, 261–69.

7. Alan I. Leshner, "Addiction Is a Brain Disease—and It Matters," *National Institute of Justice Journal,* October 1998, 2–7.

8. David Deitch, Presentation at the 132nd Congress of Corrections of the ACA (Anaheim, Calif.: 2002, unpublished).

9. Sally L. Satel and Frederick K. Goodwin, *Is Drug Addiction a Brain Disease?* (Washington, D.C.: Ethics and Public Policy Center, 1998), 21.

10. The Harvard Mental Health Letter reported that most cocaine addicts are successful in breaking their habits. It cited a federal study indicating that crack cocaine addicts were "more successful at staying clean than alcoholics." That same publication stated, "At least 50% of alcoholics eventually free themselves, although only 10% are ever treated." "Cocaine Abuse and Addiction—Part II," *Harvard Medical School Mental Health Letter,* 16, December 1999, 1. See also "Treatment of Drug Abuse and Addiction—Part III," *Harvard Medical School Mental Health Letter,* 12, October 1995, 3.

11. The role of alcohol as a facilitator of criminal behavior should not be underestimated. Dr. David Deitch noted that more crimes, including violent crimes, are committed by people who are drinking than those using any other substance. Presentation at the 132nd Congress of Corrections of the American Correctional Association (Anaheim, Calif.: August 2002, unpublished).

9. *"Getting Over on the Shrinks"*

1. American Psychiatric Association, *Diagnostic and Statistical Manual-IV* (Washington, D.C.: 1994), 612–13.

2. American Psychiatric Association, *Diagnostic and Statistical Manual-IV* (Washington, D.C.: 1994), 614–15.

3. James T. Reese, "Obsessive Compulsive Behavior: The Nuisance Offender," *FBI Law Enforcement Bulletin* (Washington, D.C.: August 1979).

4. American Psychiatric Association, *Diagnostic and Statistical Manual-IV* (Washington, D.C.: 1994), 615–18.

5. Mark Potenza et al., "Pathological Gambling," *Journal of the American Medical Association* 286, July 11, 2001, 141–44.

6. Sigmund Freud, "Some Character-Types Met Within Psycho-analytic Work," in *Collected Papers,* vol. 4 (London: Hogarth, 1946), 318–344.

7. Sigmund Freud, "The Ego and the Id," in *The Complete Psychological Works of Sigmund Freud,* vol. 19 (London: Hogarth, 1961), 12–68.

8. "Poison in Drugs," *Rocky Mountain News* (Denver), October 6, 1982, 58.

9. A letter to the *Los Angeles Times* described a tragic case when an attempt to feign

mental illness failed. At the Juvenile Hall, a fifteen-year-old boy was told by other kids that if he faked psychosis he could be sent to a hospital, where he could suddenly regain his sanity and be released. That scheme worked. Later, the youth was arrested and confined in a county jail, where he planned once again to convince the authorities that he was mentally disturbed. He knew when the guard would bring lunch, and so he planned to hang himself just at that time so he could be cut down. He would have succeeded had not a telephone rung and diverted the guard's attention. The fifteen-year-old boy died of strangulation while the guard was on the phone ("A Cry for Help, But No One Listened," *Los Angeles Times*, January 14, 1978.

10. David Wechsler, *The Measurement and Appraisal of Adult Intelligence* (Baltimore: Williams & Wilkins, 1958), 7.

11. *Atkins v. Virginia*, 536 U.S. (2002).

12. The State of Virginia passed a bill establishing procedures for determining whether a defendant in a capital murder case is mentally retarded. The defendant "bears the burden of proving mental retardation by a preponderance of the evidence." From Virginia Division of Legislative Services, "Session Highlights," February 25, 2003, 2.

10. Locked Up

1. Dept. of Justice, "Prisoners at Midyear 1982," *Bureau of Justice Statistics Bulletin*, October–November 1982, 1.

2. "Inmates Number Over 2 Million, a Record for U.S.A.," *USA Today*, April 7, 2003.

3. U.S. Department of Justice, *Juvenile Offenders and Victims: 1999 National Report*, 16.

4. In the federal system, the end of the road at one time was the government prison at Alcatraz. Now inmates requiring the tightest security are housed at the facility in Florence, Colorado, opened during 1995.

5. Craig Haney and Mona Lynch, two professors, are extremely critical of these facilities, which they regard as part of "a new era of repressive prisoner control" emanating from a "politically inspired punishment wave." Craig Haney and Mona Lynch, "Regulating Prisons of the Future: A Psychological Analysis of Supermax and Solitary Confinement," *Review of Law and Social Change* 23: 496, 553.

6. Stephen Gettinger, "Informer," *Corrections Magazine*, April 1980, 17–19.

7. From "Commitment to Change: The Power of Consequences," videotape produced by Recovery Direct, Inc.: Carpinteria, Ca., 2002.

8. American Correctional Association, *Summer–Fall 2003 Product Catalog* (Lanham, Md.: American Correctional Association), 9, 11.

11. The Criminal as Terrorist: Implications for International Terrorism

1. *The Random House Dictionary of the English Language*, 2nd Edition Unabridged (New York: Random House, 1987), 1960.

2. "16 Die in Explosions at Russian Concerts," *Washington Post*, July 6, 2003.

3. "The Mind of the Terrorist" (interview with Carl N. Edwards), *Forensic Examiner*, May–June 2003, 23.

4. "Wall Street's Verdict," *Time*, August 19, 2002.

5. Chandrahas Choudhury, "After the Fall" (review of Riccardo Orizio, *Talk of the Devil: Encounters with Seven Dictators* (New York: Walker & Co., 2003), *Washington Post Book World*, May 4, 2003, 9.

6. "The Saddam Files," *Newsweek*, April 28, 2003, 20–27.

7. James Reston, "Seeking Meaning from a Grand Imam," *Washington Post*, March 31, 2002.

8. Stanley Bedlington, "Not Who You Think," *Washington Post*, October 28, 2001.

9. Kenneth L. Woodward, "In the Beginning There Were the Holy Books," *Time*, February 11, 2002, 57.

10. "Furry Worries," Tashbih Sayyed, quoted in *Newsletter of the Ethics and Public Policy Center*, Spring 2003.

11. Dinesh D'Souza, "Sell U.S.A.'s Virtue to Muslim World," *USA Today*, May 1, 2002.

12. King Abdullah II, "The True Voice of Islam," *Washington Post*, December 7, 2002.

13. David Bamber, news.telegraph.co.uk, November 11, 2001.

14. "Conviction of a Brutal Killer Leaves Afghan Justice on Trial," *Washington Post*, October 23, 2002.

15. "An Unusual Odyssey: U.S.-Born Latino Turns Islamic Terror Suspect," *Washington Post*, June 11, 2002.

12. The Criminal's Self-Image: "Decent People"

1. Willard Gaylin, "On Feeling Guilty," *The Atlantic Monthly*, January 1979, 78–82.

2. "Anticrime Ads Focus on Mothers," *Wall Street Journal*, September 15, 2003.

3. David A. Vise, *The Bureau and the Mole* (New York: Atlantic Monthly Press, 2002), 70.

13. The Total Failure of the Conventional Wisdom

1. "Can What a Man Eats Turn Him into a Rapist?" *Daily Mail*, London, August 2, 1989.

2. "TV Blamed for Attack on Jogger," *Dallas Morning News*, May 4, 1989.

3. "Violent Song Lyrics May Lead to Violent Behavior," *Monitor on Psychology*, July/August, 2003, 15.

4. "Will Global Warming Inflame Our Tempers?" American Psychological Association *Monitor*, February, 1998, 8.

5. "Studies Suggest Link Between Lead, Violence," *Baltimore Sun*, May 9, 2000.

6. "Study Links Violence Rate to Cohesion in Community," *New York Times*, August 17, 1995.

7. "Day Care, Aggression Link Is Reinforced," *Washington Post*, July 17, 2003.

8. Nonwhite prisoners under state and federal jurisdiction in 2000 represented 64.3 percent of the total U.S. prison population. "Prisoners in 2000," *Bureau of Justice Statistics Bulletin*, August 2001, 11.

9. Commission on Law Enforcement and Administration of Justice, *The Challenge of Crime in a Free Society* (Washington, D.C.: Government Printing Office, 1967), 5, 6.
10. William Healy and Augusta F. Bronner, *New Light on Delinquency and Its Treatment* (New Haven: Yale University Press, 1936), 201.
11. David Cohen, *Stranger in the Nest* (New York: John Wiley & Sons, 1999), 9, 43.
12. William Carey, *Understanding Your Child's Temperament* (New York: Macmillan, 1997), xix, xx.
13. In 1937, Samuel Beck stated that psychopathy was a vague category and called it "the wastebasket of psychiatric classification." See Samuel Beck, *Introduction to the Rorschach Method*, American Orthopsychiatric Association Research Monograph no. 1 (Menasha, Wisc.: George Banta, 1937), 4.
14. "Antisocial Personality—Part I," *Harvard Mental Health Letter*, 17, December 2000, 4.
15. "Bullying behavior may be genetic, a study in twins finds," American Psychological Association *Monitor*, May 1999.
16. Sharon Begley, science writer for the *Wall Street Journal*, pointed out that the "one-gene-at-a-time" approach to identify a particular trait or disease is unproductive. A more fruitful approach is to look at how genes interact, referred to as "systems biology." Sharon Begley, "DNA's Double Helix Isn't So Golden Now, But Happy 50 Anyway," *Wall Street Journal*, February 23, 2003.
17. Dan W. Brock and Allen E. Buchanan, "The Genetics of Behavior and Concepts of Free Will and Determinism," in Jeffrey R. Botkin, et al., *Genetics and Criminality* (Washington, D.C.: American Psychological Association, 1999), 72.
18. Rebecca Dresser, "Criminal Responsibility and the 'Genetics Defense,' " in Jeffrey R. Botkin, et al., *Genetics and Criminality* (Washington, D.C.: American Psychological Association, 1999), 171.
19. In 1992, a federally funded conference focusing on genetic factors in crime was canceled because the idea generated so much controversy. American Psychological Association *Monitor*, December 1992, 18.
20. Mary Sykes Wylie, "Enemies?," *Family Therapy Networker*, May–June 1998, 26, 37.
21. "Beating the Odds" American Psychological Association *Monitor*, February 2003, p. 43.
22. Stanton E. Samenow, "Cryptorchism and Character: A Case Study," *Medical Arts and Sciences* 25, 1971, 9–22.

14. Coping with Criminals: Dusty Trails and Dead Ends

1. The White House Conference for a Drug-Free America, *Final Report*, June 1988, 76.
2. U.S. Department of Justice Office of Justice Programs, *Juvenile Offenders and Victims: 1999 National Report* (Washington, D.C.), 94.
3. U.S. Department of Justice Office of Justice Programs, *Combating Violence and Delinquency: The National Juvenile Justice Action Plan* (Washington, D.C.), 12.
4. "Victims Target Thieves' Parents," *Washington Post*, July 26, 2003.

5. American Probation and Parole Association, "Guest Editorial," *Perspectives*, Summer 1995, 6.
6. "Md. Prisons to Expand Treatment, Schooling," *Washington Post*, November 6, 2003.
7. "The Prison That Drugs Built," *Corrections Today*, August 2002, 88–90.
8. Pennsylvania Correctional Industries, *Guide to Products and Services* (Camp Hill, Pa: Pennsylvania Correctional Industries).
9. American Probation and Parole Association, "Guest Editorial," September 1995, 17.
10. "Tutor Teaches Reading and Self-Respect," *Corrections Today*, August 2002, 12.
11. "An Investment in a Long Shot Pays Dividends," *Washington Post*, May 1, 2002.
12. This quotation, though dated, reflects a still-current philosophy. Sub-Committee on the Penitentiary System in Canada, *Report to Parliament* (Ottawa: Supply and Services Canada, 1977).
13. Probation was regulated by statute for the first time in the United States in 1878, when Massachusetts provided for a probation officer's being appointed to serve Boston courts that had jurisdiction in criminal matters. David Dressler, *Practice and Theory of Probation and Parole* (New York: Columbia University Press, 1959), 18.
14. "Probation and Parole in the United States—2002," *Bureau of Justice Statistics Bulletin*, August 2003, 1.
15. Kahn and Chambers reviewed results of five programs treating juvenile sex offenders. Within two years, 44.8 percent were convicted of subsequent crimes not of a sexual nature. Cited in *Virginia Child Protection Newsletter 48* (Summer 1996), 8.
16. U.S. Department of Justice Office of Justice Programs, "Boot Camps for Juvenile Offenders: An Implementation Evaluation of Three Demonstration Programs," May 1966, 6, 7.
17. "Scared Crooked," *Harvard Mental Health Letter*, January 2003, 7.
18. U.S. Department of Justice Office of Justice Programs, "Recidivism of Prisoners Released in 1994," June 2002, 1.
19. U.S. Department of Justice Office of Justice Programs, *Sourcebook of Criminal Justice Statistics 2000* (Washington, D.C.), 4.
20. National Academy of Sciences, *The Rehabilitation of Criminal Offenders: Problems and Prospects* (Washington, D.C.: National Academy of Sciences, 1974), 11, 34.

15. To Change a Criminal
1. Ben Stein, "Taking the Lumps, Calling Them Sugar," *Los Angeles Herald-Examiner*, July 27, 1978.
2. Paul Hauck, *The Rational Management of Children* (New York: Libra, 1967), 100, 101.

16. "Habilitation" or More Crime?
1. Marc Renzema, "Satellite Monitoring of Offenders: A Report from the Field," *Journal of Offender Monitoring*, Spring 1998, 7–11.

2. William Raspberry, "They're Depraved, or Maybe Deprived, and I'm Confused," *Washington Post*, January 23, 1984.

3. Stanton E. Samenow, *Before It's Too Late: Why Some Kids Get Into Trouble and What Parents Can Do About It* (New York: Three Rivers Press, 2002).

4. In the 1984 edition of *Inside the Criminal Mind*, I cited a figure of $18,000 to confine one juvenile offender in a California Youth Authority facility (see page 256 of that edition). The amount of $35,000 to $64,000 was cited in an article written in 2003. Tori DeAngelis, "Youth Programs Cut Crime Costs," *Monitor on Psychology*, July/August, 2003, 50.

INDEX

ABOUT THE AUTHOR

STANTON E. SAMENOW, Ph.D., is the author of six books, including *Before It's Too Late: Why Some Kids Get into Trouble and What You Can Do About It* and *Straight Talk About Criminals*. A clinical psychologist with a practice in Alexandria, Virginia, he has spent thirty-four years as a researcher, clinician, consultant, and expert witness specializing in criminal behavior. For the past twenty years he has also served as an independent evaluator in adversarial child-custody disputes, and is the author of *In the Best Interest of the Child: How to Protect Your Child from the Pain of Your Divorce*. He has been appointed to three presidential task forces on law enforcement, victims' rights, and a drug-free America. In October of 2003, Samenow was appointed by the Circuit Court of the City of Chesapeake, Virginia, as a mental health expert for the prosecution in the trial against accused "Washington Sniper" Lee Boyd Malvo, aka John Lee Malvo.